CULTURES IN CONFLICT

CULTURES IN CONFLICT

An Essay in the Philosophy of the Humanities

Otto A. Bird

University of Notre Dame Press
Notre Dame   *London*

Library of Congress Cataloging in Publication Data
Bird, Otto A   1914–
  Cultures in conflict.
  Bibliography: p.
  Includes index.
  1. Humanities. 2. Science and the humanities. 3. Learning and scholarship.
4. Civilization—Philosophy. I. Title.
AZ101.B57   001.3   76–638
ISBN 0–268–00713–6

Manufactured in the United States of America

Magistro meo
Etienne Gilson

Cum Musis, id est,
cum humanitate et doctrina

CONTENTS

ACKNOWLEDGMENTS

For the making of this book I am indebted to more people than I can begin to thank. In the course of it, many books and articles are referred to, cited, and quoted, and I have tried to be as fair and conscientious as possible in acknowledging my indebtedness to them in the notes and bibliography. But this mode is insufficient to indicate the extent of it and, in some cases, misses it entirely. Perhaps the simplest remedy for this defect is to provide a brief narrative of the major stages in the development of the book.

Its origin dates from the fall of 1936, when I began graduate work in philosophy at the University of Chicago. At that time the newly established Committee on the Liberal Arts had just come into being under the leadership of Mortimer Adler, Scott Buchanan, and Richard McKeon. As a student of all three professors and the friend of many of the younger members of the committee, I was at once in the midst of discussions about the theory and history of the liberal arts. This interest continued and further developed when I went on to the Institute of Mediaeval Studies at the University of Toronto to complete my doctorate. It gained added impetus from the lectures that Etienne Gilson gave there during 1939–40 on the continuity of classical culture from Cicero to Erasmus. Although I had by then departed from Toronto, through the generosity that was characteristic of Gilson toward his students, I was able to obtain a copy of his lecture notes. The war interrupted my plans to work on a history of the liberal arts in the Middle Ages, and this project resulted only in a few papers on mediaeval logic many years later.

The next turn came in 1950 with the establishment at the University of Notre Dame of the General Program of Liberal Studies, a program of integrated studies based largely on the great books and of which I was the first director. With its students and faculty, I had the privilege of devoting many years of learning and teaching to the liberal arts and humanities. Without these years this book would have been immensely poorer than it is. However, it began to assume the first lines of its present shape during the late 1960s, when, on leave from the university, I served as a member of the planning committee responsible for prepar-

xi

ing the new fifteenth edition of the *Encyclopaedia Britannica* under the direction of Dr. Mortimer J. Adler. In this capacity I worked especially on the "Organization of Knowledge" that ultimately resulted in the introductory volume now known as the *Propaedia*. On returning to Notre Dame, I was able to offer courses on the theory and history of the humanities, out of which I drew the materials that appear in the article, "Humanities," in the *Encyclopaedia*, as well as a fairly detailed plan for the structure of this book.

For the time and place of its actual writing, I am beholden to the Benedictines of St. John's Abbey in their sylvan retreat in Minnesota, where I was privileged to be a fellow at their Institute for Ecumenical and Cultural Research for the academic year 1973-74.

Among my colleagues I owe a special debt of gratitude to Professor Jerome Taylor of the University of Wisconsin for many conversations about the book and its concerns. To my son, Otto Bartholomew Bird, I am obligated for the compilation of the bibliography and the index as well as the checking of all the references. Finally I am especially indebted to the Institute for Philosophical Research not only for the stimulation, insight, and encouragement generously given to me by my colleagues there, but also for a grant-in-aid that has helped to defray the cost of publication.

A POLEMICAL PROLOGUE

Ideals of Intellectual Culture

Distinction, separation, conflict—these are among the principal features of the history of learning in the West. The Greeks began the process by distinguishing philosophy from myth, thereby initiating the separation of *logos* from *mythos*. Within the domain of *logos*, they also determined many of its most fundamental divisions. Rhetoric, logic, grammar, literary criticism, arithmetic, geometry, astronomy, harmonics, physical and biological science, ethics, politics, metaphysics, and history are among the fields that they marked off. The application of reason to the matter of religion, especially by the Christian thinkers of the mediaeval West, eventually resulted in the distinction of philosophy from a theology based on faith in a divine revelation. The modern world has brought about the separation of the sciences from philosophy with the establishment, first, of the autonomy of the natural sciences and then, only within the last century or so, of the social sciences. In our own day the separating off of new sciences has continued at an even faster rate until the resulting fragmentation sometimes seems more of a curse than a blessing.

With distinction and separation, there also arises the possibility of difference, disagreement, opposition, and conflict. Once there are various and distinct kinds and ways of knowing and expressing, there is occasion for rivalry and competition, for priority and primacy. Is one way of knowing better and more important than another? If so, is it such as to set a standard or norm of excellence and perfection by which all other works of mind are to be measured and judged?

The history of learning shows that all these possibilities have been realized in fact. Differences have led to opposition and conflict. Questions of priority and importance have been answered by the formulation of ideals of intellectual culture that proclaim one form of knowledge to be the best and the criterion for all others. Three such ideals have attained especial prominence and enjoyed supremacy to such an extent that they can be said to have provided paradigms of intellectual cutlure. Each of them has tended to set the intellectual tone of an entire

1

age and has reverberated throughout that age's length and breadth. Thus the ancient classical world had as its paradigm the literary-humanistic ideal of which Cicero and Quintilian were eminent spokesmen. The Middle Ages followed a theological ideal of knowledge, of which Augustine and Thomas Aquinas are among the greatest representatives. The modern world has seen the rise to supremacy of the scientific ideal, of which Francis Bacon was the first great publicist and Comte and the positivists perhaps its most vigorous proponents.

There are still other ideals of the best knowledge, of "the knowledge most worth having." But a strong case can be made for the claim that none of them has ever attained the position, power, and general acceptance that each of these three enjoyed in its heyday. Philosophy may appear to be the most glaring omission. There is certainly no doubt that philosophers from the time of Plato and Aristotle down to the present have proclaimed the superiority of their discipline over any of its rivals. But while this much cannot be denied, it can still be argued that philosophy has never succeeded to the same extent as the three ideals just named in providing the dominant cultural form of an age. For the most part, philosophers have made good their claim only among their fellow philosophers and have failed to persuade the general literate public. Nevertheless, it must also be noted that, although philosophy may not succeed in its own cause, its presence and support are always needed for the establishment of the other ideals as paradigms. To claim paradigmatic value for any form of knowledge is, ipso facto, to put forward a philosophical assertion, i.e., one that ultimately has to seek its justification in philosophy.

A cultural paradigm makes manifest its presence by many different signs. One kind or way of knowledge, often accompanied by one particular form of expression, comes to enjoy a highly privileged and preferred position in comparison with other forms. The practioners and representatives of the dominant form tend to receive greater honor than others in the world of learning. It attracts the "best brains," receives the most attention, and has the greatest "production." Thus, for example, the so-called knowledge explosion that has occurred since the end of World War II has taken place largely in the sciences and the disciplines that imitate them, whereas the comparable "explosion" that occurred in the thirteenth century was a feature of the theological ideal in its scholastic form.

The dominance of one cultural form shows up also in the control that it exercises over the educational curriculum in its texts and methods as well as in the goals at which it aims. Thus, in antiquity, the form of education that attracted the most resources was the literary culture of the orator-lawyer; in the Middle Ages, it was the theological training of the religious; and in the modern world, it is the research training of the scientist.

Sometimes, but not always, the universities are the centers of the paradigmatic intellectual activity. They are now, as they were in the scholastic Middle Ages. Yet it was not so in antiquity, nor in the early modern period, from the sixteenth to the nineteenth centuries, when, almost without exception, high achievement in both the sciences and the humanities took place outside of the the universities: witness such figures as Erasmus, Shakespeare, Cervantes, Descartes, Leibniz, Locke, Newton, Goethe, Wordsworth, Faraday, Darwin, and Mill, none of whom did their main work within the structure provided by the university.

Each of the three paradigmatic ideals originally won its position of supremacy only as the result of overcoming and replacing another claimant to the title of primacy. The theological ideal at first converted to its own purposes the classical literary ideal and then later replaced it with the scholastic form of theology. The scientific ideal at first opposed and then conquered both the literary and the theological ideals. Usually, forms of intellectual culture become paradigm only as a result of conflict, and the conflict has been most intense during those periods when one ideal is challenging another. Such was the case in the time of the early Fathers of the Church, especially when St. Augustine was writing such books as *The City of God* and *On Christian Doctrine*. An analogous situation occurred with the rise of the new science and was expressed, for example, in the opposition of Descartes and Bacon to both the literary culture of the humanists and the scholastic culture of the theologians. The fact that in recent years there have been outbreaks of controversy between the sciences and the humanities, in which even religion and theology are once more participants, may be an indication that we are again at a time of significant cultural change. Certainly, the scientific ideals and its technological achievements no longer enjoy the unquestioned approval, if not adulation, that they had only a few years ago. Science and its remaking of the world have come to be recognized as not entirely unmixed blessings; appeals and demands are put forth in favor of a "counter-culture" that is directed mainly against a culture based on science; and for the first time in many generations, there is again widespread interest in religion. If such manifestations should prove to be more than passing fads, there will be no doubt that we have been undergoing a cultural crisis, a crisis in which one of the great and central issues is a conflict of ideals of intellectual culture.

Such a conflict becomes most intense—one is tempted to say, most vicious—when one form of knowledge lays claim to the exclusive title to all knowledge and thereby denies the value of any other form. Such intellectual imperialism has occurred under all three cultural paradigms, but today it is met most frequently in works expounding the positivist ideal of science. With the appearance of intellectual imperialism, we come to the reason for the polemical character of this prologue and, indeed, of the book. If there is any single contention of the book as a whole, it is that this imperialism is not only harmful to the intellectual life, but also unnecessary and wasteful. Differences there are among the various ways and kinds of knowing and expression, differences that are real and important, as I shall endeavor to show. Differences may give rise to a certain tension. But differences need not as such entail opposition and conflict, and certainly do not imply imperialist aggression aiming at total destruction.

Intellectual imperialism is not the only evil at large in the world of learning. Another one, although admittedly a much less harmful variety, consists in claiming for one kind of knowledge a place of centrality and supremacy, thereby relegating other kinds to a secondary position of less importance and maintaining this as a matter of right, not just of fact. The existence of paradigm ideals of knowledge, as considered above, are matters of historical and sociological fact. But it is an entirely different matter, and one with more serious consequences for the health and welfare of our intellectual life, to claim that one of the ideals—whether the literary-humanistic, the theological, or the scientific—is by right and principle the supreme and best form of intellectual activity and the criterion by which all others are to be judged.

Although the three ideals achieved their positions as paradigms in different historical periods, it seems to be a fact that once a cultural ideal achieves such a position, it never ceases to possess the power to attract and influence the mind of man, even though it may have lost its historic position in the society at large. Thus, although neither the literary nor the theological ideal is paradigm in today's scientific world, each of them continues to have followers who maintain the most exalted claims for their intellectual ideal. It thus appears at least a likely hypothesis that each of the three ideals answers to a deeply felt cultural need of man and to aspirations that are native to the human spirit. Each thereby responds to a permanent need, even though the fact that one enjoys a position of supremacy in a given society is relative to a definite time and place in history.

Cultural Conflicts and Issues

Conflict among these cultural ideals has been recurrent, if not continuous, in the intellectual history of the West. How very rich and manifold that history has been becomes evident merely from a listing of the more famous cases that have occurred since "l'affaire Socrate," which has been called the first recorded example of a "counter-culture."

In our time we are most familiar with the conflict between the sciences and the humanities, particularly in the form that it took in the Snow-Leavis controversy over the *two cultures*, in which the claims of the scientific and literary ideals met one another. The nineteenth century witnessed not only the same conflict, but also the confrontation of science and religion, as well as that of the *Naturwissenschaften* and the *Geisteswissenschaften*. Still earlier, the French Encyclopedists had called for junking all the old in favor of science and technology, Vico opposed his "new science" to the new sciences of Galileo and Descartes, and the quarrel of ancients and moderns culminated in a battle of the books. The Renaissance and Reformation saw an even more complex and confusing struggle, in which humanists and Scholastics, Protestants and Catholics, old learning and new learning of many sorts met and opposed one another on various fronts. The earlier triumph of scholastic theology did not go uncontested even in its heyday: scriptural exegetes opposed the scientific theologians, and grammar and logic each led their forces in a battle of the seven arts. Even the Dark Ages had its conflict of dialecticians and antidialecticians, while the age of the Fathers of the Church found the cause of Christian culture turned against the classical pagan learning. Although this culture may have appeared as all one to the Fathers, it was not without its own divisions, of which the deepest was that between poetry and eloquence on one side and philosophy and science on the other.

The list of conflicts, restricted as it is to the better-known instances only, is a long one. To consider each of them in any detail would require a long book indeed. It would also be a repetitious one, at least in the sense that many of the same questions and issues would keep reappearing under only slightly different forms. The conflict of cultural ideals has been a recurrent one, and there are certain constants that keep appearing in the issues that are the cause of controversy. Hence, by turning our attention to these issues it is possible to delimit and narrow the field of investigation.

For this purpose I shall consider four prominent historical forms that the conflict has taken. Although historical exposition is not the principal aim, as will soon become clear, I shall follow a chronological order and begin consideration of the issues in the conflict with "the ancient quarrel between philosophy and poetry" that Plato reported in the tenth book of *The Republic*. For the mediaeval form of the conflict of cultural ideals, I shall consider the battle of the seven arts, primarily as described in the thirteenth-century poem of that title by the French trouvère, Henri d'Andeli. I shall then turn to the quarrel of ancients and moderns, especially in the form in which it emerged toward the end of the eighteenth century as a battle of the books, as Swift called it. I shall conclude consideration of the issues in the conflict with an analysis of the Snow-Leavis controversy concerning the sciences and the humanities.

Although in each case I shall begin with an actual historical instance of a conflict of cultural ideals, the focus of interest will be the issue itself and not the historical controversy about it. Thus, after locating and identifying a prominent historical form of the conflict, I shall show that the issues involved have been recurrent ones in our intellectual history and are, in fact, still with us and deserve analysis and understanding on their own. The history, in short, will at most provide an occasion for locating an issue that will then become the object of theoretical and philosophical consideration. The philosophical, as distinguished from the historical, intent of the work becomes still more pronounced once the ulterior purpose of this consideration is taken into account. The paradigm ideals of intellectual culture and the conflicts and issues with which they have been involved and concerned are not only of considerable interest and importance in themselves. They also provide the means, and I would argue the very best and indeed indispensable means, for developing a theory of the humanities that will establish them as a unified field of study, distinct from that of the sciences, of great value in itself, and an essential and integral part of the world of learning. My concern then with these intellectual conflicts is not only or mainly for the purpose of exposing the differences that have been their cause in the hope of moderating, if not of eliminating such conflicts, however important and worth attempting this may be in itself. Rather, it also has the further and higher aim of developing a philosophy of the humanities.

Plan of the Work

There are three principal tasks lying before us, corresponding to the three parts of this book. The first task is the exposition from representative figures of the three great historical paradigms of intellectual culture to see the account that each has to give of itself and to locate at least some of the sources of the strength and power of each.

The second task is to provide an account and analysis of some of the more important and typical conflicts in which the differing intellectual ideals have become engaged. In each case, I shall begin with an instance of actual historical conflict, but, once this factual basis has been established, the principal concern will be to identify and analyze the major issues underlying the conflicts and to consider possibilities of their resolution.

The third task is to bring together the results that have been obtained in order to formulate a theory of the humanities that will show where they stand within the world of learning as well as the reason for believing that that world can constitute one world in which the sciences and the humanities form an intellectual community devoted to peaceful and fruitful cooperation.

PART I: *Major Ideals of Intellectual Culture*

CHAPTER 1: The Literary-Humanistic Ideal of Antiquity

The oldest as well as the first ideal of intellectual culture to become a paradigm was the literary-humanistic ideal. As with so much of our culture, it had its roots in the intellectual curiosity of the ancient Greeks and their tempestuous life. Conquering Rome was itself captured by this ideal and, by making the ideal its own, gave it currency throughout the ancient Mediterranean world. Although it lost its primacy to the religion and theology of Christianity, it continued to exert great influence, contributing significantly to the formation of a Christian culture and even leaving on one type of this culture its own indelible stamp. With the advent of the humanists in the fourteenth century, it acquired champions who again claimed supremacy for it and who were successful, in many cases, in gaining positions of power from which they could establish educational programs that assured the continuation of the ideal into the twentieth century. Despite the fact that another ideal has long been dominant, it still continues to make its power felt by attraction and influence.

For the exposition of this ideal, I shall look to the work of its two most eminent Latin spokesmen, who not only described and extolled the ideal, but who also prescribed a program of studies for achieving it and gave to it a proper name. The name in Latin is *humanitas*, and, since its representatives in the Renaissance came to be called *humanists* for their teaching and practice of the *studia humanitatis*, it is accurate to name the ideal after them, especially inasmuch as the program on which it is based is strong in those studies now known as humanities.[1] In word as well as idea, both humanism and humanities derive from the *humanitas* that is praised and analyzed by Cicero and Quintilian.

The Ciceronian Ideal

The ideal is an extremely literary one in that it represents a culture in which the word is central. Cicero's dialogue, *De oratore (Concerning the*

11

Orator) and Quintilian's *Institutio oratoria (The Education of the Orator)* are classical expressions not only of the ideal, but also of the art of the spoken and written word known as rhetoric. Yet it should be noted at once that Cicero himself was critical of rhetoric as a merely verbal and formal art. His ideal was the union of eloquence with philosophy. Nor is *eloquentia*, as he used the term, to be identified or confused with a formal art of words. Eloquence, for Cicero, was a wisdom, and he maintained that there was a time when eloquence was in fact identical with philosophy. The separation of the two, with distinct names, was the result of a development that he looked upon as a disastrous mistake. To make good this claim, he resorted to a curious history of culture.

According to Cicero, what the Greeks called wisdom (in Latin, *sapientia*) was the art and power of thinking and speaking that was exercised upon matters of public concern by such statesmen as Lycurgus and Solon, among the Greeks, and Cato and Scipio, among the Romans. But then there arose a new class of men. Although they were equal in ability to the former leaders, they chose to follow a life of quiet and leisure and turned their backs upon a life of action devoted to concern for public affairs in order to seek learning and knowledge alone. Thence resulted the disastrous separation. The older learning had taught together, under one and the same master, both living rightly and speaking well. Achilles, for example, was given one companion in war to teach him to be "both a speaker of words and a doer of deeds."[2] But the new men broke asunder this union by devoting themselves exclusively to specialized pursuits. Some took to the study of poetry, some to geometry, others to music, some even to dialectic, but, in any case, all were averse to civil affairs and its business and despised and derided the art of speaking. The climax of this development was reached in the person of Socrates, of whom Cicero wrote:

> He, who, according to the testimony of all the learned and the judgment of all Greece, was the first of all men in wisdom and penetration, grace and refinement as well as in eloquence, variety, and copiousness of language on any subject he took in hand, deprived of their common name those who handled, treated, and gave instruction in those matters that are the object of our present inquiry, although they had previously been comprised under one appellation: all knowledge in the best arts and sciences and all exercise in them was denominated·*philosophy;* but he separated in his discussions the ability of thinking wisely and speaking gracefully [*sapienterque sentiendi et ornate dicendi scientiam*] although they are naturally united. . . . Hence arose that divorce, as it were, of the tongue from the heart, a division certainly absurd, useless, and reprehensible, that

one class of persons should teach us to think and another to speak rightly.[3]

It is certainly surprising to find Socrates cast in the role of the villain, since we know him from the dialogues of Plato as the sage and gadfly of Athens, the founder of moral philosophy, something of a mystic contemplative, and a martyr to freedom of thought. Cicero, however, was perfectly clear about the reasons for his own animosity toward him. As he saw it, it was Socrates who introduced men to the excitement and joys of intellectual speculation and persuaded, when he did not actually seduce, them to undertake its pursuit, thereby turning their attention and efforts away from political and social life, preferring a life of contemplation to one of action, and thus divorcing eloquence from philosophy to the ruin of both.

Cicero's declared ambition was to restore the union of eloquence with philosophy. His program for achieving that union demanded a severe retrenchment for philosophy from the great scope that it had acquired in the works of Plato and Aristotle. His conception of philosophy is indicated by the fact that he spoke of a divorce between tongue and heart and not between tongue and mind. His preferred philosophy had to be one that would be useful to "a person of authority in public councils, a leader in the administration of government, a consummate master of thought and eloquence, as well in the senate as in popular assemblies and in public causes." Hence he frankly acknowledged that he wanted in philosophy "not that which is truest, but that which is most suitable to the orator."[4] This admission, which condemns Cicero in the eyes of the metaphysician and the technical or professional philosopher, accounts for the superficiality of his own philosophical writings. In Cicero's favor, it should be noted, however, that the truths of the metaphysician offer little of use in the public forum.

In thus subjecting philosophy to the needs of the orator-lawyer-statesman, Cicero also made clear that his conception of the union between eloquence and philosophy was one in which philosophy would take second place. All the arts and sciences were to be "attendants and handmaids of the orator"—(*comites ac ministratrices oratoris*).[5] Philosophy was to be the handmaid of eloquence.

Not to be misled and unjust to Cicero, I should note that philosophy was thereby reduced to *eloquentia*, not to *rhetorica*. Cicero was no less critical of the professional rhetoricians than he was of the professional philosophers. He found them equally guilty of a mistaken and perverse specialization in claiming that a purely formal verbal art, removed from any concern with content or matter, could by itself produce eloquence. Against the rhetoricians, he argued that no man could be truly eloquent who was not also wise and learned in many branches of knowledge, i.e., a philosopher. In making philosophy essential to eloquence, Cicero thus raised eloquence above mere rhetoric.

Yet Cicero also called for the closest relation between philosophy and rhetoric. His philosopher must be an *orator*, a *rhetor*. Thus in a passage that provides a summary expression of his ideal, he declared:

> Some may prefer to call the philosopher who can supply us copious matter for our eloquence an *orator*, whereas others may prefer to call the orator whom I have defined as uniting wisdom with eloquence a *philosopher*. But to me the name matters little provided it is recognized that praise is due neither to the man who knows his matter but cannot give it expression, nor to the man who is never at a loss for words, but has no matter to give. Were I forced to choose, I would prefer to be wise and unable to speak than to be a talkative fool. But if we seek the most excellent of all, then the palm is to be given to the learned orator [*doctus orator*]. If we grant that such a man is a philosopher, the controversy is at an end. But if, to the contrary, one separates philosopher from orator, then the philosopher will be inferior, for the perfect orator possesses all the science of the philosophers, whereas the philosophers with all their knowledge do not necessarily possess eloquence, and this, although they despise it, nevertheless does seem to add a certain crown to their arts.[6]

Such was the ideal at which to aim. The program of studies for achieving it is most succinctly described by the one word, *humanitas*. Cicero used this word in many different ways in his writings. Sometimes, like the English word *humanity*, it refers to that which makes man uniquely human and distinguishes him from the brutes. Cicero did not hesitate to identify the power of speech as that which is most proper to man (*magis proprium humanitatis*) and which raises him above all the other animals; thus, in effect, man is to be defined as the talking animal.[7]

Then again *humanitas* was used to refer to learning and especially to a certain kind of learning. Thus the ideal orator was described as one who is "perfect in every kind of speech and *humanitas*."[8] For this sense of the word we possess an invaluable ancient witness in a text from the second-century gramamrian, Aulus Gellius. Because of its unique importance for our investigation, it merits quotation in full.

> Those who have spoken Latin and used it correctly do not give the word "*humanitas*" the meaning that it is commonly thought to have, namely what is called *philanthropaeia* by the Greeks, signifying a kind of friendly spirit and benevolence towards all men without distinction; but they give

to *"humanitas"* about the force of what the Greeks call *paideia*, or what we call learning and education in the liberal arts [*eruditionem institutionemque in bonas artes*], since those who earnestly desire and seek after these are the most highly humanized [*maxime humanissimi*]; for the care and discipline of this knowledge has been given to man alone of all animals. That the ancients used the word in this way, and especially Varro and Cicero, is clear from almost all their books. Limiting ourselves to one example, we find that Varro, in the beginning of his first book on human things, writes: "Praxiteles, who for his great art is unknown to no one who is even a little *humaniori*," where *humaniori* does not mean as commonly used easy-going, tractable, and benevolent—for this meaning does not at all fit the context—but rather that anyone trained and learned would know from books and from history who Praxiteles was.[9]

Humanitas, then, was for the Latins what *paideia* was for the Greeks, and *paideia*, as Werner Jaeger has eloquently shown, summed up in a word an ideal of general and liberal culture as well as a program of studies for achieving it that reaches back to the time of the Sophists.[10] In Aristotle, for example, we find *paideia* contrasted with *epistéme*, the scientific knowledge of the specialist, and the man with *paideia* is described as one who is "able to form a fair off-hand judgment of the goodness or badness of the specialist's presentation . . . and who in his own person is able to judge critically in all or nearly all branches of knowledge and not merely in some special subject."[11]

From this it is clear that in developing his ideal of culture Cicero was drawing upon an already long-established tradition. Cicero never attempted to hide his debt to the Greeks, and, since he coined Latin words for Greek philosophical terms, he may well have had *paideia* in mind when he wrote about *humanitas*.

The Greek term gains added significance from the fact that it enters into the compound term *enkuklios paideia*, from which we derive our word *encyclopedia*.[12] Scholars dispute about the original meaning of this term and sometimes deride those who take it to refer to encyclopedic knowledge, just as Newman was criticised for seeming to imply in his *Idea of a University* that *universitas* meant a place of universal knowledge. Yet there seems to be little doubt that *paideia* referred to a general knowledge, i.e., a knowledge of many different subjects, not to one speciality, and also that it was a knowledge that was conceived of as propaedeutic to any further knowledge. Cicero clearly distinguished a lower and an upper level in the education of his ideal orator. The first is called *puerilis institutio* ("the education of boys"),[13] and the second, *politior humanitas* ("the more polished *humanitas*")[14] which implies that the former is a less polished or ruder *humanitas*; it was this more elementary and general learning that was referred to as *enkuklios paideia*, as Quintilian noted.[15]

Given the object of the present inquiry, these terminological distinctions are important. They serve to emphasize the distinction between the elementary general learning that is needed, as it were, to provide a man with his humanity—such being the force that is carried more or less implicitly by calling this learning *humanitas*—and that further and additional learning that confers a more polished humanity upon its possessor.

What, we may now ask, is the difference in content between the two levels of learning? There are many indications in Cicero's writing of the way he conceived of them, but a much more systematic presentation of the whole program of studies is to be found in the work of Quintilian.

The Program of Quintilian

The *Institutio oratoria* (*The Education of the Orator*) has been recently described as "the finest statement of ancient rhetorical theory."[16] But while it may well be that, it is also a textbook of the Ciceronian ideal. Quintilian was a Ciceronian, among the earliest of a long line of near idolators of Cicero, but he was not Cicero, and the ways in which he differed from his master had significant effects upon his work. In the first place, although, like Cicero, he was trained for the bar and actually pleaded some cases, he was for most of his life the professor of a famous school of rhetoric in Rome, and his main work took the form of a textbook, not that of a philosophical dialogue. Then too the fact that he lived and wrote under the government of the empire, and not as Cicero had under the republic, may explain why he emphasized less the training of the orator as a statesman and a maker of policy and placed greater stress on its literary character and its moral value.

The program of studies established by Quintilian can be divided into three parts: the studies that fall under the direction of the master of grammar, the *grammaticus*, which correspond to the *puerilis institutio* of Cicero; the professional training in the art of oratory given by the master of rhetoric; and the final studies that the student should pursue on his own which constitute the *politior humanitas*.

Under grammar was included the whole circle of elementary studies—the *enkuklios paidea*—and Quintilian remarked that he meant by the term *grammatica* what the Latins called *litteratura*.[17] It comprehended not only reading, writing, and speaking correctly both Greek and Latin, but also the reading and interpretation of the poets in both languages, as well as any knowledge needed for that purpose. Grammar thus encompassed all the disciplines that had already begun to be called the liberal arts, and in the course of his first book, which is devoted to the work of grammar, Quintilian named all of the seven that later form the mediaeval trivium and quadrivium: grammar, rhetoric, and logic; arithmetic, geometry, music, and astronomy.[18] The entire arts program could thus be brought under grammar as the art charged with reading and understanding a text, although Quintilian himself warned against the aggression of grammar in claiming more of rhetoric than it should and failing to recognize and admit that each art has its own proper sphere.[19]

All but the first and last of the twelve books of the *Institutio oratoria* are devoted to the art of rhetoric, and in his account of it, Quintilian drew upon a tradition that was already more than five centuries old. The art in its general lines was first systematically analyzed by Aristotle, whom Quintilian followed for the most part. The actual content of the art lies outside the scope of the present inquiry, yet it is worth noting at least its general divisions for the light they throw upon the ideal of culture that was served.

In any speech or discourse, besides the speech itself as a linguistic structure, three distinct elements can be distinguished: (1) the speaker and the impression that he makes as a person, i.e., his character; (2) the subject on which he speaks; and (3) the audience he addresses and wishes to influence.

With respect to the audience, three kinds of rhetoric or oratory can be distinguished according to the way the speaker wishes to influence it: (a) as regarding the future and what is to be done, which is the field of political or deliberative oratory; (b) as regarding the past and how it is to be judged, which is the province of forensic or judicial oratory; and (c) as regarding the present as praiseworthy or blameworthy, which is the concern of epideictic or panegyric oratory.

Rhetoric as an art consisted in the knowledge and skill in the use of the means for achieving these various ends. The study of the art was divided into five parts: (1) invention—the discovery of arguments concerning the subject or matter of the speech; (2) disposition—the arrangement of the arguments to achieve the desired purpose; (3) elocution—the fashioning of the appropriate style for the purpose; (4) Memory; and (5) delivery—the learning and delivering of the speech.

The first part of ancient rhetoric, devoted to invention, has recently experienced something of a revival in the so-called new rhetoric, which is largely the work of the Belgian professor, Chaim Perelman.[20] This part dealt with the topics or commonplaces of argument as forms or types adaptable to different situations. Hence, it was concerned with how to think and reason about moral and practical questions and thus was based on the principle that matters such as these constitute a proper concern for reason, even though they may be closely implicated with our tastes and emotions. Rhetorical *inventio*, in effect, provided a defense of practical reason in its claim that our actions and the values on which they are based are not merely and solely the product of our emotions.

Elocutio, the third part of the art, included the study of "the flowers of rhetoric," i.e., of the various figures and devices of speech, considered as ornaments and embellishments of language. This part received great development through the extensive classification and naming of the many different figures of speech. It is also the part that is hardest for us to appreciate today, since we fail to take the great delight in this feature of rhetoric that our ancestors seemed to have had from ancient times through the Renaissance, if not into the nineteenth century.[21]

Study of the art included not only learning the rules, but also extensive reading and analysis of literature to understand how they work in actual practice as well as imitation of the best models as a means of acquiring skill in applying them. For this purpose it was necessary to have select lists of the best writers and best books. This need was expressed by Quintilian as follows:

> If there were a single word for every single thing, words would require less care, for all would then at once present themselves with the things to be expressed. As some, however, are more appropriate, or more elegant, or more significant, or more euphonious, than others, they ought all, not only be known, but to be kept in readiness . . . so that when they present themselves to the judgment of the speaker, the choice of the best of them may be easily made. . . . But this object we shall effect by reading and listening to the best language.[22]

Here, we have in principle the idea of *classic*, although Quintilian himself does not use the word. He spoke instead of "ranking authors in an order and even omitting some altogether."[23]

This is no place to get into the vexed question of the meaning of *classicism*. Nor is there any need, since for our purpose it is important only to note how this literary ideal of culture contained from the beginning the note of the classic as a criterion. The standard at first, as the text just cited reveals, was predominantly verbal. Not all usages of language are equally good for accomplishing the purposes for which they are intended. Every person knows this from his own experience and the many times in which his utterances elicited far different responses from those he intended. Quintilian went further than this in his idea of the classic, in which he implied that some usages are more correct than others and not merely more effective. This ideal of correctness of speech was especially prominent in antiquity. But it has ever since held its place and retained its followers. In fact, the standard of correctness adopted by the recent *American Heritage Dictionary of the American Language* not only accepts that of Quintilian, but actually quotes him, in declaring that correctness depends upon "the custom of speech, which is the consent of the learned, as custom of life, which is the consent of the good."[24] Hence, in determining questions of good usage, the editors of the dictionary proceeded on the principle that "good usage can usually be distinguished from bad usage even as good books can be distinguished from bad books," and they appealed to the best authorities, these being "not the scholarly theoreticians, not the instinctive verbalizers of the unlettered mass," but rather "those professional writers who have demonstrated their power to wield it effectively and beautifully."[25]

Interpretation of this rule can be excessively narrow and rigorous, as it was with some of the Latin pedants of the Renaissance who refused to employ any word except those to be found in the writings of Cicero. Quintilian showed more sense. He recognized that even the best writers have their low points that even Homer nods at times. Nor did he limit his recommendations to any one author. The list of great books that he presented as containing models of excellence includes many Greek and Latin authors. He called them "the thinkers of the best thoughts, the speakers of the best language" (*optima sentientem optimeque dicentem*). This phrase recalls Matthew Arnold's definition of culture as knowing "the best which has been thought and said in the world."[26]

One feature of the selection is worth noting for its bearing on the quarrel of ancients and moderns. It was the practice of the ancient critics, especially those of the great *Mouseion* at Alexandria, to exclude anything of their own age, which usually meant anything less than a hundred years old, thus giving a definite preference for the ancients against the neoterics.[27] Again, Quintilian was not as strict in his demands. He admitted writers of his own time into his list of recommended readings, although the ancients admittedly predominate. The strongly literary cast of the list is obvious from the fact that of the eighty writers mentioned (forty-seven of them Latin, thirty-three Greek), over half of them are poets (twenty-five Latin, twenty Greek), with supreme praise bestowed upon Homer and Virgil; seventeen of them are orators (twelve Latin, five Greek); eight are historians (four from each language); and ten are philosophers (six Latin and four Greek, although he acknowledged that in philosophy the Latins lagged far behind). It should cause no surprise that literary excellence provided

the controlling criterion of the list, inasmuch as the writers were recommended primarily as models of literary style.[28]

Education and learning for Quintilian was the work of a lifetime.
The orator, Cicero had noted, needs to have knowledge not just of the
arts but also of the great concerns of man (res magnae).[29] Hence, after a
person acquired the arts of learning through making the circle of
learning and achieved his professional formation through the study of
rhetoric, he was expected to continue his education by himself and
acquire a politior humanitas. For this purpose, Quintilian recommended, as Cicero before him, the study of history, law, and
philosophy. But the two men understood by philosphy somewhat
different things, and the difference had its effect upon the formulation of their ideal of culture.

For Cicero, as we have seen, philosophy was necessary to the doctus
orator inasmuch as it formed an integral part of the union of eloquence
and wisdom. But for Quintilian the ideal was not the doctus orator, but
the bonus orator, in which bonus meant the morally virtuous man. The
change from doctus to bonus is indicative of the greater importance that
Quintilian placed upon morality so that his ideal tended to stress the
inseparability of eloquence and morality rather than that of eloquence
and wisdom. So too, whereas Cicero condemned the philosophers for
so specializing their interests that they abandoned eloquence and public affairs, Quintilian criticized them for theorizing about morality and
abandoning the practice of it. His ideal was the good man expert in
speaking (vir bonus dicendi peritus). Greater value was attributed to
moral goodness than had been the case with Cicero.[30] The whole of
Quintilian's educational program is summarily described as the training of such a man.

> The orator whom we will educate is the perfect orator, and he can only
> be a good man. Therefore, we demand of him not only an excellent power
> of speech, but all the moral virtues as well. Nor can I admit that the science
> of the moral and honorable life should be left to the philosopher. For the
> man who is a true citizen, fit for the affairs of private and public business,
> capable of guiding cities by his counsel, establishing them by his laws, and
> reforming them by his judgments, can certainly be none other than the
> orator.[31]

Enduring Features of the Ideal

For today's reader it is unfortunate, if not actually misleading, that
the ideals of Cicero and Quintilian are expressed in terms of oratory
and the orator. The term rhetoric has acquired a pejorative ring as

connoting vain and useless verbal display. We have grown so accustomed to a plain style that it is hard for us not to consider inflated the high style that Cicero and Quintilian admired and recommended. The worth and importance of the ideal, however, by no means depends upon the current status of oratory and the orator. In closing this preliminary account of the ideal, it may be useful to indicate those features of it that have tended to retain a perennial value.

I have called the ideal a literary one because of the great importance it places upon the word, both written and spoken. Words are but words, one may say, a mere *flatus vocis*, a breath of voice, and of no more worth than that. Lest this provide a reason for underrating the ideal, it is well to emphasize the very great importance of words and language in intellectual activity and achievement. It still remains true for us as it was for the ancients, despite the careless usage of some ethologists in referring to apes and bees as possessing a "language," that language provides the surest evidence that man differs in kind from other animals.[32] Then too, language, while not the only means of communication that we possess and not always the most effective, is still the only way we have of overcoming the temporal and spatial bounds of our present existence so as to communicate with those far removed from us in time as well as space. Through their writings Cicero and Quintilian have continued to speak to anyone with the ability to read and the willingness to listen.

That men have continued to listen is certainly the result not only of what those writers had to say, but also of the way in which they said it. This is especially true of Cicero, of whose writings Petrarch—the first Ciceronian of the Renaissance—declared that as a boy when he could understand nothing of their meaning, he was "held fast by a certain sweetness of the words and their sonority so that anything else seemed grating and dissonant."[33] Such testimony as this isolates as one of the essential features of the literary ideal its delight in verbal beauty and the conviction of the value of that beauty. Not everyone values it as highly as Petrarch, and some may even be as deaf to verbal music as to any other, but of such persons the literary ideal maintains that they are ignorant of the good they are missing. The aesthetic value of words is one constant in all variants of the literary ideal of culture.

Another feature of the ideal is the great importance attached to knowing languages other than one's native tongue. For Cicero and Quintilian, of course, there was no choice. The materials of the ideal, as well as its first expression, came to the Latins in Greek. Rhetoric and the other verbal arts as well as philosophy and the sciences received their first great developments from the Greeks in the Greek language. We do not know whether many of the greatest of these even knew any language other than their native Greek. A barbarian was literally one who did not speak Greek, and the Greeks by the sheer quantity as well as the quality of their achievements in the work of mind succeeded in persuading the Latins that it was so in fact. The result was that for generations no man was considered learned unless he knew Greek as well as Latin. The transference of learning from Athens to Rome thus brought with it, in fact as well as idea, the introduction of a learned language. Greek remained the learned language of the ancient world. It was then replaced in the West by Latin, which long enjoyed that exclusive privilege until the rise of the modern languages finally pushed it aside, although in the case of the liturgical practice of the Catholic Church and its theology, this deflation of Latin was not accomplished until the mid-twentieth century.

The more general issue that is raised by this linguistic fact concerns the place and importance of the knowledge of languages in intellectual life. Is the failure to know more than one's native tongue a serious lack, a defect? There is no doubt that the disappearance of a standard language for learning places an additional burden upon scholars in that it requires time to be spent in learning a variety of languages that could otherwise be given to other studies. D'Alembert, himself no admirer of the literary ideal, noted this disadvantage in his preface to the *Encyclopédie*.[34] The more significant question, however, is not the ease and facility of learning, but the cultural value of foreign language study.

Assertion of the value of a knowledge of languages has long been a feature of the literary-humanistic ideal. In part, this emphasis is based on the importance attributed to language itself. Since no single language in itself ever exploits all the possibilities open to speech, a knowledge of many languages is needed to understand fully and appreciate the nature and power of speech. For a scientific study of language, knowledge of at least three foreign languages is recommended: one dead language, one modern language that belongs to the same group as the native language, and one language from outside that group. This argument, however, is more proper to the scientific ideal than to the literary ideal of culture. The latter stresses rather the aesthetic and humanistic value of language study. Thus T. S. Eliot argued, for example, that since languages undergo different developments, the possibility of some kinds of literary and poetic excellence are limited to certain languages and not found at all in others. Latin, he claimed, provided the supreme example of the classic, especially in the work of Virgil.[35]

Accordingly, to one who knows only his native language, the way is closed to an understanding and appreciation of the kinds of power and beauty that are unique to other languages. On this point John Stuart Mill is a valuable witness, since in the nineteenth-century conflict between Oxford and Edinburgh regarding the merits of the literary and scientific ideals, he tended to side with Edinburgh. Yet, on the virtues of the ancient classical writers, he had this to say:

In purely literary excellence—in perfection of form—the pre-eminence of the ancients is not disputed. In every department which they attempted,—and they attempted almost all,—their composition, like their sculpture, has been to the greatest modern artists an example, to be looked up to with hopeless admiration, but of inappreciable value as a light on high, guiding their own endeavors. In prose and in poetry, in epic, lyric, or dramatic, as in historical, philosophical, and oratorical art, the pinnacle on which they stand is equally eminent.[36]

The advantages of knowing foreign languages, however, are not limited strictly to the literary and aesthetic order. They also possess great value in the logical and analytic order. It may be a moot question whether thought is possible at all without language. Yet one need not go to the extreme of a Whatmough, who claimed that thought is completely determined by language habits, to acknowledge that there is an extremely close relation between language and thought. The danger to one who knows only his native tongue is that of mistaking words for things and believing that he should think about things as he does because that is the way they are, whereas in fact it is only the way his language has of talking about them. To keep from worshiping such idols of the market place, as Bacon called them, the knowledge of foreign languages provides a strong support.[37] It can make us aware of the extent to which our way of seeing the world depends on the linguistic habits we have acquired in learning to speak our native tongue.

To be limited to one language is a restriction, but so is it to be limited to the present. To see the world only through the interests, knowledge, and needs of the present time is to limit drastically our human possibilities. Hence, the literary-humanistic ideal has never ceased to emphasize the great achievements of the past. Great works of literature overcome time in that they can continue to speak to men from age to age. The temporality in which they exist is thus significantly different from that of other forms of human activity. They exist in and possess a different temporal dimension as it were, which is a feature that will receive further consideration when I come to consider the quarrel between ancients and moderns.

The literary ideal of culture, as we have seen from the exposition of it in Cicero and Quintilian, rivals philosophy in the generality of knowledge that it demands. But where it differs from philosophy, and indeed from the pursuit of any knowledge for its own sake, is in the moral and political demand that it makes of learning. It seeks a prudential wisdom—involving the senses, emotions, and will as well as intellect—that understands men and their actions in all their individual concreteness. "The best which has been thought and said" is not to be only an object of admiration and comtemplation, but it is intended to provide a criterion for assessing the quality of life and society as well as a means for improving it. From Cicero and Quintilian in antiquity, through John of Salisbury, Petrarch, and Erasmus in the Middle Ages and the Renaissance, through Matthew Arnold and Saint-Beuve in the nineteenth century, to T.S. Eliot and F.R. Leavis in our own time, the ideal has been both extolled and put to work as a humanizing and civilizing force. The word of man is to be prized and treasured not only for the beauty and knowledge that it brings, but also for the great power that it has over human affairs.

CHAPTER 2: The Theological Ideal
of the Middle Ages

The theological ideal with which this chapter is concerned is the ideal of intellectual culture that was predominant in the Christian Latin West during the Middle Ages. The Middle Ages, wherever one sets their limits, covered a long span of time during which the religious ideal of knowledge assumed many varying forms, Jewish and Islamic as well as Christian. Here, however, I shall be concerned only with the Christian form of the ideal. As providing a paradigm for mediaeval culture, this ideal was based on the belief that God has revealed Himself to man, not only through inspired writings, but also in the person of his Son, Jesus Christ, whose Spirit continues to vivify the world through the Church that He established. The entire purpose of the ideal was to study, investigate, and deepen understanding and appreciation of this faith. Although this faith provided a basis for unity, the ideal of culture to which it gave rise received many diverse forms. I shall present the two forms considered to be the most important and representative: the patristic version of the ideal as expressed in the writings of St. Augustine and the scholastic version of it represented in the work of St. Thomas Aquinas.

Christianity, of course, did not enter the world as an ideal of intellectual culture. Its first disciples were not learned men as the world understands learning. Indeed, from the start and continuing to this day, there has never ceased to be among some Christians a doubt and question about the value of intellectual learning. Did not St. Paul, speaking with the authority of Sacred Scripture, declare that God "shall destroy the wisdom of the wise and bring to nothing all the learning of the learned"?[1]

Thus, at its very source, this theological ideal raised an issue regarding the relation between religious faith and intellectual learning. This is an issue of obvious consequence for an ideal of intellectual culture, since some resolutions of it would reduce to a scant minimum any concern at all with the work of the intellect. Consideration of this important issue will be postponed until the analysis of issues in Part

Two. In this chapter I shall confine myself to resolutions of the issue that not only admit, but also foster and promote, the compatibility of faith and reason.

The Augustinian Ideal

The first dominant form of the Christian theological ideal was one that was based on the literary ideal of Cicero and Quintilian. There is nothing surprising in this fact, since all the Fathers of the Church received the same intellectual formation as other educated men of the Roman Empire and bore the stamp of its rhetorical literary culture. The mark of its impress is evident throughout their writings as Christian teachers and often was of decisive influence even in their conversion to the Christian faith.

How pervasive the influence of this rhetorical training could be is eloquently revealed in the account that Augustine gave of his conversion. As a youth, he was sent off to Carthage to study rhetoric. Pursuing the usual course of readings in the *libris eloquentiae*, he discovered his vocation to the intellectual life from reading Cicero's praise of wisdom. He turned then to read the Bible, since from his mother he had learned to associate wisdom with the name of Christ. In this move, obviously something more than his rhetorical education was at work. But the result of his first reading of the Scriptures was typically literary: their style was repellent and utterly "unworthy to be compared with the stateliness of Cicero." It was not until several years later, while a teacher of rhetoric at Milan, that he learned how to read them from the example of St. Ambrose, who was also known for his eloquence. From Ambrose he learned that the Scriptures are to be interpreted spiritually and not always in a material and literal way. He then began in earnest the study of the Bible, which he continued for the rest of his long life, bringing to it and exploiting to the full all the literary arts that he had acquired from his early education.[2] Finally, when in the fullness of wisdom and sanctity he came to put in writing his formulation of the Christian intellectual ideal, the result is accurately described as a transformation of that same Ciceronian-Quintilian ideal that remains predominantly literary in character into one baptized, as it were, and ordained to a religious and supernatural end.

All of Augustine's vast work contributed to the formulation and communication of his ideal of theological culture. But there is one work in particular that explicitly addressed the task of defining that ideal and drawing up a program for achieving it. For this reason, this work, *De doctrina christiana*, has deserved to be known as the founding charter of Christian education in the West.

According to Augustine, everything that a man needs to know is contained in the Sacred Scriptures: "For whatever a man may have learned from other sources, if it is harmful it is there condemned; if it is useful, it is therein contained. And although anyone may find there everything useful that he has found elsewhere he will also find there in much greater abundance things that are to be found nowhere else, but can be learned only from the wonderful sublimity and wonderful humility of the Scriptures."[3] But although all the knowledge that one needs may be contained there, it is not immediately available, patent, and clear to anyone who opens the book. Augustine knew from his own personal experience that one needs to be taught how to read the book. In order to teach a person how to read the Bible, to understand it, and to communicate it to others, Augustine wrote his work *On Christian Doctrine*.

If such was his aim, it might appear that his ideal of learning is, if anything, even more literary than that of his classical models, insofar as his attention was focused even more intently than theirs upon the task of reading and understanding a text. Up to a point, such a judgment is true, and this book of his is recognized as a classic of hermeneutics. But it is not the whole, nor even the most important, truth about the book and the ideal of culture that it expressed. Everything that is most important here turns upon what Augustine means by reading.

Augustine himself took great care to make clear what he understood by reading the Scriptures. The first of the four books in which the *Christian Doctrine* is divided is devoted entirely to explaining the aim and purpose of studying the Bible. That purpose is not limited to achieving an intellectual understanding of what the text says, whether it be the wonderful history of the Jewish people, their laws, ceremonies, and beautiful psalms, or even the account of the life, suffering, and death of Jesus Christ, his teaching and that of his Apostles. While it is true that a person has not understood the Bible if he has not learned about these persons and events, still that is not the purpose of the reading. The whole purpose of reading the Bible, according to Augustine, lies in fulfilling the Lord's great command to love God and neighbor. "If anyone thinks that he understands the holy Scriptures, or any part of them, yet in his understanding does not build up the twofold love of God and neighbor, he does not understand them at all," he wrote. For his part, Augustine did not hesitate to prefer a misreading of the text that led to an increase in charity to a correct reading without charity.[4]

Love is the purpose of the reading, and its main rule is to pursue along the road of the affections the proper order of love. Augustine, accordingly, was concerned during most of his first book with love, its kinds, and their proper order, all by way of providing an analysis of the Lord's commandment. His commentary, incidentally, provides a *locus classicus* for one of the crucial positions in the controversy regarding *agapé* and *eros*. Since man's loves are disordered, the pursuit of love calls for moral reformation and the purging of the soul, the medicine for which is Christ, the incarnate wisdom of God, who serves as both physician and cure.[5]

Reading the Scriptures as they ought to be read, according to Augustine, is thus an activity and a task that is at one and the same time affective, as moving the emotions; moral, as reforming the will; religious, as worshiping and seeking an ever more intimate union with God; and intellectual, as understanding a text and its meaning. The goal and purpose of the Augustinian ideal thus differs transcendentally from that of the literary ideal. The wisdom at which it aimed and which it sought was not the eloquent and moral, but still human and worldly, wisdom extolled by Cicero and Quintilian, but a wisdom that was identified with the transcendent God Himself. The possession and achievement of this wisdom cannot be achieved in this life, where at best men can be only *in via*, or on the way to eternal life. Nor does the achievement of this goal require as a necessary condition the acquisition of a literary and intellectual culture. Before Augustine presented his proposed course of studies, he emphasized that the Scriptures themselves are not absolutely necessary, "except for the instruction of others." A man by himself could do without them, provided he is "supported unshakeably by faith, hope, and charity." For these virtues the Scriptures are not an indispensable means. Indeed, the very reverse is the case: faith, hope, and charity are necessary for a proper understanding of the Scriptures.[6]

Augustine allowed that there is one case in which the Bible is needed and indispensable, namely, "for the instruction of others." Inasmuch as an intellectual ideal, like that of any cultural activity, is meant to be shared and communicated, the Bible thus forms an integral part of the Augustinian ideal, even though its end lies always beyond it in its divine author. The Bible, in other words, is to be used to achieve an end beyond itself. But since it is a book, the knowledge, arts, and all the intellectual tools and devices needed to use it well are predominantly those of a literary culture. For his program Augustine drew explicitly and unashamedly upon the resources available in the

Ciceronian ideal.[7] The main interest in it for us, however, lies not so much in its classical antecedents as in the new theological function and orientation given to these antecedents that resulted in the formation of a new and distinct ideal of intellectual culture.

The exegetical part of Augustine's manual begins by declaring that the interpretation of the Scriptures depends upon two things: "A way of discovering [*inveniendi*] what is to be understood and a way of expounding [*proferendi*] what has been understood."[8] Corresponding to this distinction, which derives from the classical ideal, Augustine also proposed the same twofold way as his classical model: a program of preparatory culture—an *enkuklios paidea*—for acquiring the means of understanding and a training in rhetoric for gaining skill in expression.

The preparatory program that he recommended comprises the liberal arts crowned by philosophy. First comes grammar, for, since God has revealed Himself through the intermediary of human language, it is necessary to know the language used for the communication, whether in the original form or in translation. For Augustine's readers, Latin is the first requirement, but he also called for a knowledge of Hebrew and Greek, the original languages of the Bible.[9] Command of language also includes skill in interpreting tropes and the various figures of speech so as to avoid confusing the figurative with the literal.[10]

In addition to grammar, but annexed to it as indispensable aids to the art of reading and writing, several diverse studies are called for. According to the order in which they are named by Augustine, the first is history, conceived primarily as a chronology of world events helpful in placing the events narrated in the Scriptures;[11] geography, the natural history of animals, plants, and stones; astronomy, but only a little, with a special warning against the superstitious use of it in astrology;[12] and some knowledge of mechanical arts and techniques as useful for interpreting images and figures of speech drawn from them.[13] The rational sciences of dialectic and mathematics are especially emphasized as being objectively grounded in the nature of things rather than, like language, the result of human institution and convention. Dialectic (*disputationis disciplina*) is useful not only for distinguishing valid from invalid reasoning, but also for handling the questions that any profound study of Scripture is certain to raise so as to assure coherence of thought and avoidance of error.[14] A knowledge of mathematics, including arithmetic, geometry, and music, considered as a study of rhythmic proportion, is declared to be useful, especially that of the properties of numbers for the light it can throw upon the numbers mentioned in the Bible.[15] Rhetoric too is to be studied, although its special utility is emphasized more in connection with the discussion of expression. Rhetoric, like logic and mathematics, is held to have an objective basis: "Men did not themselves institute the fact that an expression of charity conciliates an audience, or the fact that it is easy to understand a brief and open account of events, or that the variety of a discourse keeps the auditors attentive and without fatigue."[16] The study of philosophy, "especially the Platonists," is to form the crown of the whole program of studies.

The Platonic philosophy is singled out for having "said things that are true and well accommodated to our faith."[17] In this recommendation, Augustine revealed his superiority to Cicero as a philosopher. The latter preferred not the truest philosophy but that most useful to the orator. Hence he chose the philosophy of the second Academy, since its position of skepticism made it easy to talk on either side of any question. In the life of Augustine, as well as in his work, philosophy was a far more powerful influence than it was in Cicero's. In fact, the reading of the work of Plotinus, who was the foremost of the Platonists for Augustine, provided crucial intellectual illumination on his road to conversion by enabling him to throw off his deeply rooted materialism and rise to the conception of a purely spiritual reality. For this contribution he never ceased to be grateful to the Platonic philosophy.[18]

In calling for the study of philosophy as well as that of the other liberal arts and sciences, Augustine was recommending the study of pagan authors and hence, it might be claimed, exposing his readers to temptation. To meet this charge, Augustine appealed to a scriptural example: Just as the Israelites, at God's command, took with them in their exodus the gold and silver of the Egyptians, so Christians should not fear to put to their own use the intellectual treasures of the pagan world. He mentioned especially "the liberal disciplines suited to the use of truth, most useful precepts concerning morals, and even some truths concerning the worship of one God."[19] Yet he warned that pagan knowledge should be used with care. Not only should we repudiate and detest its "association with demons," but we should also understand that no study "taught outside the church of Christ can lead to the blessed life," and always observe in this study the maxim, *ne quid nimis* ("nothing in excess").[20]

The course of studies just sketched was clearly modeled upon the program of the ancient *grammaticus*, but it has been given a different direction and ordered to a new end. So too, Augustine's treatment of rhetoric in his consideration of the task of expression reveals the influence of Cicero, but subjects rhetoric to a Christian inspiration and orientation.

The question posed in the fourth and final book of *On Christian Doctrine* is whether a Christian should study the art of rhetoric in order to strive to be eloquent. He answered by claiming that rhetoric in itself is neither good nor bad and becomes so only by the use that is made of it. If it can be put to a bad use, that is no reason why it should not also be put to a good use, as it can be when it serves to make the truth more fruitful by making it more accessible, more agreeable to receive, and more moving.[21] The goal to be striven for is the union of eloquence with wisdom, an ideal that has already been achieved, according to Augustine, by many ecclesiastical writers, especially St. Paul. He accordingly devoted a long analysis to show that the arts and devices of the rhetoricians had been used by St. Paul to achieve the very excellences that they had extolled.[22]

Thus far Augustine's prescriptions for rhetoric followed his classical models. He parted company with them, however, with regard to the relation of rhetoric to eloquence. While he admitted that rhetoric could be useful to the Christian speaker and hence merited study, he held that it is not itself indispensable for eloquence. In fact, it is possible for a person to become eloquent merely by studying and imitating the models of eloquence to be found in the Scriptures. Moreover, for a mature person it is even a waste of time to bother with learning the rules of rhetoric.[23] Truth is more important than expression, since it is only through truth that the goal of charity can be attained: "For charity itself, which is the end and fulfillment of the law, cannot be right if the things loved are not true but false."[24] Thus, in the end, Augustine's directions for the study of rhetoric amount to much the same as his advice regarding the arts and sciences. The controlling principle for all must be *ne quid nimis*.

Such, in brief, are the main lines of the program of studies that Augustine proposed for his ideal of Christian culture, lines that he in his own life and work did much to establish and promote. The end at which it aims is religious and theological, and ultimately is one that transcends this world. But the program for moving along the way to that end is predominantly literary in its character and emphasis. It is exegetical insofar as it is focused upon reading and interpreting the Bible. Augustine's practice in his own writing was always profoundly scriptural, whether he was commenting directly upon the sacred text and writing a *psalmorum enarratio* comparable to the *poetarum enarratio* of the ancient grammarians, defending his faith against criticism and attack, thereby producing incidentally a theology of history, or rendering an account of his own religious life for his edification as well as that of his readers. In all of it, he was always engaged profoundly in the interpretation of Scripture. The shape of his program was determined by its exegetical function. Hence his conception of biblical exegesis was the controlling principle behind the program. In this conception a major, if not predominant, influence was his doctrine of the multiplicity of meaning.

Scripture, as already noted, is rightly read only if it encourages charity. But this aim is more readily attained once it is recognized that the text is always open to a number of readings and a multiplicity of meanings. The principle and the need for it as well as the use to which it is put can be seen from Augustine's handling of figurative expressions. It is essential, he emphasized, not to confuse them with literal expressions and to mistake a figurative use for a literal one or vice versa. The general rule for distinguishing the two derives from the purpose of the Scriptures and the reason for studying them: "Whatever appears in the divine word that cannot refer literally [*proprie*] to virtuous behavior [*morum honestatem*] or the truth of faith must be taken as figurative [*figurata*]."[25] Most of the third book of *On Christian Doctrine* is devoted to the consideration of examples of applying the rule. But rather than looking at one of these, it is more pertinent to take one from the *Confessions* in which he also explicitly answered objections to his doctrine of multiple meaning.

In the context, he is engaged in interpreting the beginning words of *Genesis* and has offered many meanings of them. He then raised as an objection the question: But what did Moses, the human author, mean by the words? The implication was that Moses meant only one sense. To this, Augustine replied as follows:

> When one man says to me: "Moses meant what I think," and another, "Not at all, he meant what I think," it seems to me more reverent to say: Why should he not have meant both, if both are true; and if in the same words some should see a third and a fourth and any other number of true meanings, why should we not believe that Moses saw them all, since by him the one God tempered Sacred Scripture to the minds of many who should see truths in it yet not all the same truths. Certainly—and I say this fearlessly and from my heart—if I had to write with such vast authority I should prefer so to write that my words should mean whatever truth anyone could find upon these matters, rather than express one true meaning so clearly as to exclude all others, though they contain no falsehood to offend me."[26]

As an example of Augustine's own use, we may consider his interpretation of the biblical injunction to "increase and multiply." Literally, it can be understood as applicable to all creatures that reproduce. But Augustine argues from the fact that the biblical text applies it only to "creatures of the sea and of men," that it is meant to be interpreted figuratively; he then applies it to words and meanings.

> In this blessing I take it that you granted us the faculty and the power both to express in many ways what we understand by one single idea, and to understand in many ways what we find expressed obscurely in a single way. Thus the waters of the sea are filled, and their waves stand for the various meanings of signs; and the land is filled with new generations of men; its dryness is shown in its thirst for truth, and reason rules over it.[27]

Because of the possibility of multiple meanings, various and abundant information becomes of great importance for the help it can provide in the discovery of meanings, especially inasmuch as Augustine counseled his reader to find meanings for all proper names as well as for all numbers, stones, plants, animals, and so forth that occur in the text even if only in the guise of an image or figure. The things signified by the words of the text are to be read as symbolic of a further reality beyond themselves and ultimately of the mysteries of the Christian faith.

The great importance attributed to the figurative, allegorical, or spiritual reading of the text diminishes, if it does not counteract, the literary emphasis of the Augustinian program. It is not that ancient pagan critics did not also employ such a mode of interpretation for there was a long tradition of so reading the Homeric poems, but in the hands of Augustine this interpretation was to be governed by the rule of faith. In this respect, which is the controlling factor, the Augustinian ideal is theological and religious: theological in ever seeking to know God better and religious not only as founded on religious faith, but also in its worship and love of God. Yet it also remains true that the ideal has a decidedly literary cast from the importance that it gives to the literary arts: to grammar for reading and understanding a text and to rhetoric for providing the means of persuasion.

The Didascalicon

Augustine completed his work *On Christian Doctrine* about the year 427 in a world in which the Roman Empire was still dominant and paganism a present and powerful force. Some seven hundred years later, in the 1120s, Hugh of St. Victor, in Paris, wrote his *Didascalicon*, a work that has the same general purpose as Augustine's, but written in a vastly different situation. In the long interim, during the Benedictine centuries, the Augustinian ideal had been monasticized. The principal intellectual activities of the monks were *lectio* and *meditatio* ("reading" and "meditation").[28] The reading continued to be primarily in the Scriptures, for which Augustine's work provided the main exegetical guide. In establishing and developing the program of studies that he had described, the monks preserved and transmitted the classical literary heritage as a part of their theological ideal.

The *Didascalicon* calls for notice because it provides a transition from the patristic and monastic form of the theological ideal to its scholastic form. Hugh's work continued to conform to the Augustinian ideal. *Lectio* and *meditatio*, he wrote in his preface, are the two principal ways of advancing in knowledge, and the Bible remained the most important book to be read.[29] But the differences from Augustine's book are considerable and significant in foreshadowing the scholastic form of the theological ideal.

The *Didascalicon*, like Augustine's book, is a guide to reading, a book on how to read and ultimately on how to read the Bible. Hence it too is hermeneutic. Hugh's work, however, is markedly more intellectualistic than Augustine's. Its ultimate intent remains the same in being religious, and, in this respect, it is affective and moral as well as intellectual in aspiring to that wisdom which is Christ and to union with God. Yet it is significant that Hugh's work restricted its concern to *lectio* alone and left consideration of "so great a matter as *meditatio*" to another book.[30] Concerned only with reading, Hugh accordingly gave much more attention than Augustine to the consideration of the arts and of knowledge for their own sakes. The first half of his work is entirely devoted to them, and it is not until the second half that he comes to consider the Sacred Scriptures.

Hugh was also much more systematic than Augustine, which was another respect in which he was more intellectualistic. He worked out an elaborate division of the whole world of knowledge into four different groups of arts: theoretical, practical, mechanical, and logical.[31] It is a highly interesting and useful map of the world of learning, one to which we will return in chapter eight.

Hugh's interest in system also extended to the study of the Bible, and his work is viewed as marking an important step in the shift from positive to systematic theology.[32] He compared Sacred Scripture to a building for which the foundation is provided by a literal or historical reading and on which the superstructure is raised by an allegorical reading that reveals the mysteries of faith. "The whole of divinity" is said to be contained in eight mysteries: the Trinity, Creation, sin, nature, law, the Incarnation, the New Testament, and man's own resurrection.[33] Although his theology remained scriptural, it was obviously already aspiring to a systematic organization in its ideal of constituting divinity as a whole.

Hugh continued to describe his ideal of culture as the union of eloquence and wisdom, but, in contrast to Augustine, he assigned little importance to rhetoric. It is included among the liberal arts, but is grouped with argumentative logic as dealing with probable argument.[34] There is nothing in his book that corresponds to the entire final book of Augustine's manual.

In all these respects, Hugh's book marked a departure from the Augustinian formulation of the theological ideal and revealed anticipations of the scholastic formulation. Yet it remained still a far remove from that version and much closer to Augustine's, as becomes plainly evident when compared with that of St. Thomas Aquinas.

The Thomistic Ideal

The shortest, most direct way to an understanding of the vast difference of the scholastic ideal from that of Augustine's is to consider how Thomas began his great *Summa Theologica*. After a brief prologue, the work opens with a consideration of "The Nature and Extent of Sacred Doctrine." This topic comes at the beginning, he wrote, "in order to place our purpose within definite limits." To this end, ten questions are proposed for discussion.

1. Whether besides philosophy any further doctrine is required
2. Whether Sacred Doctrine is a science
3. Whether Sacred Doctrine is one science
4. Whether Sacred Doctrine is a practical science
5. Whether Sacred Doctrine is nobler than other sciences
6. Whether this doctrine is a wisdom
7. Whether God is the subject of this science
8. Whether Sacred Doctrine is argumentative
9. Whether Sacred Scripture should use metaphors
10. Whether in Sacred Scripture a word may have several senses

Thomas's teaching on sacred doctrine in these articles has generated much controversy.[35] Yet from the questions themselves and the manner in which they are phrased, it is obvious at once that we are in a very different intellectual world from that of Augustine and Hugh. A distinction is drawn between Sacred Scripture and sacred doctrine, and since his work is with the latter, the implication is clear that the theologian has more to do than to study Holy Writ. The notion of philosophy, science, and argumentative method is given great prominence, while the propriety and utility of metaphor and multiple meanings —principles especially dear to both Augustine and Hugh—are put to question. The way in which he answered the questions, the form of his exposition, departed still further from the ways of the earlier writers. Although in adopting this method Thomas was following the practices of his contemporaries and not inventing it himself, he was known even in his own time for the innovations he introduced.[36] The first feature of the method is the fact, as well as the style, of the questioning. Everything is thrown into the form of a question. The basic unit into which the vast *Summa* is divided takes the form of a question, the consideration of which is called an "article." The *Summa* consists of 2,669 of these articles, grouped together in 512 *quaestiones* ("questions"); these form "treatises," that are in turn grouped together into "parts." There are three parts: the first deals with God and the *exitus* of all creatures from Him; the second with man's movement toward Him, the *reditus*; and the third with Christ as man's way to God.

This questioning of everything, even matters of faith, was frequently found upsetting, and Thomas was once asked whether it is not dangerous to one's faith to question it and dispute about it.[37] Thomas obviously did not think so. Yet it had one undeniable effect in that it tended to turn men away from the study of the textual sources of faith in the Scriptures. The development of the *quaestio* as the typical intellectual approach as well as the prevailing literary form of the scholastic ideal can be traced back to the ancient *lectio* of the sacred text.[38] The effort to interpret and understand it led to the raising of difficulties that needed resolving until in the course of time the difficulties came to be considered for themselves without reference to the text in which they had originated. This development did not take place without opposition, the leaders of which were often followers of Augustine. Roger Bacon, for example, complained in 1267 that the taste for *quaestiones* had led to the abandonment of the text of the word of God and a preference for disputation over exegesis.[39] Evidence of the existence of this conflict appears in these first questions that Thomas raised about sacred doctrine. This is especially true of articles 2 and 8, asking whether sacred doctrine is a science and should be argumentative.

To many, in Thomas's day no less than in our own, it would appear preposterous even to think of equating religious doctrine with science. By *science*, Thomas understood primarily the Aristotelian conception of certain knowledge, which is not, at all points, the same as our understanding of the term today. Yet the two still meet at several points, and at all of them science is usually sharply set off from religious doctrine. Thus by *science* we commonly understand a kind of knowledge that is based on evidence that is objective and public, that is available to anyone able to handle its terms and methods, that addresses itself to general and recurring patterns of events rather than concrete singulars and unique individuals, that reasons from that evidence in ways that aim at greater precision or certitude than that of common opinion, that develops a precise terminology for achieving clarity of thought and expression which avoids ambiguity and the poetry of metaphor, and that spurns argument from authority. All these are traits of thought and expression that we would expect to be held up, at least as an ideal, by any knowledge claiming to be science. But they are traits that Thomas also demanded of science, as he made clear in his discussion of first ten articles.[40] How then could Thomas also maintain that sacred doctrine is a science since religious knowledge seems to differ so widely on many of these points?

Thomas based his assertion that sacred doctrine can rightly be called a science primarily upon two aspects that are prominent in the Aristotelian conception of science: (1) the ideal of science as an axiomatic system; and (1) the hierarchical relation among the sciences, especially the relation of subalternation. Both are features that are still strong in mathematics and the highly mathematicized sciences. Of the two, that of subalternation is the more important. No science ever proves all its principles, but some of them are either taken for granted as evident ("posited," as we would say today), or else they are taken over from another science in which they are proven. A subalternate science is of the latter sort, a good example of which is provided by optics. This science studies the properties of visual or light rays, using for this purpose the theorems about lines and angles that are proven in geometry. Geometry is thus a "higher" science than optics, since the latter depends upon the former for its geometrical theorems. This dependence, however, does not destroy the autonomy of optics as a distinct science, since it still retains its own method and object. A visual or light ray is not in every respect the same as a geometrical straight line, nor does it always have the same properties and act in the same way, but such features can only be known from the physical investigations that are undertaken in optics, and are not known to geometry.[41]

The axiomatic structure of Aristotelian science is based upon the fact that it is "argumentative," which is to say that it proceeds from principles by arguing according to the rules of logic to demonstrate its conclusions and to organize them systematically according to their logical dependence upon one another. In this schema two points are significant for Thomas's purpose: (1) a science does not prove its principles, and (2) the entire science is contained virtually in its principles so that the demonstrations from them are, in effect, an unfolding and explication of what is already contained within them.[42]

Such are the leading features of the Aristotelian conception of science upon which Thomas based his claim that sacred doctrine is a science. The fact that sacred doctrine is based upon the revelation of God does not prevent it from being a science, Thomas argued, because as we have just seen, a science does not prove its basic principles, and the revelation of God functions as the principles of sacred doctrine. These principles are contained in the articles of faith, which comes to man from God, i.e., from God's science (scientia Dei) as given to man by God Himself. Proceeding from these principles as received from a higher science, sacred doctrine then uses reason to show the truths that they contain. Sacred doctrine is thus a science subalternated to God, just as optics is a science subalternated to mathematics, since it receives its principles on authority from outside itself.[43]

There remain, however, striking differences between the two—all the difference between the authority of God, on the one side and that of mathematics, on the other, and the differences in the way the two are accepted. The one depends ultimately only upon natural evidence and human reason and the propositions based upon them, whereas sacred doctrine goes beyond these in requiring faith in God and his revelation, commitment to a person and a belief that He has made known these truths about himself that are contained in Sacred Scripture and the teaching of the Church. If then there are certain respects in which sacred doctrine is a science, there are other respects in which it differs radically from the science of the philosophers and the scientists.

That Thomas should have wanted to claim the status of science for religious knowledge was a scandal to followers of the Augustinian ideal, just as it has remained so to some Christians down to this day. That ideal, as we have seen, was centered upon the study of the sacred text; it reveled in the multiple meanings of figurative language, and it sought always a knowledge that would increase the fervor of charity. Its preferred method was not argumentativus and inquisitivus, but revelativus in concentrating upon revelation, praeceptivus in commanding men to action, orativus in its practice of prayer, and symbolicus since only the concrete symbol and not the abstract concept could accommodate and suggest in any way the ineffable, inconceivable mystery of God.[44] Furthermore, although Augustine was always liberal in his use of language, he frequently opposed science, as an inferior knowledge restricted to the transitory things of this world, to wisdom, which reaches to the eternal things of God.[45] In all these respects Thomas differed from Augustine. It is not surprising then that the Augustinians reacted strongly and fought back against what appeared to them to be a resurgence of ancient pagan reason against the Christian faith.

There is also no doubt that in the work of Thomas the focus of theological study is transferred from the study of Sacred Scripture to the consideration of God. He asserted as much in his discussion of the question whether God is the subject of sacred doctrine. In declaring that "God is truly the subject of this science," he noted that Augustine and his followers sometimes seemed to assert otherwise, and he referred to Augustine's *On Christian Doctrine* as well as Hugh's work *On the Sacraments*. Thomas accounted for their concentration upon Scripture, Christ, and the work of salvation by saying that they were "looking to what is treated of in this science, and not to the aspect under which it is treated [*rationem secundum quam*]."[46] He did not deny, in other words, that sacred doctrine would be concerned with Scripture and, indeed, be based upon it, but he asserted, in effect, that the purpose of the study would not be exegesis, but reasoning about God. Between Augustine's *doctrina christiana* and Thomas's *sacra doctrina*, the issue was thus clearly exegesis vs. science, the biblicist vs. the philosopher-theologian.

To avoid radical misunderstanding, however, it must be noted at once that sacred doctrine for Thomas remained a scriptural, not a philosophical, theology. "There are two kinds of theology," he wrote, "the kind of theology pursued by the philosophers that is also called metaphysics," based on natural reason, and "another theology that investigates divine things for their own sake, . . . and this is the theology taught in Sacred Scripture."[47] But although it remains a scriptural theology, sacred doctrine is not exegetical, like Augustine's, but speculative, and it is this feature, this emphasis, that lies at the root of the difference between the two theologies.

Whereas Augustine's theology was ordered to charity and accordingly moved in the affective, moral, and religious order, Thomas's was frankly "speculative rather than practical, because it is more concerned with divine things than with human acts, although it does treat even of these, according as man is ordered to them by the perfect knowledge of God."[48] Since it is speculative and aimed primarily at knowing, its preferred method is an argumentative one. This concern for rational argument, in turn, dictates that the kind of language to be used should aim at clarity, the avoidance of ambiguity, precision in terminology, and strict observance of the conditions and rules of logical argument. Metaphorical and figurative language, multiplicity of meanings, and poetic delights are to be avoided as infirmities, if not corruptions, of the argumentative mode, since poetry is the very lowest form of learning according to Thomas.[49] The Platonic philosophers may resort to such devices, but, in the eyes of Thomas, theirs was a bad way of teaching.[50] While admitting that such use of language is appropriate in Sacred Scripture, given its purpose, Thomas maintained that it is not proper to the work of theology as he conceived it.

In what sense, then, is Thomas's sacred doctrine a scriptural theology? How can there be a science based on a religious faith? With these questions we come to the very heart of the Thomistic ideal, since the answer to them will reveal how he thought speculative reason should be used on matters of faith. The answer is contained entirely within one brief sentence, but it is a sentence so compact that it would take a book to unpack it completely. The sentence, which forms the conclusion to the argument that sacred doctrine is one science, reads as follows:

> Because Sacred Scripture considers some things according as they are divinely revealed [revelata] everything whatsoever that is divinely revealable [revelabilia] shares in the one formal object of this science and, therefore, is comprehended under sacred doctrine as under one science.[51]

The controlling distinction is clearly that between what is *revealed* and what is *revealable*. In fact, it has been claimed that Thomas coined the word *revelabile* to make his point,[52] and it is certainly true that, as he used it, it marked a profound departure from Augustinian theology by allowing a much larger scope for rational speculation. It would be wrong, of course, to think that Augustine had not used his reason to its utmost and without stint in the service of his faith. Thomas, in fact, appropriated a statement of Augustine's to characterize sacred doctrine as the science "whereby saving faith is begotten, nourished, protected, and strengthened."[53] But for Augustine the work of reason was always directed to the understanding of the revelation contained in Sacred Scripture, i.e., to the *revelata*. It did not extend to the revealable, as Thomas understood it.

The *revealable* contains, in the first place, all that has been actually revealed, "the revelation made to the apostles and prophets who wrote the canonical books."[54] This consists of two sorts of truths: truths that exceed the power of human reason and that, consequently, would not have been known if God had not revealed them, such as the mystery of the trinity and of creation in time. Revelation contains, in addition, truths that are within the reach of reason, although only with difficulty and the danger of error, such as the existence of God Himself. The *revealable*, however, is not limited to the *revealed*, but contains also what God might have revealed about Himself, but, in fact, did not, such as the implications and conclusions that can be derived from the *revealed*.

In its study of God as *revealable*, sacred doctrine has a fourfold task to perform: to seek to understand and protect the revealed mysteries beyond its grasp; to prove by reason whatever is rationally demonstrable within the *revealable*; to derive new implications and conclusions from the *revealed*; and to organize all into a rational structure. This last task calls for much more than merely the deduction of previously unstated conclusions. The *Summa* is a vast rational structure, but strictly formal deduction is only a small part of it. It employs many other forms of reasoning, informal as well as formal, reductive as well as deductive. Although its ideal may be the scientific model of a deductive axiomatic system, in its actual result the reasoning of the *Summa* is more reductive and hypothetical than it is deductive. It explains the revealed truths by means of theological propositions that yield these truths as conclusions and bind them together into a network of rational relations. Thomas himself noted this fact in giving his theory of the Trinity, the logic of which he compared to that of the Ptolemaic theory of astronomy. This theory, he observed, is "considered as established because thereby the sensible appearances of the heavenly movements can be explained; not, however, as if this reason were sufficient, since some other theory might explain them."[55] The use of such reductive reasoning has led one logician to claim that the *Summa* in its logical structure is closer to that of modern physics than it is to a purely deductive science like mathematics.[56]

In its study and exploration of the revealable, theology takes its start from faith, accepting as principles the statements of Sacred Scripture as revealed by God. Its purpose and goal is the God of salvation, known as such, and to be attained only through faith in a revealing God. Its source, its continuing inspiration, lies in the religious apprehension of the revealing God. Sacred doctrine, as the truth revealed by God, is participation in the divine-revealing operation, since through faith God is working within man to make Himself known. This knowledge is most perfect among the angels and blessed in heaven; it first reached man through the prophets and apostles, who handed it on to all the faithful, by whom it continues to be studied and treasured as an endless source of life and illumination. Since its principles are given by and in revelation, sacred doctrine teaches nothing that was not taught by the prophets and apostles, but since its subject is the infinite God, the search for understanding is a never-ending one.[57]

One Ideal, Two Formulations

The Thomistic ideal of intellectual culture differs in many significant respects from the Augustinian ideal. Seized upon with a factional spirit, these differences have frequently led to fierce disputes. Yet there is a fundamental identity between the two ideals in source, inspiration, and end: they are both concerned with the same God, the same revelation, and the same faith. For both theologians this identity is much the most important fact. For Thomas, no less than for Augustine, all the arts and sciences are the handmaids of theological learning.[58] For both, the ideal of intellectual culture is theological, in service to the same God and the same faith. Their work, then, represents not so much two ideals as to two different formulations or versions of the same ideal. The differences between them lie in the means and methods that they use, not in either source or end, and they are differences that occur in many contexts other than the theological one.

The most obvious difference between the two appears in the style of writing, and this reveals a preference for different intellectual arts. The theological ideal of Thomas is clearly under the dominance of logic in that its aim throughout is *argumentativa*: to arouse the mind to a question; then, having raised a question, to observe that there are good and authoritative arguments on both sides of the question, but that one side is stronger and truer; and, finally, to clinch the argument by showing where the truth is contained in the opposing arguments. Such, in fact, is the structure of the article form, Thomas's favorite literary genre.[59] The Augustinian ideal is no less clearly under the dominance of rhetoric. Augustine too wants to know, but he wants to know in such a way as to move the heart toward God by persuading man of his misery without God, inciting him to undertake the search for Him, urging him to pray, trying to bring him to prayer in the very act of reading. In its strongly rhetorical emphasis, the Augustinian ideal reveals its affiliation with the literary ideal of culture, just as the emphasis upon logic and science in the Thomistic ideal looks to a scientific ideal.

Still another way of characterizing this difference is provided by Pascal's observation that the intellect and heart follow two different orders.

> The heart has its own order; the intellect has its own, which is by principle and demonstration. The heart has another. We do not prove that we ought to be loved by enumerating in order the causes of love; that would be ridiculous. Jesus Christ and St. Paul employ the rule of love, not of intellect; for they would warm, not instruct. It is the same with St.

Augustine. This order consists chiefly in digressions on each point to indicate the end and keep it always in sight.[60]

Augustine's is a theology of the heart; Thomas's a theology of the intellect. But the difference should not be allowed to conceal the underlying similarity. Heart and head, after all, do not live in complete separation, but both live by one and the same life. The same holds true of these two forms of the theological ideal. Both are ways of faith seeking understanding (*fides quaerens intellectum*).

CHAPTER 3: The Scientific Ideal of the Modern World

The idea of science and of scientific knowledge is not a modern discovery. Like much of our intellectual life, it too has its roots in the ancient Greek world. Plato's idea of reasoned knowledge in which thoughts are linked together as by so many chains, Aristotle's syllogistic as an axiomatic system, the mathematics of Eudoxus, Euclid, and Apollonius, the physics of Archimedes, and the astronomy of Ptolemy are all "scientific" in a way that well accords with meanings that the word has today, just as there is good reason for the assertion that Lucretius's poem is the epic of positive science. It remains true nonetheless that science did not come to be the paradigm of intellectual culture until modern times. It boldly and unmistakably laid claim to that position in the seventeenth century and quickly established its right to it, at least in the opinion of those who would agree with Whitehead that the combined labors of Galileo, Descartes, Huyghens, and Newton have "some right to be considered as the greatest single intellectual success which mankind has achieved."[1]

This statement, however strong or exaggerated it may be, does not by itself amount to an assertion that science is the paradigm of intellectual culture. For that, it is also necessary to add that it provides a model of knowledge by which all the rest should be judged. Whitehead himself did not go this far, and, in fact, he devoted the philosophical efforts of his late years to an attempt to bridge the gap between the sciences and the humanities in order to overcome the "bifurcation of nature" brought about by the success of science.[2] Science, however, has had many champions who have not hesitated to claim for it the position of paradigm. At the very beginning of the seventeenth century, in the person of Francis Bacon, it found perhaps its greatest spokesman and publicist, and since his day there has been an unbroken line of writers who have acknowledged his leadership and pursued the way he opened: from D'Alembert and the French Encyclopedists, through Auguste Comte and the logical positivists of the *Encyclopedia for Unified Science*, to B. F. Skinner, P.B. Medawar, and Jacques Monod in our own time.

It would be false as well as misleading to identify science and the scientific enterprise with the interpretation given to it by this positivist school of thought. Science is susceptible to more than one philosophical interpretation. Scientists of great repute, now as well as in the past, have denied that positivism provides an accurate account of their work and purpose. Often the loudest proponents of the positivist view of science have not been especially noted for their scientific achievements. The positivist version of science is admittedly an extreme one. Yet it is this very feature that gives it an advantage for our purposes. By emphasizing and even exaggerating the claim of science to be considered the paradigm of knowledge, it throws into relief the main features of that ideal, thereby revealing more clearly the issues and reasons underlying the conflict between the sciences and the humanities.

Science, according to the positivist view of it, has every right to be paramount in the intellectual world. Nothing else, in fact, deserves to be counted as knowledge. With this claim we have reached not only an extreme position, but one that is also chemically pure as it were. In the history of thought, many different kinds and ways of knowing have established their value, and some have even attained positions of supremacy. But never before has one kind of knowledge claimed for itself the exclusive right to all that deserves the name of knowledge. Yet this claim has been made in the name of science. For this reason, if for no other, it is worth investigating how the claim has come to be made and on what grounds it has been based.

The Baconian Dream

Francis Bacon was not a scientist. He was Lord Chancellor of England, and Harvey, who was a scientist and also Bacon's physician, said of him that he wrote science "like a Lord Chancellor."[3] In making the remark, Harvey is reported to have been "speaking in derision," as indeed he may well have been. His words, however, were prophetic of Bacon's influence if they are understood to imply that his main concern was that of a statesman working to secure science's political, social, and economic advancement. In his work he used all the arts of eloquence that Cicero had recommended for the statesman and won for himself a secure place in history as the first great publicist of science.

His fame for this accomplishment rests primarily upon two books: *The Advancement of Learning* (1605) and the *Novum Organum* (1620). In the first of these he undertook to survey all the learning of his time, to assess its condition by determining its strong and weak points, and, in particular, to indicate areas in which it was deficient. To make such a survey, he had to draw up a map of the world of learning, and the one that he produced was one of the most influential ever constructed. Jefferson used it as the system for organizing his own library, which later became the first Library of Congress. The French Encyclopedists adopted it as the plan for their work. On his map, Bacon noted places unknown and in need of exploration and thus became the prophet of new sciences that awaited future development, particularly literary history and business management.[4]

In intent, the *Novum Organum*, was even more ambitious than *The Advancement of Learning*. As the title indicates, it was meant to provided a new organon for science and philosophy that would replace the organon of Aristotelian logic. Bacon, in common with Ramus, Descartes, and many other men of his time, was confident that method was the key to all knowledge. In this endeavor, however, he was much less successful than he was in the *Advancement*. There are many reasons for his failure. Although he dabbled in experimenting, he was not a practicing scientist. In fact, he was not only unacquainted with the method that the new scientists were actually using, but what he did know he misinterpreted. Thus, he belittled the achievements of Gilbert and Harvey on the magnet and the circulation of the blood, refused to accept the theories of Copernicus and Kepler, and misunderstood the work of Galileo. The experimental and inductive side of science he understood and appreciated, but he overemphasized its role and failed to see the importance of hypothesis and reductive reasoning in formulating the questions to be answered as well as in the work of constructing theories to provide answers. He also underestimated the contribution of mathematics to the task of achieving a scientific understanding of the world. In short, the *Novum Organum* was a failure in its announced purpose of providing a new instrument, a new logic, and a new method of reasoning for science. But where it did succeed, and that on a grand scale, was in its promotion of science as an ideal and in winning friends and influence for it.

The first book of the *Novum Organum* indicates how Bacon was able to achieve this feat, and many of its arguments continue to be used today in the cause of science. The structure of the book owes much to the ancient rhetorical tradition, a feature of Bacon's work that has only recently come to be appreciated.[5] It is organized to win adherence to a certain point of view and to gain acceptance for the new science. To this end, the first book is divided into two parts: a "pulling down part" that attacked the prevalent forms of learning, especially in philosophy, by allegedly exposing their weaknesses, the causes of their errors, and the reasons for hope that these causes could be overcome; and a part producing arguments designed to dispose the mind to receive the new science and to have confidence in its ultimate success.

The truth as well as the worth of learning, according to Bacon, is to be judged by its results: "For fruits and works are as it were sponsors and sureties for the truth of philosophies. . . . Wherefore, as in religion we are warned to show our faith by works, so in philosophy by the same rule the system should be judged of by its fruits, and pronounced frivolous if it be barren, more especially, if in place of fruits of grape and olive, it bear thorns and briers of dispute and contention."[6] Thus, at the beginning of modern science, the pragmatic note is struck that still resounds today: Science is to be judged by what it does, what it produces and accomplishes. In fact, Bacon did not hesitate to identify truth in science with utility as "the very same things" (*ipsissimae res*).[7]

By this criterion, Bacon foresaw the most brilliant future for science: Great discoveries and inventions would benefit all men throughout the world and not just the few in a few countries and thereby would "extend the power and dominion of the human race itself over the universe." Such far-reaching changes had already begun, he claimed, with the invention of printing, gunpowder, and the magnet: "For these three have changed the whole face and state of things throughout the world," Bacon wrote, "the first in literature, the second in warfare, the third in navigation, whence have followed innumerable changes, insomuch that no empire, no sect, no star seems to have exerted greater power and influence in human affairs than these mechanical discoveries." But even more important than these, and still more far-reaching, would be the discovery yet to come of the method of discovery itself, "by means of which all things else shall be discovered with ease!"[8]

Although technological change for the control of the world is an important aim, it is not the only goal and purpose of science for Bacon. Knowledge and truth are no less important, he emphasized: "Building in the human understanding a true model of the world [*verum exemplar mundi*], such as it is in fact, not such as a man's reason would have it to be."[9]

Such, in brief, is the hope, the dream, that Bacon had for science. We know now, 350 years later, with the flowering of science and technology, that in large part his promise has been fulfilled. But what reason did Bacon have for his confidence that it would be? The basis of his hope is worth noting for what it can tell us about the scientific ideal itself.

His hope was grounded, in part, upon the fact, noted above, that the scientific revolution was already under way in his own time. This fact led him to ask why it was that, after many centuries, even millennia, of human learning and speculation, so little progress had been made toward the hoped-for goal. One main reason he attributed to the fact that men had not been thinking about these matters or had been thinking about them in the wrong way. He claimed that more progress had been made in technology and the mechanical arts than in speculative understanding because the former were founded on nature whereas man's learning had been primarily bookish: "For what is founded on nature grows and increases, while what is founded on opinion varies but increases not."[10] Looking back over twenty-five centuries of learning, he concluded that "you can hardly pick out six that were fertile in sciences or favorable to their development."[11] Hence, although learning may already have had a long history, very little of it had been devoted to science. During the Christian ages, "the best wits applied themselves to theology," whereas in the preceding Roman age, "philosophers were principally employed and consumed on moral philosophy, . . . and the greatest wits applied themselves very generally to public affairs." Natural philosophy had flourished only among the Greeks, Bacon asserted, and that was "but a brief particle of time."[12] Thus, Bacon maintained that science had progressed little up to his time and little time had been devoted to its cultivation because it had not constituted an ideal of intellectual culture. To overcome that disability and establish science as such an ideal was the goal to which Bacon turned his efforts.

Bacon described his conception of that goal in words that recall those that Cicero had used for his radically different ideal. Thus Bacon wrote that he wanted to establish "forever a true and lawful marriage between the empirical and rational faculty [empiricam et rationalem facultatem], the unkind and ill-starred divorce and separation of which has thrown into confusion all the affairs of the human family."[13] For Bacon as for Cicero, the source of the trouble lay in a disastrous divorce for which the only remedy was the reestablishment of the union that was meant to be. But whereas the partners for Cicero were eloquence and philosophy, for Bacon they were experience and reason. The change is highly significant, especially with respect to the first partner. Philosophy is readily enough correlated with reason in Bacon's terms, but his *experience* is certainly not the same as Cicero's *eloquence*. This displacement bodes ill for the literary ideal. The same holds true of the theological ideal, since *experience* here also excludes faith.

The hope for the future, according to Bacon, lay in bringing about "a closer and purer league between these two faculties, the experimental and the rational." Learning throughout its history, he charged, had been in the hands either of "men of experiment or men of dogmas," the former of whom he compared to the ant (they "only collect and use") and the latter, to spiders (they "make cobwebs out of their own substance"). The new man of science is to imitate the bee, that "takes the middle course: it gathers its material from the flowers of the garden and of the field, but transforms and digests it by a power of its own."[14] Experience, as Bacon understood it, demands more than mere observation and the accumulation of facts. Experiments must be devised that put the question to nature inasmuch as "the secrets of nature reveal themselves more readily under the vexations of art than when they go their own way."[15] For this purpose, both reason and sense observation are needed in order to secure understanding as well as utility by providing "experiments of light" (*lucifera*) and not only "experiments of fruit" (*fructifera*).[16]

Bacon was convinced that for the achievement of this ideal an entirely new inductive logic was needed to replace the old logic that he mistakenly thought was deductive only, and he was also confident that he possessed the secret of this new logic, a confidence in which he was also mistaken. But although wrong in this respect about the method demanded by science, in another he was eminently right, namely, in seeing that the promise of science could not be achieved without the collaborative effort of many specialists and an encyclopedic organization of knowledge. It was his lifetime ambition to establish a "Great Instauration" so as to make it possible that "the entire work of the understanding be commenced afresh, and the mind itself be from the very outset not left to take its own course, but guided at every step; and the business be done as if by machinery."[17] Although Bacon did not live to complete more than the beginning of this ambitious project, he did not lack successors to take up his venture and to continue it.

The Encyclopedists' Program

In order to gain control over nature and establish the "kingdom of man," science had first to be organized into a program for social reform and even for revolutionary action.[18] The first "giant step" toward that goal was taken a century after Bacon's death by the *Encyclopédie Française*. Its editors and writers were, for the most part, men of letters, not scientists, but they knew well and welcomed with enthusiasm the achievement of the first great physical synthesis resulting from the work of Galileo, Kepler, Descartes, and Newton. They were, if anything, still more enthusiastic over the technical applications of science, which already demonstrated, they believed, the possibility of remaking the world in the social and political as well as in the economic and industrial orders. Science, in short, was seen to contain the promise of revolutionary progress. But if this promise was to achieve fulfillment, the public had to be enlightened, a task that called for a great diffusion of knowledge. The schools and universities, in their opinion, were not only inadequate for this task, but actually opposed to it, since they were still controlled by men devoted to the literary-humanistic ideal or to the theological ideal. For the achievement of their program, they produced the mammoth *Encyclopédie ou Dictionnaire Raisonné des Sciences, des Arts et des Métiers* in thirty-eight large volumes published between 1751 and 1772.

The term we have already met in the *enkuklios paideia* of the ancients, where it referred to the circle of studies providing the arts of learning and a general culture. The Encyclopedists used the term in the sense it still bears as applied to a set of books containing articles that attempt to deal in some way with most, if not all, of human knowledge. The French work, however, differed from most recent encyclopedias in espousing a definite point of view and actively promoting the scientific ideal of culture.

For its plan of organization the editors adapted the division of knowledge drawn up by Bacon in *The Advancement of Learning*. Bacon was their acknowledged leader, to such an extent that D'Alembert said of him in his *Preliminary Discourse*, that "one would be tempted to regard him as the greatest, the most universal, and most eloquent of philosophers."[19] Like their master, the editors directed much of their attention to the "pulling-down" task, and criticized the literary-humanistic ideal no less than the theological ideal of culture. D'Alembert provided in his *Preliminary Discourse* "a philosophical history of the origin of our ideas," as he described it, which amounts to a Cartesian reading of Bacon. After a rapid, general, and, it must be said, highly fanciful account of the rise of the arts and sciences, he reviewed the history of learning. According to his story, enlightenment began only with the Renaissance, but once that had been reached, progress continued without a break, with one triumph after another for the cause of science. The implication was that it will so continue in an unending stream of success.

The Encyclopedists wanted to extend as widely as possible the applications of science, and their accounts of technological processes, which included many beautiful, detailed engravings, have won them a place in the history of science and technology. They were also convinced that science constituted man's most important knowledge as providing a basis for ultimately encompassing "the infinitely varied branches of human knowledge in a truly unified system."[20] Yet, along with Bacon, they recognized and admitted that science does not constitute the only important and genuine kind of knowledge. Other kinds of learning also deserve to be called knowledge. The next step in the development of the scientific ideal as a paradigm of intellectual culture came with the assertion that empirical science is not only the best knowledge, but the only form of learning that deserves the name. This step was taken, definitely, confidently, and proudly by Auguste Comte in his philosophy of positivism.

The Positivist Ideal

Comte considered his work as the culmination of "the great movement imparted to the human intellect . . . by the combined influence of the precepts of Bacon, the conceptions of Descartes, and the discoveries of Galileo."[21] His work, as he viewed it, was a continuation along the same line and differed from theirs only in extending the positive methods of science to the study of man and the social world, thereby completing the task of science by providing a comprehensive knowledge of everything. This account of the evolution of science and of his own place in it at the climax was based on Comte's conviction that he had discovered the key that unlocked the plan of history. According to this "great fundamental law," human progress in all fields passes through three stages that are related to one another as beginning, transition, and culmination. Each stage represents a definite state of intellectual knowledge which determines a corresponding form of political government as well as a specific type of literary, artistic, and economic organization. His position was thus the very inverse of Marx's in holding that the form of intellectual knowledge determines everything else in human life, including the form of economic organization.

This law of development is based on the proposition that "the human mind, by its very nature, makes uses successively in each of its researches of three methods of philosophizing, whose characters are essentially different and even radically opposed to each other."[22] These methods and stages are: (1) the theological or fictitious, (2) the metaphysical or abstract, and (3) the scientific or positive. The theological stage is described as that one in which "the human mind directs its researches mainly toward the inner nature of beings, and toward the first and final causes of all phenomena . . . [and] therefore represents these phenomena as being produced by the direct and continuous action of more or less numerous supernatural agents." At the metaphysical stage, the supernatural agents are replaced by "abstract forces, real entities, or personified abstractions." At the final and positive stage, the mind "gives up the search after the origin and hidden causes of the universe and a knowledge of the final causes of phenomena. It endeavors now only to discover, by a well-combined use of reasoning and observation, the actual laws of phenomena—that is to say, their invariable relations of succession and likeness."[23]

The same three stages, according to Comte, are to be found in the development of each individual mind, of each science, and, so too, of all the sciences taken together. Hence, the law of the three stages is held to provide men with the principle not only for understanding the development of history, but also for organizing knowledge and putting it to work for the reconstruction and reorganization of society.

Positive science is the final and culminating stage in all these developments. The word *positive* is used to express the opposite of the chimerical or unfounded. It is based on fact; it is empirical or experimental in starting from fact and returning to fact for verification, and it reasons in a way that is open to all to see and to follow. It holds to the phenomena capable of public observation and spurns any appeal to introspection as "pure illusion."[24]

There is only one method that can be truly called positive, and it is fundamentally the same in all the sciences: it is the method of the empirical sciences based on mathematical reasoning of which physics provides the model. All the sciences are branches from one and the same trunk, but each science in its development to the positive stage has made its own special contribution to the development of science as a whole. Mathematics was the first science to develop, and Comte, who was more of a mathematician than Bacon, made it the logical basis of all the other sciences. Astronomy, the next science to arise historically, added to mathematics the methods of observation and hypothesis for the purpose of prediction and thereby established the first scientific laws. Physics then built on astronomy by adding the methods of experiment and controlled observation. Chemistry revealed the importance of nomenclature and worked out the basic principles for its development. Biology, at the positive stage of the science, contributed the comparative method and the principles of classification. Sociology, or social physics, as Comte frequently called it, is said to complete the development of positive science by providing a scientific understanding of man and society, the most complex of all objects and the end for the sake of which all the others are studied.[25]

The tree of science, according to Comte, thus grows from the most general, simple, and abstract stage, represented in mathematics, to culminate in sociology, the study of the most complex and concrete object. It is this science, Comte declared, "which from every point of view marks the completion of the positive method" and the end for which all the others have been only the preparation. Once sociology has become established and proven its success, "the old philosophy must be doomed to extinction," since the ground and reason for its existence will be exposed, as this science discloses "the laws of the continuous variation of human opinions."[26] The completion of positive science will also bring with it the possibility of organizing all of knowledge into one rational system and so eliminating any need for historical knowledge. Since science is progressive and cumulative in method and result, there is no need to know its history; one needs only to be educated up to the point at which science is carrying on its investigations so as to continue on from there. Any truths previously discovered belong to the present of science, so its past consists only of errors discarded.

Comte believed that the science of his day had reached the point where it could establish a definitive program for the future. Such a program would have three main tasks: (1) to complete the circle of the sciences by developing the social sciences; (2) to reform the entire educational system by making positive science its basis and central concern; and (3) to undertake with the help of science the systematic restructuring of society. To carry out such a program Comte called for the formation of a scientific elite to provide the direction for science and education as well as society as a whole. Science by its specialization and division of labor had failed to obtain a view of the whole and had thereby frustrated the triumph of positivism. The great and urgent need, Comte wrote, is

> a new class of properly trained scientists who, instead of devoting themselves to the special study of any particular branch of science, shall employ themselves solely in the consideration of the different positive sciences in their present state. It would be their function to determine exactly the character of each science, to discover the relations and concatenation of the sciences, and to reduce, if possible, all their chief principles to the smallest number of common principles, while always conforming to the fundamental maxims of the positive method.[27]

The work of this elite would result in the formation of a general culture of positive philosophy, "a new general and really rational education," that would replace all previous education that remained "essentially theological, metaphysical, and literary."[28]

Such an educational reform, Comte believed, would assure a brighter future for all mankind by eliminating the moral and political crises that have continually convulsed the world. "The world is governed and overturned by ideas," he wrote, and "as long as individual minds are not unanimously agreed upon a certain number of general ideas capable of forming a common social doctrine . . . the nations will necessarily remain in an essentially revolutionary state."[29] It would continue to remain so, he argued, as long as anarchy rules the intellectual world as a result of "the simultaneous employment of three radically incompatible philosophies—the theological, the metaphysical, and the positive." Peace, he held, could only come with the rule of one, and he was confident that "the positive philosophy is alone destined to prevail in the ordinary course of things."[30]

Comte left no room for doubt that his ideal was based on the claim that there is only one true knowledge, that of positive science using mathematical and empirical methods for understanding and controlling the phenomenal world. The theological ideal of intellectual culture is explicitly repudiated, as is clear from the place assigned to the theological and metaphysical stages in the evolution of humanity. Comte admitted that those stages were once important and even necessary for human development, but that was long in the past, and their lingering on in the age of positive science was seen as only obstacles to progress.

With regard to the literary ideal of culture, Comte's position is somewhat more ambiguous. He allowed that poetry as well as the fine arts are among "the most important agents of education, intellectual and moral, that we can conceive."[31] In the list of classics that he compiled for his "positivist library," he included many works of imaginative literature from Homer and the Greek tragedians down to Goethe and Scott in his own day.[32] He also promised a flourishing future for literature and the fine arts under the positivist regime.[33] Yet he held that "the aesthetic faculties relate more to the affective than to the intellectual life," and he denied that they had ever constituted a paradigm of intellectual culture, claiming that even in antiquity "the social influence of poetry and the other fine arts was secondary to the theological, to which it lent aid, and by which it was protected, but which it could never supersede." Still more emphatically, he declared that "the faculties of expression have never directly overruled those of conception; and any inversion of this elementary relation would directly tend to the disorganization of the human economy, individual and social, by abandoning the conduct of our life to faculties which can do no more than soften and adorn it."[34] In other words, the literary and aesthetic faculties always have been and always should be secondary to the scientific, conceptualizing mind. Thus, although Comte claimed to reconcile all our ways of knowing in a new synthesis, he did so, in effect, only by denying and ruling out much that others would count as genuine and important knowledge, poetic as well as theological and metaphysical. Metaphysics, it should be noted, did not include all of philosophy. Comte recognized and admitted that positivism constituted a philosophy, but he claimed that it was not a metaphysics, since it posited nothing beyond the phenomenal. Philosophy had to be "radically one" with science, and he believed that this would win general acceptance once positive science had conquered the moral and social realm as it already had the natural world.[35]

The Encyclopedia of Unified Science

Comte died in 1857, and since then science has made immense progress. However, it has not yet achieved the unification of all knowledge that he foretold and called for, although plans to achieve that goal have not been wanting. One of the most recent is the Movement for the Unity of Science, which has resulted in two preliminary volumes of an *International Encyclopedia of Unified Science*. The first of the twenty fascicules composing the work is a programmatic manifesto of the movement. Written in the 1930s, it betrays the enthusiasm and optimism of the logical positivists. The moving spirit behind the *Encyclopedia* was the sociologist Otto Neurath, and in his introductory essay he placed the work squarely in the tradition of Bacon, the Encyclopedists, and Comte, but claimed that it went beyond them in attempting to "organize a logical synthesis of science."[36] The distinguishing term in the phrase is *logical*. For between the time of Comte and the 1930s, progress toward unification appeared to be greatest in logic and mathematics, especially in the attempt of Russell and Whitehead to comprehend all of mathematics in one logical system, that of the *Principia mathematica*. The *Encyclopedia* proposed to extend the work of synthesis and unification to all of science, indeed to all of knowledge.

Neurath was explicit in claiming that nothing besides science deserves to be counted as knowledge. "If one takes the thesis seriously," he wrote, "that in the field of knowledge one only has to deal with scientific statements, the most comprehensive field of statements must be that of unified science."[37] The same claim was made even more emphatically by C.W. Morris, writing in the same number: "All knowledge forms in principle one unified whole, and there exists no system of knowledge (such as metaphysics, aesthetics, ethics, religion) alongside of or superior to unified knowledge." Although he asserted that science was not opposed to these activities, he declared that it was in opposition to "such activities as claim to usurp its own cognitive goal or which wither and die when the light of scientific investigation is turned upon them,"[38] a proviso so wide as to deny cognitive status to anything but science.

Unified science, we are told by Neurath, is to be built up from within science itself, not by the imposition of any philosophy or superscience, but with "science itself supplying its own integrating glue."[39] Connections between the various sciences are to be established by means of "systematical bridges," and axiomatization was to be pushed as far as possible, although without any expectation of achieving "a final axiomatization." Greatest hope of success was seen in the possibility of achieving a "unification of scientific language."[40] Writing on this topic, Carnap pointed out that it would be premature to look for a "unity of laws" among the various sciences: "It is obvious that, at the present time, laws of psychology and social science cannot be derived from those of biology and physics." But what can be done, he maintained, is to devise a unified language. By this he meant a language in which all scientific statements can be translated into a form in which all reference is ultimately only to physical objects—"a common reduction basis," he called it, "consisting of a very narrow and homogeneous class of terms of the physical thing-language."[41] Expressions that do not lend themselves to such a reduction are to be understood as either belonging to the apparatus of science, or else as not scientific, i.e., as not knowledge.

With the outbreak of World War II, the movement for the unity of science lost its momentum, never to regain it. The first fascicule of the *Encyclopedia* appeared in 1938, announcing the program for nineteen succeeding numbers on the foundations of the sciences. The final one did not appear until thirty years later, and the intervening years saw many departures from the original plan. It is also significant that when the whole collection was published together in two volumes in 1969-70, the series title for the whole had been reduced to a "postcolon:" "Toward an International Encyclopedia of Unified Science."[42] Confidence in the possibility of achieving that goal had obviously waned from its high point in the 30s. Yet the scientific ideal of culture that it represents is certainly still alive and not only remains strong, but is by far the most powerful in existence.

It would be well, in closing this chapter, to warn again that the version of the scientific ideal that has been presented in the strong line from Bacon through the Encyclopedists and Comte down to the logical positivists has not been offered as the best and truest statement of the nature and aim of science. The positivist version is not the only philosophy of science, nor do I believe it to be the best. It is offered here as the strongest expression of the scientific ideal of intellectual culture and the most extreme in asserting the claim of science to provide the paradigm of all intellectual endeavor. Hence, for the purpose of locating and identifying the issues that generate cultural conflict, the sharpness with which it asserts that claim is a decided advantage.

PART II: *Major Issues in the Conflict*

In the course of delineating the major ideals of intellectual culture, we have already encountered several occasions of conflict, such as Cicero's attack upon scientific specialization, the opposition between the Augustinian and Thomistic ideals of theology, and the attempt of positivistic science to overturn both the literary and theological ideals of culture. These conflicts, however, and the differences and issues on which they are based have been noted only for the help they can provide for the exposition of the ideals. They have not been studied for themselves. In this part I undertake that task.

My main purpose here is to achieve a better and clearer understanding of the causes of conflict. Hence, my main concern will be with the differences—real or imaginary—that have divided men in their intellectual pursuits. I shall attempt to express the issues as sharply as possible, even at the risk of overemphasizing the extent of the differences among the various positions. It will be left to Part Three to correct any such distortions when the similarities and common foundations and purposes within the intellectual world and the basis of unity and community are considered. This part, however, will be devoted primarily to the discussion of intellectual conflict and the issues and differences that have given rise to it.

CHAPTER 4: The Quarrel between Philosophy and Poetry

Plato's Criticism of Poetry

The earliest explicit account that we possess of a conflict of cultural ideals is Plato's discussion of the quarrel between philosophy and poetry. I begin with this account, not only because it is the first, but principally because Plato remains an unfailing source of suggestion and insight for anyone seeking to understand the issues that pose such conflicts as well as the basic positions that can be taken upon them.

Plato in many of his writings was centrally concerned with questions about the best form of culture and education, or, in short, with *paideia*. What knowledge is best? What is the range of the choices open to us? How are we to judge and distinguish the best among the various contenders? If one form of knowledge is better than others, how is an educational program to be organized to lead to the acquisition of that knowledge? Plato not only raised and argued these questions, but he also provided definite answers to them. There is also no doubt that, despite the fact that he was one of the greatest literary artists the world has seen, Plato vigorously opposed a literary ideal of culture represented by poetry and rhetoric in favor of an ideal that is mathematical and scientific as well as philosophical.

According to Plato, the quarrel was already ancient in his day, with many "signs of ancient enmity between philosophy and poetry." The quotations cited as proof of the antiquity of the quarrel are no longer traceable, although they seem to be directed at philosophy from the side of poetry.[1] The opposite attack, from philosophy upon poetry, is said to go back to Pythagoras, and this is not unlikely, since it is the mathematicizing reason that is frequently held to be hurt by poetry. Plato's criticism of poetry with its accompanying defense of philosophy would not make sense if poetry did not somehow constitute a rival and competing ideal of intellectual culture. That it did so is clear from the statement put in the mouth of Socrates, that "we hear persons saying that the tragedians and Homer, who is at their head, know all the arts and all things human, virtue as well as vice, and divine things too."[2] From this it is evident that, while Plato's understanding of what is meant by "poetry" may not coincide with ours at every point, it does to the extent that for both of us poetry includes Homer and the tragedians. So too, although his concept of philosophy was more extensive than is usual today, what he does in his dialogues still counts as philosophy.

Plato's criticism of the literary ideal is based on a metaphysical position regarding the nature of reality. Many of the charges that he made, however, have no necessary connection with that philosophy and, in fact, have been advanced by thinkers who do not share it. Still, it is useful to begin with a discussion of the philosophical basis of his criticism, since it contains much that bears upon other aspects of our project besides the quarrel between philosophy and poetry.

The shortest, if not the simplest, description of Plato's ideal *paideia* is contained in his account of the various kinds and objects of knowing. This occurs in the discussion of the famous image of the divided line in the the sixth book of the *Republic*.[3] We are told to draw a line to represent all the objects that we can know and to divide it into two unequal sections standing for the visible and the intelligible world. Each of the sections is to be divided again according to the same proportion (see below).[4] The diagram is used to make three kinds of discriminations: ontological, regarding the kinds or levels of being that there are; epistemological, regarding the kinds of knowing; and pedagogical, regarding the parts of the educational curriculum. The two lower segments are shorter than the upper two, since the visible world is less extensive than the intelligible world; our knowledge is not limited to what can be seen. Within the visible world, Plato was concerned to draw a sharp distinction between images and reflections on the one hand and the material things that are their originals on the other, since he held that just as images are imitations of material things, so the whole material world is an imitation of the intelligible world. The reason for dividing the latter also into two is based on the distinction between two different kinds of intellectual activity: hypothetical reasoning, of which mathematics provides the clearest example, in which given certain assumptions, we reason from them to conclusions; and intellectual insight or intuition that results from the investigation of assumptions and tests a theory ultimately by the apprehension of the idea or form.

The Divided Line[4]

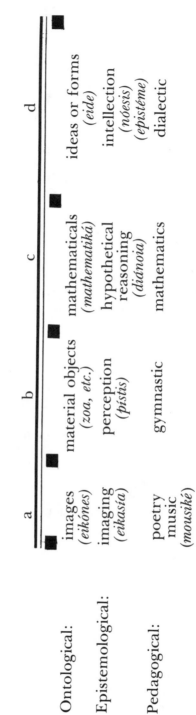

	the visible		the intelligible	
	a	b	c	d
Ontological:	images (*eikónes*)	material objects (*zoa, etc.*)	mathematicals (*mathematiká*)	ideas or forms (*eide*)
Epistemological:	imaging (*eikasía*)	perception (*pístis*)	hypothetical reasoning (*diánoia*)	intellection (*nóesis*) (*epistéme*)
Pedagogical:	poetry music (*mousiké*)	gymnastic	mathematics	dialectic

The aim of both education and life itself, at least for the philosopher, is to move up the line, and, according to the allegory of the
cave (in book seven), to turn away from the things and images of this
material world by looking to the invisible objects of abstract thought,
through training in mathematical thinking, and then to turn from
and transcend this realm by a critical investigation of our knowledge
through dialectic until we gain an insight into the highest ideas that
rule all the worlds. In other words, it is to move from many beauties
to beauty itself, the cause of all the others—from particular goods
that at best are partial to the good itself that makes all others good.

Metaphysically, Plato's position is based on the principle that
things here are not all that they appear to be and that this world of
appearance depends on a higher and better reality that is invisible
but reachable through philosophical thought and moral virtue.
Epistemologically, the position draws a sharp distinction between
sense and intellect, between the apprehension of sensory images that
yields at best conjecture (*eikasía*) and the apprehension of their material originals that results in belief (*pístis*), and between hypothetical
reasoning (*diánoia*) and dialectical or philosophical though (*nóesis*).
Pedagogically, the curriculum that Plato elaborated was unashamedly intellectualistic. Critical, abstract, conceptual thinking is held up as
the highest, most valuable knowing that man can have short of the
intuition of the ideas that rule both the intelligible and visible
worlds. The curriculum for educating the philosopher-king embodies an ideal of philosophical culture that would preside over the
city of men as well as the city of the soul. Just as this phenomenal
world is itself only an imitation and not the really real, so too any
knowledge that stops short of philosophical knowledge of ideas fails
to reach the best.

Of all imitations, poetry is held by Plato to be the lowest and the
worst. It is lowest because it is the furthest removed from the really
real; it is worst because it is the most deceptive. How far removed it
is from the real is illustrated by the example of the three beds.[5] The
bed that the poet presents in a poem is like a painting of a bed in
being an image of a bed, an imitation of the bed that is a product of
the carpenter's art. But the carpenter's bed is itself also an imitation
inasmuch as it is made to conform to the idea of bed by which all
beds are beds. This last bed, the archetype of all beds, is declared to
be the work of God, and its construction presumably followed
mathematical forms, since we are told in the *Timaeus* that the world
itself was patterned after the mathematicals, especially the regular
solids.[6] The ideal bed, the mathematical form that it integrates, and

the material bed on which men sleep are all more real than the poetic image of a bed, which presupposes all the others. Poetic construction is thus at three removes from the really real and, hence, cannot possibly provide more than a semblance of the truth.[7]

What is worse, poetic construction is a lying and deceiving imitation. Not only do poets not know the true nature of the things that they write about, but they always prefer to write about the more exciting and passionate things, since these more readily move and please their audience. In thus inciting and playing upon the emotions, the poet, Plato charged, "awakens and nourishes and strengthens the feelings and impairs the reason . . . for he indulges the irrational nature which has no discernment."[8]

In order to remove the sting from Plato's criticism, it is sometimes urged that it misses the mark by overlooking the poem as a linguistic structure and concentrating exclusively upon the extralinguistic object that is imitated. For Plato, however, this appeal to language would do little to alter the situation, since he maintained that language itself is at best only an imitation and, ultimately, always inadequate for grasping and expressing the truth. Writing in his *Seventh Letter* why no written exposition of his philosophy was possible, he distinguished five elements that enter into true knowledge: words, their meanings, the material images words denote, the knowledge in the soul, and the truth known. To take a circle as an example, there is first "that very word which we just uttered. The second thing is its meaning . . . as that which has the distance from its circumference to its center everywhere equal. Third comes that which is drawn and rubbed out again, or turned on a lathe and broken up—none of which can happen to the circle itself. Fourth comes knowledge, intelligence, and right opinion about these things . . . of which intelligence comes closest in kinship and likeness to the fifth," which is truth itself.[9] Fitting these stages to the divided line, the first two that represent language will fall on the lowest segment, standing for images, where poetry also falls. Thus emphasizing poetry as a linguistic structure will not affect its place on the scale of knowledge. It remains in the lowest place.

Since the highest truth is ineffable, poetry and language are necessarily inadequate. "It does not admit of exposition like other branches of knowledge," he wrote. "After much converse about the matter itself and a life lived together, suddenly a light, as it were, is kindled in one soul by a flame that leaps to it from another and thereafter sustains itself."[10] Thus the highest and best knowledge of the highest and best is not only a vision such as the intuition of beauty that comes at the top of the ladder of love in the *Symposium* or the sight of the good described in the *Republic*, but it is also a life lived by and of itself as well as with others.[11]

To illustrate the various elements in the Platonic ideal, it is helpful to consider how the various parts of the divided line can serve to show the different ways in which the *Republic* itself can be read. As a text, it consists of a series of marks on a collection of writing materials, which are themselves imitations of words, although they do not actually function as such until their meaning is grasped. The marks and their meanings, as we read them, then provide us with an imitation, a verbal image or icon, of a conversation that Socrates had with some of his friends about justice and the good life. It is literally an imitation in words of the kind of conversation that Socrates might have had, but, as Aristotle pointed out, we have no name for an "imitated conversation."[12] For any adequate reading of the dialogue, some account must be taken of its dramatic structure, the characteristics of its *dramatis personae*, the significance of their interventions in the course of the dialogue, as well as the overall "plot" of the intellectual and dramatic discourse. But after we have done all that and have come to some understanding of what the dialogue has to tell us about justice, we will still have at most only an opinion about justice, namely, of what it is said to be in the *Republic*. To begin to think for ourselves about justice, the discourse must puzzle us, as it did Thrasymachus in book one, and encourage us to seek further as it did Glaucon and Adeimantus in the second book, until we take its account of justice as a model to follow in our own pursuit of justice, reasoning from our assumptions until we know them well enough to put to the test the presuppositions not only of Plato and of others, but also our own, and not only in thought, but also in practice, in our individual spiritual life as well as in our social relations; then we can move, dialectically, as Plato would say, from ideas, through ideas, until we are reaching out toward the idea of justice itself—beyond the reach of any book, and beyond even the reach of language, for that matter. *The Republic* provides a verbal imitation or image of a discourse about justice—the first stage. It can be read and understood as expounding as a second stage a theory about justice. It can be used as a third stage to aid us in our own thinking about justice as we reason about what justice is and test models of it by following up the conclusions to which those widely lead. Finally, we can criticize our basic assumptions about justice at the same time that we endeavor to live and act accordingly in the hope of knowing and living justice as it is in itself.

Against Plato, or against this interpretation of his thought, it might be argued that it was at least inconsistent of him to devote so much of his life to writing when he held such a low opinion of language. T. E. Hulme once observed that art would be useless "could reality come into direct contact with sense and consciousness,"[13] a statement that would seem to sum up Plato's position regarding poetry. But to conclude so would be overly hasty. Both St. Augustine and St. John of the Cross believed that union with God is possible in this life; yet neither gave up writing, and the latter even wrote poetry. The possibility of a knowledge that is ineffable does not imply its actuality. Recourse to words may be needed, by ourselves no less than others; in order to point the way to such knowledge. After all, language is needed if only to warn of the inadequacies and dangers of language. It was in writing that Plato complained of the shortcomings of writing: it is one with paintings, poems, and speeches, in that "if you ask them a question, they preserve a solemn silence."[14] It is a failing of words, especially in their written form, that they will stop and frustrate inquiry rather than encourage and promote it.

> Nobler far is the serious pursuit of the dialectician, who, finding a congenial soul, by the help of science, sows and plants therein words which are able to help themselves and him who planted them, and are not unfruitful, but have in them a seed which others brought up in different soils render immortal, making the possessors of it happy to the utmost extent of human happiness.[15]

For this reason Plato preferred the dialogue above all other forms of writing, since it is an image and imitation of dialectical activity.

Nonetheless, there still remains a fundamental irony in Plato's attitude toward poetry. Although he criticized it harshly and banned poets from his ideal republic, he is still the most poetic of the great philosophers, master of the written word and of the dramatic form of the dialogue, maker of images, metaphors, analogies, and myths. So too, although he extolled the value of mathematical reasoning, he refused to confine his attention, interests, and hopes within the limit of the cognitive conceptual order. The wisdom that he sought and expounded as an ideal of human life had to satisfy the will and heart as well as the intellect. Hence, although he criticized poetry for sacrificing idea and thought to image and feeling, in his own practice he refused to give up either image or feeling. His theory and practice thus raises in a way that is unique the issues regarding the relation between image and idea and between feeling and thought,

issues that still remain with us, and to the consideration of which I
now turn.

Two Kinds of Language Use

Plato, of course, is not the only philosopher to be critical of words
and images. In fact, Plato's fellow philosophers have at times turned
the criticism against him. Aristotle, for example, parted company with
his master regarding the use of metaphor in philosophy and declared
that there was no place for it in scientific demonstration.[16] Developing
the same point, Thomas Aquinas declared: "To argue from various
similitudes and representations is proper to poetry," but poetry is
ranked as "the lowest form of learning [infima doctrina]."[17] Plato held
the same opinion, as we have just seen, but Thomas turned the charge
against Plato, claiming that his method was bad for philosophy in that
he "everywhere teaches by figures and symbols, and means by his
words something different from what they say."[18] Thomas made the
same criticism of the theologia symbolica of the Pseudo-Dionysius in
words that also apply to Augustine's work. That method is to be
avoided, he wrote, because "tropes, i.e., metaphorical language, provides no basis for argument; symbolic theology is non argumentativa,"
whereas, as we have seen, theology according to his ideal should be
eminently argumentativa.[19]

Aristotle and Thomas, at least in principle, wanted nothing to do
with metaphor. Yet Plato and Augustine were equally emphatic in their
resort to metaphor. Many more instances of this same opposition could
be cited, but these are enough to raise the question: What are we to
make of such an extreme opposition? What basis or sense is there to it?
Why should there be such a difference and conflict of opinion over the
value of metaphor? This is not the place for an extended analysis of
metaphor. Nor is there any need. If we attend to only the obvious
features of metaphor, we can see why different evaluations are given of
it.

A metaphor involves a juxtaposition or comparison of two or more
items. Plato, as we have seen, compared poetry to painting—ut pictura
poesis, as Horace said.[20] We are asked to think of a poem as a picture
and to see its words as somehow presenting an image for us in a way
that words in nonpoetic uses do not; and, as a picture is sometimes
worth a thousand words, so a poem may somehow present something
much more vividly than words ordinarily do. Since Plato wanted us to
believe that poetry is an imitation or image of something else, it obvi-

ously served his purpose to compare a poem to a picture, since the comparison fortified and compounded his claim about poetry by its reference to painting.

The advantages of such a procedure are obvious, especially when we are attempting to understand something that is obscure or removed from our ordinary experience. The difficult and obscure can be illuminated by comparison with something that is better known, and it may call our attention to something that we had not noticed before, or that we had forgotten or overlooked because it had become so familiar.

Metaphor implies that the two items brought together are somehow alike or can be considered as being alike in some respect. But no two things are ever completely alike: any metaphor always limps. For some purposes the difference between the two, i.e., the location of the limp, may be more important than the similarity. This is especially true of logical argument, since formal validity depends upon singleness of meaning and purpose. Metaphor declares: A *is like* B. But this will not suffice for logic, which demands nothing less than A *is* B. To argue validly from A *is* B and B *is* C to A *is* C, the meaning of the terms must remain the same. It will not hold that if A *is like* B and B *is like* C, then A *is like* C. For A may be like B only in respect to B_1 whereas B is like C only with respect to B_2, and hence there is no basis for concluding anything about the relation of A to C.

Thus we have located one reason for a difference in attitude toward metaphor. What is good for poetry can be a trap for formal logic. The difference, even opposition, between the two attitudes is based on the different uses or purposes for which language is employed. The poetic use is not the logical use, and language functions differently in the two cases. In fact, it has been claimed that these two represent the two extremes among the many uses of language. The contrasting characteristics of the two have been described in many ways, as illustrated in the accompanying table.

Two Kinds of Language[21]

poetic	scientific
metaphorical	literal
ambiguous	unambiguous
analogical	univocal
many-meaning	single-meaning
mysterious, inexplicable	plain, explicable
obscure	clear

indefinite	definite
vague	precise
nontechnical	technical
extra- or non-logical	logical
nonargumentative	argumentative
nonconceptual	conceptual
nonreferential	referential
nonpropositional	propositional
nonverifiable	verifiable
expressive	descriptive or designative
imaginative	nonimaginative
contextual	noncontextual
presentative or intuitive	discursive
concrete	abstract
synthetic	analytic
organic	mechanical or logical
subjective	objective
uniting subject-and-object	separating object from subject
personal	impersonal
aesthetic	nonaesthetic
language for its own sake	language for communicating
unique, untranslatable	translatable

There is admittedly something faintly ridiculous, if not actually misleading, in attempting to capture the distinctive features of the poetic and logical (or scientific) uses of language by drawing up a list of contraries. Such a list tends to exaggerate the differences between the two and to draw boundaries where often none can be drawn. The Platonic writings, for example, straddle both columns. Although Plato's criticism of poetry would appear to express a preference for the kind of language represented by the second column, his actual practice has many of the features listed in the first. Yet the very fact that Plato's writing straddles both columns can also serve to justify drawing up such a list. For in the eyes of Aristotle or Thomas, that very fact indicates why the Platonic method is a bad one for philosophy. According to their ideal, philosophy should be done in the kind of language characterized by the second column and abstain from that of the first. The lists thus enable us to identify two different ideals of philosophy. But, more than that, they also serve to indicate the basis for a still greater conflict of cultural ideals. They provide one way of distinguishing not only the Aristotelian way of philosophy from that of Plato, but also the Thomistic and scholastice form of theology from the

Augustinian and patristic form, and, still more generally, the scientific from the literary ideal of intellectual culture.

Besides this issue regarding language, and indeed already implicit in it, there is also an issue regarding the relation between feeling and thought, which demands attention before proceeding further with regard to language and poetry.

Feeling and Thought

If feeling can be an obstacle and hindrance to thought, as Plato charged, feeling must be distinct in some way from thought. Yet sometimes they are not clearly and definitely distinguished from one another. William James, in seeking for a generic term that would cover "mental states at large, irrespective of their kind," finally narrowed his choice down to "either FEELING or THOUGHT," before he settled upon the latter.[22] More recently, Susanne Langer has posed the same question and decided in favor of "feeling," for any intraorganic process of which one is aware: "an appearance which organic functions have only for the organism in which they occur, if they have it at all."[23] Thinking is then taken as only a very complex form of feeling with the result that, if thinking can be opposed to feeling at all, it is only as one feeling is opposed to another.

Yet it cannot be denied that in our ordinary experience we speak frequently of feeling being opposed to thought, since it is a fact that our feelings do sometimes get in the way of thinking. The objection sometimes urged against the sexual passion is that it monopolizes attention to the exclusion of all else. It is also a fact that some uses of language attempt to avoid as much as possible any appeal to feeling or involvement with it, whereas other uses do all they can to arouse and play upon the emotions. This can be seen from several of the items in our table of contraries. Objectivity and impersonality are ideals of science, while subjectivity and concern for what is happening to the person are characteristic of poetry. Thus Neurath, for example, in adverting to the question of the value of the emotions in comparison with science, declared that science could have nothing to say on such a subject.[24] But if this extreme would exclude emotion entirely from science, the other one would identify poetry, and indeed all art, exclusively with the emotions. John Stuart Mill is a good representative of this position, and the expression he gave to it is especially pertinent to our concern in that he also attempted to show where poetry and art are to be located on the map of learning.

The great value of poetry, according to Mill, lies in the education of the feelings and cultivation of the sentiments that it can provide. Mill spoke from his own personal experience. After an excessively rationalistic education, based on the principles of Bentham's utilitariansim, he suffered a nervous breakdown at the age of twenty, the recovery from which he attributed in large part to the reading of poetry. His previous education had been seriously deficient, he concluded, in its complete neglect of the aesthetic order, and, as a result, he had been stunted and crippled in the affective and emotional side of his life.

In conceiving of poetry as essentially the expression and representation of the emotions, Mill did not restrict it to verbal and linguistic utterance, but extended it to include music, painting, sculpture, and all the fine arts. Poetry is thus equated with the aesthetic order, considered as correlative with the intellectual and moral sides of human life and "not less needful to the completeness of the human being."[25]

Poetry, however, is not mere emotion without thought and knowledge. In poetry, no less than in science, the mind is at work, but it is working in a different way. Knowing poetically, according to Mill, is knowing through the emotions. Poets, he wrote, "are so constituted that emotions are the links of association by which their ideas, both sensuous and spiritual, are connected together."[26] Poets, in this respect, are not unique, except in the degree to which they think through their emotions. Mill pointed out that the "capacity of strong feeling which is supposed necessarily to disturb the judgment is also the material out of which all motives are made—the motives, consequently, which lead human beings to the pursuit of truth" through science as well as to the making of poems.[27] Feeling, Mill was claiming, provides the ground of all motivation in all of us. But while feeling may motivate the scientist, when he comes to *do* science and especially in communicating his results, he endeavors to leave feeling behind and attend purely to the demands of thought. Not so the poet. His thinking, Mill claimed, continues to be done through the emotions: "The poetry of a poet is Feeling itself, employing Thought only as the medium of its expression."[28] The poet possesses, in Wordsworth's phrase, "the feeling intellect."[29] It is not surprising then that the poet's language has a character and emphasis that is strongly affective.

It makes good sense to claim that feeling provides a motive for thought. The stronger the interest and attention that we bring to the activity of knowing, the easier and better we know. The art of teaching, as any teacher knows, demands more than a knowledge of subject matter, since to communicate it successfully, he has also to motivate and delight the student so as to bring him to the task of learning. Feeling obviously can be an aid to thought, but is there such a thing as thinking and knowing through feeling? That, certainly, is a much larger claim.

It is significant that the Angelic Doctor would agree with the saint of rationalism, as Mill has been called, in maintaining that there is a way of knowing through feeling that is distinct from conceptual knowledge. St. Thomas described this knowledge in various ways. In fact, from his works it is possible to compile a list of contrasting terms describing the two kinds of knowledge that corresponds to the list of terms drawn up for the two uses of language.[30] Thus one kind of knowledge is variously described as affective, experiential, by way of connaturality, inclination, and the will, through love and virtue from the depths of the self, without discourse. Contrasted with this there is a knowledge that is speculative, by way of reason, rational inquiry, and the intellect, through study and teaching that is discursive and ratiocinative. This series of terms is obviously similar to our previous one. Yet Thomas, in making these distinctions, was writing not about the difference between poetry and science, but about different ways of possessing moral and theological knowledge.

We have two different ways of judging according to Thomas. One is "by way of inclination," and it is thus that the virtuous man "judges rightly of what concerns that virtue by his very inclination towards it." Without recourse to rational deliberation and the weighing of pros and cons, but merely from the way he feels, the man who is temperate, courageous, just, and prudent knows in any given case the virtuous thing to do. Another way of judging is provided by rational knowledge, as is seen from the fact that "a man who knows moral science can judge rightly about the virtuous act even though he does not have the virtue." Thus a judge, not particularly just in his own acts, might still be able to render a just decision in a given case from his knowledge of the law and its applications. The same distinction holds with regard to knowledge of divine things according to Thomas: "The first way of judging about divine things pertains to the wisdom that is included as one of the gifts of the Holy Spirit" and is taught "not by mere learning, but by suffering divine things."[31] This way of knowing is said to be based on love and to consist in an experiential knowledge (*experimentalem notitiam*). For this reason, according to an etymology that mediaeval authors were fond of, *sapientia* ("wisdom") is so called because it is a *sapida scientia* ("a savorous science").[32]

Whether or not there is a "feeling intellect" and an affective knowledge depends on whether there is such a thing as knowledge in and through love. No one would deny that love can supply a motivating factor for study that results in a closer, more detailed knowledge. The question at issue is whether love itself can be cognitively revealing. In describing this knowledge as connatural and achieved in the depths of the self through affinity, Thomas was claiming, in effect, that love achieves a closer union with its object and in that union sees and knows more than speculative reason alone can. The union through love and affection reaches to the individual as a unique individual, whereas the speculative, conceptualizing intellect of science is interested in the individual only as an instance of a general type. Love is not only directed toward the object in all its unique singularity, but it also makes the lover like the loved, "connatures" him to it.

Knowledge through connaturality is taken by Maritain as the common link that binds together moral knowledge, mystical experience (supernatural as well as natural) and art and poetry.[33] In all three there is

> an obscure knowledge through inclination—born in the preconscious of the spirit—in which the world is known *in* and *through* the subjectivity, grasped both together and inseparably by means of an emotion become intentional and intuitive. Such knowledge is utterly different from what we ordinarily call knowledge, it is more experience than knowledge. It is neither conceptual nor conceptualizable; it is ineffable in itself. . . . But precisely because it is not abstractive nor rational, it has no intelligible boundaries, and expands, as it were, to the infinite.[34]

Maritain also suggested that connatural knowledge is not confined within these regions. "It can come into play everywhere—in science, philosophy, big business, revolution, religion, sanctity, or imposture," wherever, in short, the power of discovery manifests itself.[35] Thus connatural knowledge has in the thought of Maritain much the same function as the creative imagination in Shelley's *Defence of Poetry*. It is the creative principle in man, the source and inspiration of discovery, invention, creation in any order—"not like reasoning, a power to be exerted according to the determination of the will," but, in Shelley's words, a power that "arises from within, like the color of a flower which fades and changes as it is developed, and the conscious portions of our natures are unprophetic either of its approach or its departure."[36] Shelley and Maritain differ in their psychologies, but Maritain is certainly right in refusing to identify the power with imagination to the exclusion of intellect. The intellect is at work here just as it is in science, but in a different way. In any case, as St. Thomas once observed, it is not the intellect that knows, but man through the intellect, and the same holds true of man's other powers.[37]

The Defense of Poetry

At this point poetry might enter an objection, not only on its own behalf, but on that of all the fine arts. If poetry is so extended and generalized in scope as to become a way of knowing found at work in every region of human life, it has ceased to possess a home of its own and has lost its especial claim upon the aesthetic order. Yet it is certainly here that it bases its claim to fame and right to autonomy. Poetry as a verbal art makes a linguistic structure comparable to the structures produced by the other arts that can be known, enjoyed, and contemplated entirely for itself; it is an intrinsic good that, in this sense, can be said to exist for itself. It may provide knowledge, and knowledge that is of a special kind; it may also be a means of educating the emotions. But in addition it is something that is worth considering for itself, an object of art that is a source of joy that demands and merits admiration and praise for its own sake.

The importance of poetry as making has been emphasized at least since Aristotle seized upon that feature in his defense of poetry against Plato's criticism of it. It is the point underlying the claim that "A poem should not mean / But be."[38] The significance and import of the distinction is illuminatingly explained by an example that Valery gave in his essay, "Poetry and Abstract Thought." One man asks another for a light for his cigarette, and his request is granted. With that his words have accomplished their purpose; they have died and are forgotten. The words of a poem refuse to die in this sense; they have a concrete form that "asserts itself and makes itself, as it were, respected; and not only remarked and respected, but desired and therefore repeated." Language can thus "produce effects of two quite different kinds. One of them tends to bring about the complete negation of language . . . . Language is transformed into nonlanguage." But in its poetic use language remains language but refuses to die, continuing to live a life of its own. Between the two uses there is all the difference that there is between walking and dancing.[39]

What then are we to say in response to Plato's criticism? that he was just wrong and misconceived the nature of poetry? It might seem so, since the defense of poetry has seized upon the particulars of his criticism and argued that they are not failings, but virtues. Poetry, so goes the defense, should be praised and honored, not criticized, for its use of images, its concern with the emotions, and its delight in language for its own sake. Yet such an abrupt dismissal may be too quick and mistake the object of Plato's criticism. Perhaps his attack was directed not so much against the poets for their craft as against the claim that poetry constitutes the highest knowledge and the paradigm of all knowledge.

It has been argued, notably by Professor E. A. Havelock, that Plato was the first to state the case for a literate culture and to celebrate its rise as one based upon abstract conceptualization, distinguishing diverse intellectual enterprises expressed in a prose of ideas that can be preserved in books. His criticism of Homer is to be taken seriously and literally inasmuch as the epic poet represented and summed up in his work all the preliterate culture of the previous "oral-aural" society in which the epic poetry of the image-makers was the "preserved communication" of the entire cultural inheritance.[40] So understood, the quarrel between philosophy and poetry recorded by Plato reflects a conflict between cultures as ways of life as much as, if not more than it does a conflict of intellectual ideals. Poetry in a preliterate society can enjoy a centrality of position and power such as it can never attain in a literate culture. The quarrel then is to be seen as nothing less than a power struggle for the control of society, a struggle that can end only with the disappearance of the loser.

By this accounting, the growth and development of a literate society, completely replacing the old preliterate culture, should be counted as a victory for Plato and philosophy (including under this term science as well). Yet, as we have seen from our consideration of the literary ideal, rhetoric and poetry continued to dominate all of ancient classical culture, even to the extent of attacking philosophy for its pretentions. Of course, the literary culture was bookish and, hence, literate, not exclusively "oral," as in a previous age. Yet, as we also saw, it continued to place great importance upon the value and power of the spoken word. Furthermore, even under a literate form, poetry continued to exercise its function of image-making, working through the emotions in an affective way that is nonconceptualizable and achieving expression only in and through the poem itself. The poetic mind can carry on in a literate society as well as in an oral culture. The reasons for the quarrel, the issues on which it was based, have not disappeared then with the coming of a literate culture. Poetry and art on the one side and philosophy and science on the other still retain the differences to which Plato called attention.

Does it follow then that conflict between the two sides is inevitable? Not necessarily. Considering again the language characteristic of each (as illustrated in the table on contraries), we can admit the differences and even allow that one kind may be more useful for some purposes than for others. Yet we have not seen any reason for holding that one is the only correct and legitimate way of using language. Indeed, tabulating kinds of language by contraries would be badly misleading if it led one to believe that any use of language is ever purely and solely of one kind: ever purely cognitive or purely noncognitive, designative or expressive, communicative or self-sufficient. Any linguistic utterance constitutes an entity that can be considered for itself apart from what it communicates. If of sufficient complexity, it is also expressive of an attitude and may even reveal personal traits of the speaker, although its main purpose may be to function purely as a means of communication without calling attention to itself or its speaker. So too, any linguistic utterance is always something more than a singular entity. No matter how much it may aspire to self-sufficiency and to call attention to nothing but itself, without communicating anything beyond itself, it consists of words with meanings, and meanings transcend the utterance as a singular entity. Even when it is clear that the linguistic utterance is intended to serve only one purpose, there is nothing to prevent it from being used in a very different way. So Newton's laws, for example, surely in intent cognitive and scientific, can be read musically if we are to believe Whitehead, who once suggested that they occasionally be sung as a celebration of the triumph of science.[41]

The various functions or kinds of language can be looked upon as constituting a continuum that stretches from one extreme represented by the poetic use to the scientific use at the other extreme, with many other functions in between these two. Any use of language may focus more upon one part of the continuum than upon another, but the continuum is never broken in the sense that no language use is ever confined solely to one function. This feature of language has led W. T. Jones (to whom I owe the illustration) to claim that it provides a basis for reconciliation between the humanities and the sciences, since both fall within the same continuum, even though one prefers one part over another.[42] His suggestion is a good one, and one that I shall pursue in more detail later on. Yet it is a fact that poetry and philosophy (and their analogues) do come into conflict. Why, if there is nothing in the activities themselves to make conflict inevitable, should it continue to arise? This question is an important one for our enterprise, indeed crucially so, but before facing it I should first consider in some detail some of the other major issues that have given rise to a conflict of cultural ideals.

CHAPTER 5: The Battle of the Seven Arts

The conflict of cultural ideals takes different forms. A form that was especially prevalent during the Middle Ages is that of a battle among the arts. A poem written in old French about 1240 by an otherwise unknown trouvère, Henri d'Andeli, bears the title, "La Bataille des VII Arts," and presents an account of a conflict among the liberal arts in which the forces led by Logic put to rout those led by Grammar.[1] At issue is the question whether logic or grammar is to have the position of primacy among the arts. Behind this question lurks the larger one regarding the relation among the arts and how they are to be ordered with respect to one another. *"Ordo artium"* is, in fact, the title of another mediaeval poem in Latin, dating from the late twelfth century, that deals with the problem of the proper order to be observed among the arts when they are considered as preparatory to theology.[2]

Disputes among the arts are not unique to the Middle Ages, especially when *art* can be understood so broadly as to include any kind of learning.[3] The Renaissance witnessed disputes among the various fine arts, especially the claim of painting to be superior to music and poetry.[4] Kant wrote a little work on the strife among the university faculties.[5] In our own day the controversy over the two cultures also in certain respects involves a battle of the arts. The mediaeval version, however, is unique in at least two respects: it concerns the liberal arts conceived of as limited to a small number considered to be of unique importance for all of learning, and it raises the question of hierarchy within that world in its claim that theology is the queen of the sciences. The latter question pertains to consideration of the classification of the sciences, a subject that will be taken up in chapter eight. The present chapter will consider the question of the order among the arts and, beyond that, the wider issue of the relation between faith and reason.

The Order among the Liberal Arts

The arts that appear in the two mediaeval poems are the liberal arts that we have already encountered in considering the classical literary ideal as constituting the base of the program of preparatory culture, the *enkuklios paideia*.[6] The number of the arts and especially the personified form in which they were familiar to mediaeval writers derived for the most part from the work of the fifth-century North African writer, Martianus Capella, entitled *The Marriage of Mercury and Philology*. This is a huge work, consisting of nine books, seven of which are elementary textbooks of the seven liberal arts, presented in the following order: Grammar, Dialectic, Rhetoric, Geometry, Arithmetic, Astronomy, Harmonics (*Musica*). Each book is an elementary school textbook of not very high quality, and, in fact, has been described as bearing "comparison with a term paper written by a high school senior of good standing who has a knack of turning out papers with a minimum of effort."[7] The other two books, which introduce the work, written in some of the most difficult Latin ever written, present a highly elaborated allegorical account of the marriage of between Mercury and Philology. The first book tells of Mercury's efforts to find a wife, of the recommendation to him by both Apollo and Virtus of the maiden Philology, and of the final ratification marriage to her by the council of the gods on Olympus. The second book describes the preparation of Philology, a mortal maid, for marriage with the god, of her journey to heaven, and of the marriage itself, at which she receives as a present from her bridegroom seven fair handmaids, the seven arts. Such is the plot, but it is greatly embellished with much bizarre and curious lore.

The description of the arts as women, their characteristic features and various accounterments, determined the iconography of the liberal arts for both the Middle Ages and the Renaissance.[8] They are slaves of Mercury and are presented to Philology to serve her as handmaids. The conception of the arts and their function and relation is thus made to depend upon the interpretation of the allegorical marriage between the two principals.

Concerning Mercury, we are told that in his search for a wife, he at first thought of Sophia, Mantice, or Psyche as a possible mate, but turned his attention elsewhere upon learning that each was already attached to another god.[9] His initial preference for these ladies tells us something about his character, and this impression is strengthened when we learn that the *doctissima virgo* Philology had been responsible for their education. From this much we know that Mercury is attracted to wisdom (Sophia), prophecy (Mantice), and the soul (Psyche). He is also amenable to virtue, since it was upon the advice of Virtus that he sought out Apollo. His character is described still more explicitly in the speech delivered by Jupiter to the council of gods summoned to ratify the marriage. Mercury is lauded as the interpreter of his mind (*interpres meae mentis*) and his very word (*sermo*).[10] From this it would appear that

Mercury is to be identified with the *logos*. In fact, this principle, common to Stoic and Neo-Platonic philosophy, was frequently identified with Mercury or Hermes in late antiquity.[11] Certainly, it is appropriate that the *logos* should be joined in union with *love-of-the-logos* (*Philo +logia*).

We first hear about Philology from Apollo's highly laudatory description of her as a most learned maid (*doctissima virgo*) to whom many great ladies are indebted for their accomplishments. On her first appearance, she is engaged in the vigil before her wedding day figuring out the numerological omen for her marriage and identifying Mercury with the Egyptian god Thoth, the inventor of letters and of the arts.[12] The Muses sing her praises as their friend and the head of the arts, more learned even than Mercury: "*Est doctus ille divum, / Sed Doctior puella.*"[13] More evidence of her learning appears when, on taking the potion of immortality to prepare for the journey, she pours forth all manner of books, which the Arts, Disciplines, and even the Muses hasten to gather upon for their own use.[14] Philology's outstanding features are her learning, her diligent application to inquiry, and, upon her marriage, her possession of the seven arts.

Mediaeval readers of Martianus made him a disciple of Cicero, despite his far-from-Ciceronian style, and found in his allegory a statement of the Ciceronian ideal of learning. That ideal, as we have seen, consisted in the union of eloquence and wisdom as realized in the person of the *doctus orator*,[15] and encapsulated in the expression *littarae atque doctrinae*.[16] According to the ninth-century writer Scotus Erigena, no reader of Martianus could deny that he was a disciple of Cicero, since his work pictures the marriage of Mercury as *facundia sermonis* ("eloquence of word") with Philology as *studium rationis* ("work of reason").[17] John of Salisbury, writing in the twelfth century in a style far closer to Cicero's than that of Martianus, identified Mercury with eloquence, Philology with love of truth, and their marriage with the sweet and fruitful union of reason and word, to which he applied the biblical injunction that no man should separate what God has joined together, since Philology without Mercury is barren and childless.[18]

This interpretation of the allegory would appear to be neither forced nor farfetched. Mercury is an obvious choice to represent *litterae* and eloquence, since he was widely acclaimed in antiquity as the god of eloquence and the inventor of letters. As *logos*, he fits the role even better as the epitome of expression, a point that is further emphasized by the fact that he had formerly been married to Facundia "copiousness of speech"), who was also a student of Philology.[19] All the features attributed to Philology as the *doctissima virgo* fit her to represent *doctrinae* ("learning"). Both Mercury and Philology appear in the allegory not for themselves alone, but primarily for the celebration of their marriage, which can accordingly be read as the union of letters and learning, of eloquence and wisdom, that constitute the Ciceronian ideal. The arts then appear as serving maids because they are intended to serve as means to the ideal as an end. They are referred to by Martianus as *disciplinae cyclicae*, words that reflect their greek name of *enkuklios paideia* and corresponding to the Ciceronian expression *puerilis institutio*.[20]

The close interconnection among the arts is indicated by the fact that they are represented as sisters. Martianus did not distinguish any subgroups within the seven as later mediaeval writers did in grouping the three verbal arts together in the trivium and the four mathematical arts in the quadrivium. Nor is any one of them singled out as holding a place of preeminence, although Grammar is said to be the oldest and Rhetoric is pictured as deeply impressing the divine congress by her familiarity with Pallas and Mercury. In Martianus's own writing there is no doubt that rhetoric is the most important. In fact, one of his closest students has written that Mercury in the book, who was once "the trickster god of Italian market places . . . is once again reduced to a bag of tricks—the rhetorical arts."[21]

The representation of the arts of learning as handmaids of another, and hence not independent, was not original with Martianus. According to the second-century writer Diogenes Laertius, Aristippus (ca. 435–350 B.C.) likened the arts in relation to philosophy as handmaids to Penelope.[22] St. Clement of Alexandria (died ca. 214) used the same figure in subordinating "the encyclical branches of learning" to the study of wisdom, but then identified wisdom with God, thus making "wisdom the queen of philosophy as philosophy is of the preparatory culture.[23] His position is thus identical with that of Augustine.

In the twelfth-century poem entitled *"Ordo Artium,"* the seven arts again appear as servant maids, but they also have an added responsibility, as doorkeeper to Theology, of deciding who is to be admitted to her presence. As is indicated by the title, the poem is expressly concerned with the relation of the arts to one another and to theology. Grammar enjoys the place of priority as the oldest and "the nurse of the arts." She bears with her the tools of the art of weaving (*ars textoria*), since it is her task to weave coverings for her sisters, the books that she makes being the clothes of the arts.[24]

The importance of Grammar emerges still more clearly from an argument that Rhetoric has with Theology. Speaking for her sisters as well as herself, Rhetoric complains to their mistress Theology that the honor of liberal studies has so deteriorated that they have been compelled to prostitute themselves in order to survive. She declares that men are being admitted to the presence of Theology before they have followed the ways of the trivium and quadrivium and while completely ignorant of the arts. For this sad state of affairs, Rhetoric places the blame directly upon Theology herself.[25] Theology, in answer, expresses amazement at the charge and claims that the fault is not hers, but theirs; for they are her doorkeepers, and it is their responsibility to determine who is to be admitted. She agrees that her presence has been profaned by a crowd of vulgarians, and complains that "the scale of the disciplines has been overturned," with the result that the rude and untrained are attempting to theologize. But the remedy, she says, is clear. The need is for the proper order of knowledge and learning: first, poetry to provide the rules of grammar; then logic to furnish arms for disputation; then rhetoric for flowers of ornament; and finally the mathematical arts to provide certainty.[26]

The question of the proper order to be observed among the arts is also prominent in the poem of Henri d'Andeli, written perhaps two generations after the *"Ordo Artium."*[27] Indeed, the situation has worsened, since the arts are now pictured as engaged in open battle. Logic is accused of being the cause of the conflict. She is charged with attacking the value of Grammar and stealing her followers until "every boy runs her course ere he has passed his fifteenth year."[28] Logic is described as dominating the whole trivium and quadrivium, having even won to her side a "perverse Grammar" and a corrupt Rhetoric.[29] Even Theology, "Madame la Haute Science," although said not to be interested in the conflict, is described as "holding disputations in the schools, leaving the right learning, and trumpeting philosophy."[30]

In this situation Grammar decided that she had no course open except to wage battle. She raised her banner outside Orléans and assembled her army, consisting of the ancient grammarians Priscian and Donatus as well as Martianus Capella, the ancient classical authors Homer, Virgil, Horace, Ovid, Terence, Martial, Persius, Juvenal, Seneca, Lucan, Statius, and numerous early Christian and mediaeval Latin poets. Preparing to meet the attack, Logic marshaled her forces in Paris, consisting of all the trivium and the quadrivium, Philosophy with Aristotle and his numerous books, Plato, Socrates, Porphyry, Boethius, Macrobius, and Gilbert de la Porrée, Canon and Civil Law with their books, Medicine and Surgery represented by Hippocrates, Galen, and a number of Parisian physicians, as well as Necromancy and Astrology.

The two forces march forth, and battle is joined outside Paris. Although the poet declared that it was a great loss and a great pity that the two were at odds and could not agree about learning, his own sympathies were clearly with Grammar.[31] He noted that Logic, like Astronomy, loves lofty things, whereas Grammar loves the fountains, but then he criticized Logic for trying to teach her students to fly before they were able to walk.[32] Although many blows were struck by both sides, Grammar is defeated and forced to flee, her authors scatter and desert, and Logic is left victorious. But although Logic was clearly the victor, the poet is confident that her victory will not be a lasting one and prophesies that the succeeding generation will find Grammar restored to her place of preeminence.[33]

The poet was premature in anticipating the return of the literary ideal to supremacy within a generation. It is true that Petrarch, often considered in his own day as well as now the first of the humanists, was born (1304), within two generations and the humanists' program of *studia humanitatis* marked a revival of the literary ideal. Yet its triumphant return to the universities did not occur for some centuries. The literary revival took place, for the most part, outside of the universities, where the arts faculties which controlled the universities remained under the dominance of logic.[34]

The theoretical basis for the primacy of logic among the arts as the *ars artium* was sketched by Thomas Aquinas in the introduction of his commentary on one of the logical works of Aristotle. Logic, he wrote, is rightly called the art of arts, since it is the art that directs reason itself, and reason is the source of all the arts. Truth is always the aim of reason, but it cannot always be achieved with the same degree of certitude. The different degrees of certitude that can be reached provided Thomas with a basis for distinguishing and ranking the various arts. First, and at the top, there is the certitude of science, which is attained by means of judicative logic, or logic *tout court*. Next is the stage of belief or opinion, which is characterized by the high degree of probability that can be achieved by dialectic with its probable arguments. When the most that can be achieved is a suspicion that favors one side of an argument over another, we are in the sphere of rhetoric. Poetry comes at the bottom, since the degree of certitude that it can achieve amounts at most to a conjecture based on a representation.[35]

This scheme, in effect, amounts to a reduction of all the seven arts to logic. All the mathematical arts, in aiming at the certitude of science, fall under the rule of judicative logic. Grammar, understood as literature, was considered, as we have seen from the *"Ordo Artium,"* to consist chiefly in reading the poets, and hence falls under poetry at the bottom. The other part of grammar as the art of reading and writing is presumably propaedeutic to all.

Thomas, like Plato, thus placed poetry and the verbal arts at the bottom as the lowest form of learning (*infima doctrina*).[36] This interpretation of them may not be as disparaging as it first appears. If the arts are considered with respect to their teachability, there is much truth to the claim that mathematics is more teachable than poetry, especially insofar as the teachable implies the sayable. A mathematical demonstration within an axiomatized system approaches the limit of saying all that can and need be said, of exhaustively stating all its meaning. A poem, on the other hand, approaches the other extreme of meaning more than can ever be said; in fact, to suppose that its meaning can be completely explicated has been branded by literary criticism as the heresy of paraphrase.[37]

Before concluding this account of the mediaeval battle of the arts, we should note that the mathematical arts of the quadrivium did not lack defenders of their claim to supremacy. Robert Grosseteste and his disciple Roger Bacon both claimed that the quadrivial arts are the gateway and key to all other sciences, so that with knowledge of them one can readily acquire knowledge of everything else, while without it one cannot even know of what he is ignorant.[38] Needless to say, this position remained a minority one in the Middle Ages and did not begin to come into its own until the advent of the new science.

Issues in the Battle of the Arts

The battle of the arts has obvious similarities with the quarrel between philosophy and poetry. The case made for grammar, as we have seen, was also a defense of poetry, whereas the position of logic lies on the side of philosophical and scientific reason. There were, however, other issues. One is clearly the issue between ancients and moderns, which was in the background in the Platonic quarrel. D'Andeli, however, brought it to the fore by giving his account the form of a battle of the books, and his editor presented it as a forerunner of the more famous quarrel of the seventeenth and eighteenth centuries.[39] Another issue, and one that we have not encountered before, is posed by the appearance of a "perverse Grammar" and a "corrupt Rhetoric" fighting on the side of Logic against the forces of Grammar. Since grammar includes the study of language and literature, this fact would seem to indicate that there are two diverse ways of approaching language and literature: one way that is literary and poetic, siding with grammar, and another that is logical, even scientific. In fact, one feature of the triumph of scholasticism was the development of a *grammatica speculativa*, now considered to be an early form of scientific linguistics.[40] From this it would appear that there is a distinction to be made between two different ways of studying language and literature, one of which belongs to the humanities, the other, to the sciences.

This distinction with the possibility of opposition between the two ways is obviously an important one for understanding the nature of the humanities. It would indicate that the humanities should not be identified with definite subject matters such as the study of language and of literature, since these subject matters are also susceptible of another approach that is characteristic of the sciences. In accord with this distinction, it has been maintained by some that the humanities should be looked upon as general arts of the understanding that transcend all subject matters in that they apply to all and are used in thinking about any one of them. So considered, the humanities are then comparable to the liberal arts in the ancient and mediaeval scheme of them as the arts of learning that are propaedeutic to any and all knowledge.[41]

The division within the arts between trivium and quadrivium poses still another issue. The distinction was sometimes viewed as that between verbal arts (*artes sermocinales*) and nonverbal arts of the real (*artes reales*).[42] They are, accordingly, the arts needed for reading the books of men and those needed for reading the book of nature. These two groups of arts are sometimes considered to be different arts that are not only opposed, but are incompatible with each other, resulting in a conflict between word and thing.

The battle of the arts, however, has been mainly a battle within the trivium. At issue is the relation between them and whether one is more important than the others. Since all three arts of grammar, rhetoric, and logic are grouped together, presumably they are all necessary for the use of language. The question can then be asked, what would be the result of giving priority to one of the three in the use of language? This is a question that has already arisen in our consideration of the difference between a poetic and a scientific use of language.

All the issues just mentioned call for consideration, and I shall return to them, not once, but many times. The issue to which the remainder of this chapter is devoted is none of these, however, but rather the question of the end for which the arts are taken to be propaedeutic, and especially of their best and highest use. This, as we have seen, was assumed by our mediaeval authors to be theology, "Madame la Haute Science," queen of the arts and sciences. This claim rests on two presuppositions: one, that the classification of the kinds of learning is a hierarchy in which the supreme place belongs to theology; and, two, the more basic assumption that theology, i.e., supernatural theology based on religious faith, constitutes a valid kind of knowledge. It is this latter question that will now be considered, a question, needless to say, that has often been the cause of intense conflict, since it involves the difficult and complex problem of the relation between faith and reason.

Faith and Reason

In the conflict of cultural ideals, this issue has a special importance in that it has evoked more clearly than any other the entire range of positions that it is possible to take in regard to the conflict. Thus it has been maintained, on the one hand, that the whole conflict rests on a mistake and there is no real basis for it, and, on the other, that it is not only real but irreconcilable, short of complete capitulation of one side or the other. In between these two extremes it has been held that there is a real basis fo the conflict, but reconciliation is ultimately possible, although perhaps not without certain tension between the two. This range of positions has been represented in the conflict between the sciences and the humanities, although perhaps never so starkly as in the conflict between faith and reason. The issue, for this reason, deserves special consideration.

The first great conflict between faith and reason was a consequence of the victory of logic in the battle of the arts. The climax of that conflict can be dated precisely as occurring on 7 March 1277. On that day the Bishop of Paris, acting with the knowledge if not at the command of Pope John XXI, issued a condemnation of 219 propositions, allegedly currently taught at the University of Paris, and forbade the teaching of them henceforth as false, pernicious, heretical, and harmful to the faith.[43] Ironically, Pope John XXI, the former Petrus Hispanus, was the author of the most famous elementary textbook of scholastic logic. Many of the 219 propositions were derived from the work of Averroes, the Arabic commentator on Aristotle, who was apparently the preferred teacher of the arts faculty at the university. Several of the condemned propositions concern the relation of faith and reason:

> That the Christian religion is a hindrance to learning
> That there are fables and falsehoods in the Christian religion, just
>   as in all other

That one knows no more from knowing theology
That what the theologians say is based on fables
That true wisdom is the wisdom of the philosophers alone
That no state of life is superior to the practice of philosophy

These propositions were asserted some seven hundred years ago. Yet the same charges are still being made, the only change being that science has replaced philosophy. They reduce to the claim that theology and religion are not genuine knowledge, but, in fact, no more than a form of fable or myth.

The thirteenth-century bishop would no doubt be much surprised to learn that men of religion have now taken the position that he condemned and argue that it provides a defense of faith: it is the very strength and virtue of religion that it is a form of myth and story. This position demands our attention, not only because it has become one of the principal ways put forward to reconcile the conflict between faith and reason, but also because this would then appear to be only another form of the old conflict between philosophy and poetry.

In this case as in the older one, it has been argued that the analysis of language provides a useful approach by showing that its religious use differs so radically from that of science that there is no basis of conflict between the two. When conflicts do arise, they are held to be the result of misunderstanding, based on a misinterpretation of religious language. The most common mistake, allegedly, is to read a religious statement as though it were making an assertion about the way things are. Many religious statements, admittedly, seem to do so, e.g., that there is a God, that He created the world and its creatures, that He became man in the person of Jesus Christ, Who was put to death on a cross and arose again from the dead. But although such statements may be literal in form in seeming to assert the way things are, it is argued that they should not be interpreted in this way, but should be read as myth, parable, and story.

A clear and forthright expression of this position can be found in *Religion and the Scientific Outlook* by the English Christian writer T.R. Miles. Written within the tradition of linguistic analysis, Miles's work has the virtue of lucidity, which makes it useful as a representative statement of the position.

Miles prefers to speak of religious language as *parable*, although he admits that the word *myth* would have served just as well; presumably, the same holds true for *story*.[44] A parable, according to his analysis of it, has three main characteristics. First, "the question of its literal truth or falsity is unimportant," and it is of no significance whether the persons in the parable were actual historical persons or not; so much is obviously true of such parables in the Gospels as those about the Prodigal Son and the Good Samaritan. Second, parables contain "for the most part assertions that are empirical," that is, they talk about things, matters, and events that fall within our experience, so that "we know perfectly well what states of affairs would constitute the cash value of these assertions." Third, "and most important, parables convey a message." None of them is "a bare record of events, whether fictional or otherwise. . . . It invites us to view these events in a particular way; it gives us a new 'slant' on them, a new insight into what was happening." Therefore, if we accept the parable, "we are necessarily committed to a completely new way of life."[45]

Miles does not claim that all religious language is always to be understood as parable. There is also "the language of moral exhortation, the language of worship, and so on." But it is the parable as it occurs in the Bible as a literary form for teaching that provides the pattern for understanding the religious statements of greatest significance, and especially those that have the same form as literal statements of fact. According to Miles, however, it is a basic error to take them as such. For, in religious language interpreted as parable, there is no question of existence or of objective validity. Such concepts belong exclusively to science and the world of sense experience and are not appropriate to parable. Even when parables are opposed in content and recommend different courses of action, resolution of the differences between them is not a matter for rational argument. Reasons may be advanced for preferring one parable to another, but "whether a particular parable is a good one is a matter in the last resort for personal conviction rather than rational argument."[46] Yet the acceptance of a parable is a serious matter of consequence. "To accept the theistic parable is to commit ourselves to a particular way of life . . . a matter of supreme importance."[47] Thus the existence of God, the creation of the world, the life and death of Jesus are to be understood as parables, myths, or stories, disposing us to adopt a certain attitude toward the world and to act accordingly.

According to Miles, the great advantage of this interpretation of religious language is that it settles, "once for all," the conflict between faith and reason, religion and science. This claim, Miles writes:

> is not the presumptuous one that it sounds, for the matter is one of logical necessity, and it would be muddled thinking to claim anything less. . . . Only if what is offered in the name of religion is a factual assertion can there be any question of head-on conflict. There can be logical contradiction between two factually significant assertions. . . . But if what is

being offered in the name of "religion" is the language of parable, there can be no question of straight logical contradiction. By the laws of logic "In the beginning God created the heaven and the earth" can never be in contradition with *any* assertion that *any* scientist could ever make; and the same holds in the case of all other Christian parables. To insist that such language is parable and not literal truth is to ascribe a recognizable and legitimate function to a group of basic religious assertions, and the result is to supply a permanent guarantee that those assertions cannot be refuted by the findings of science.[48]

Behind this resolution of the conflict between faith and reason, as behind so much of modern thought, the mighty influence of Immanuel Kant can be detected. He too claimed to eliminate any possibility of conflict by assigning religion and science to such different realms that they have no common ground on which even to meet. Science operates within the realm of pure reason which provides us with factual and theoretical knowledge of the ways things are. Religion, however, dwells in the realm of the practical reason, which can provide us with directives that tell us how to live, but nothing at all about the world.

In his work *On Religion Within the Limits of Reason Alone*, Kant defined religion as "the recognition of all duties as divine commands." Since the commands are recognized as divine, religion involves some relation to God, but Kant insisted that they demand no knowledge that God exists, "no special duties having reference directly to God," and especially "no *courtly obligations* over and above the ethico-civil duties of humanity [of man to man]." Since it is strictly and only practical and moral, religion can make no statements about the existence of God, nor does it require any. "In religion, as regards the theorectical apprehension and avowal of belief," Kant wrote, "no assertorial knowledge is required. . . . Faith needs merely the *idea of God*, to which all morally earnest [and therefore confident] endeavor for the good must inevitably lead; it need not presume that it can certify the objective reality of this idea through theoretical apprehension." All that is needed for religion, according to Kant, is the minimum assertion that "it is possible that there may be a God," where by "God" we need understand no more than "the object towards which our legislative reason bids us to strive."[49]

Knowledge in the strict sense, "assertorial knowledge" of the way things are, is for Kant the reserve of science and especially of mathematical physics. It is restricted to what is given in space-time and presented in sense experience, and it is impossible to know whether there is anything at all beyond spatial-temporal existence. Hence, religion is not knowledge in this sense. Yet in our ordinary experience as men, we cannot avoid questions of what is good and right, of what we ought to do. To such questions as these no answer is provided by spatial-temporal knowledge. Such questions are questions of values, not of fact, and these two are strictly incommensurable according to Kant. That there is a God is one kind of statement; that He ought to be worshiped is another kind. And there is no way of deriving the one from the other. Nor is it of any help to claim that God Himself commands worship, for then worship would not be entailed unless we knew that divine commands ought to be obeyed. Even the threat of punishment for disobedience provides no help logically, since one would still be free to disobey if he were willing to run the risk of punishments. There are two distinct and separate realms, one of fact, the other of value, and there is no meeting between the two. Science is located in one, religion in the other. Hence, since there is no meeting place between the two, there is no ground for conflict.

The two-realms theory of Kant and Miles achieves a reconciliation between faith and reason by abandoning any claim to truth for faith and religion and holding that science alone can tell us how things truly are. Similar to this position is the theory of two truths according to which conflict is impossible because science and religion are held to express truths about completely separate orders. This doctrine may have been taught by the Latin Averroists at the University of Paris against whom the condemnation of 1277 was directed, since its introduction refers to men who say that "things are true according to philosophy but not according to the Catholic faith, as though there were two contrary truths."[50]

Still another proposal for resolution by reinterpreting the notion of truth has been more recently advanced. But instead of denying truth to religion or claiming for it a different order of truth, it maintains that science is no better off than religion when it comes to verifying its theories, since verification itself is said to rest ultimately entirely upon the subjective decision of the scientist. "Acceptance is all the verification a theory needs, wants, or can find."[51] In addition, any completely objective verification independent of personal appropriation is an illusion. But if all verification is ultimately a matter of postulation and even of personal preference, there is no reason why one should not accept one proposition in science and its contradiction in religion. Thus we seem to have in this proposal only another variant of the two-truths theory.

All three of the theories just considered, in effect, come to the same end of denying that religious faith provides knowledge of the way things are. This way of avoiding conflict between faith and reason thus comes at a high price, indeed, a price too high for many a religious person to pay. Freud was a good witness to this refusal, the more valuable since he himself opposed religion as an obstacle to the advance of science. After asserting that religion could easily end its fight with science if it would only admit the existence of two truths or two realms, Freud noted that religion has continually refused to do so, and for a very simple reason.

> Religion cannot make this admission, because if it did, it would lose all influence over the mass of mankind. The ordinary man knows only one *truth*—truth in the ordinary sense of the word. What may be meant by a higher or a highest truth, he cannot imagine.[52]

In practice, of course, one would have to admit that men often act as though the doctrine of two truths were true. Men have frequently found no difficulty in living as though one set of beliefs were true on Sunday and its contradictory set true on the other days of the week. Even in matters of thought, it often happens that we may very well not know which of two contradictory beliefs is the true one, be genuinely doubtful about both, and be ignorant of any way of deciding in favor of one over the other. But such a state of mind, common as it may be, is still not the same as accepting the doctrine of two truths. It is not the belief that both are true at the same time, but rather it is an ignorance at the time of which is the true one, an attitude of wait and see.

Logically, the doctrine of two truths is absurd. It destroys the very notion of truth as well as the possibility of rational argument, for if two logically contradictory statements can both be true at the same time and in the same respect, then any proposition at all can be true. With that, not only is there no longer any basis for reasoned thought, but, as Aristotle pointed out, we would also have to abandon speech as a form of communication.[53] Communication depends on at least a minimum of stability in the meanings of the words we use in talking; in asking for bread, for example, we are not both asking and not asking for it at the same moment.

If religious faith refuses to abandon its claim to knowledge of the truth, conflict with other kinds of knowledge remains an ever present possibility; the possibility, needless to say, has been frequently realized. There is also no doubt that the conflicts have concerned cognitive claims about the way things are (or were). Thus, for example, faith and reason have clashed over such questions as the shape of the earth, the place of the earth in the heavens, the age of the earth, origin and extinction of species, the existence of God, the historicity of Jesus, the authorship of the Gospels, the possibility of miracles, and the nature and existence of evil. On all these questions, conflict has occurred because faith and reason have proposed answers that are contradictory, one asserting what the other denies. How then is the conflict to be resolved if the way out provided by the two-truths or two-realms theory is refused?

The simplest most straightforward answer is the position that holds that resolution is possible only by complete capitulation of one to the other—either of faith to reason, or of reason to faith. For those who profess no religious faith or who deny that it is knowledge, there is no problem at all; reason must be followed as our best and only means of knowing the way things are. No less definite and dogmatic is the position that puts faith first and holds that reason must always be subject to it. Yet it must also be noted that there have always been men of faith who have asserted the primacy of reason over faith in matters of conflict.[54]

These solutions to the conflict are overly simple in that they resolve it, as it were, by an appeal to force that entirely denies the claim of its opponent. More complex, and admittedly more difficult, is the position that attempts to recognize the rights of both faith and reason and yet find a way of adjudicating between them when they come into conflict. This position requires that two conditions be satisfied: one, that both faith and reason are asserting and denying the same thing at the same time and in the same respect, so that there is a real contradiction at issue; and, two, that one cannot assert and maintain both of them. The second condition, which has been called the principle of the unity of truth, maintains that no proposition that has been validly established as true in one field can be inconsistent with any proposition validly established as true in another. This requirement does not deny that truth may be learned, expressed, and verified in different ways, or that truth in poetry, mathematics, science, philosophy, history, religion, or wherever else it may be found is in all respects the same. All the principle asserts is that however various these truths may be, they must still be mutually consistent, so that no two of them assert propositions that are logically contradictory.

This middle position regarding the relation of faith and reason has been well represented by Pascal. As a man of science as well as a man of religion, he recognized the claims of both and admitted the possibility of their conflict. The basis for resolving the conflict, he held, is provided by the principle of the unity of truth. Aiming at a reconciliation of the two, Pascal declared that the first step was to recognize that "there are three principles of our knowledge, the senses, reason, and faith," each of which has its own object, and its own kind of certitude. Hence, in considering any controverted proposition that is submitted to our examination, Pascal wrote:

> We must first determine its nature to ascertain to which of these three principles it ought to be referred. If it relates to a supernatural truth, we must judge of it neither by the senses, nor by reason, but by Scripture and the decisions of the Church. Should it concern an unrevealed truth and something within the reach of natural reason, reason must be its proper judge. And if it embrace a point of fact, we must yield to the testimony of the sense, to which it naturally belongs to take cognizance of such matters.[55]

We have here a rule for interpreting religious statements that come into opposition with those of science. It provides a way of identifying interpretations that are false, for if they are truly opposed to the evidence of sense and of reason, they cannot be true. In such cases, Pascal declared, citing the authority of both Augustine and Thomas:

> We must interpret the Scripture and seek out therein another sense agreeable to that sensible truth, because the Word of God being infallible in the facts which it records, and the information of the senses and of reason, acting in their sphere, being certain also, it follows that there must be an agreement between these two sources of knowledge. As Scripture may be interpreted in different ways, whereas the testimony of the sense is uniform, we must in these matters adopt as the true interpretation of Scripture that view which corresponds with the faithful report of the senses.[56]

So far, however, the rule is negative only. It enables us to identify as false those interpretations that contradict the senses and reason within the spheres of their competence. Yet revelation also contains statements that go beyond the competence of both sense and reason, e.g., that the world has been created in time. Is there any rule for determining the truth in these cases? If the teaching is truly revealed, then one may be sure that any rational proofs adduced of the contrary cannot be truly demonstrative. So Thomas argued in his time against the Latin Averroists that, using their own principles, their argument for the eternity of the world could be shown to be faulty. But he also argued against the Augustinians that their arguments purportedly demonstrating creation in time were also faulty. A truly revealed mystery cannot be either proven or disproven decisively by reason alone. Creation in the sense of the absolute dependence of a contingent being upon God for its very being may well be provable, but not that such a creature had to have been created in time, since there is nothing contradictory in the notion of an eternal creature, a being that has always been, but for all eternity always owes its existence to the will of God.[57]

Why then should one accept a revealed mystery as true? Ultimately, there is only the authority of Scripture and its authoritative teachers and the faith that underlies the acceptance of both. There are reasons for faith, however, reasons for accepting the possibility of revelation as well as its actuality. Also there is no good and sound reason for rejecting a revealed statement only because it cannot be attested to by either sense or reason. Neither sense nor reason are unlimited in scope, and what is not within their scope is not necessarily opposed to them, since its truth may lie outside and beyond them. Yet the decision to refrain from a priori rejction is still not equivalent to positive acceptance. Are there then positive reasons for believing such statements? Pascal thought so, and his doctrine that the heart has reasons that reason cannot know emphasizes an important truth about the sources and conditions of knowledge. In a justly famous *pensée*, he wrote:

> The heart has reasons which reason is not acquainted with [*connait*]. One knows [*sait*] it from a thousand things. I say that the heart naturally loves the Universal Being and naturally loves itself according as it gives itself; and it hardens itself against one or the other at its will. You have rejected the one and kept the other [i.e., rejected love of God and kept love of self]. But is it by reason that you love yourself?[58]

The context shows that Pascal gave at least two different senses to the expression "reasons of the heart." They can refer to immediate intuitions that we have without any discursive sequential reasoning. It is in this way, he wrote, "that we know first principles. . . . We know that we do not dream, however impossible it is to prove it. . . . The knowledge of first principles, as of space, time, motion, number, is as sure as any of those which we get from reasoning. And it is upon these reasons of the heart and of instinct that reason must base itself and found all its discourse."[59] Not everything can, or need, be proven. Reason and all of learning presuppose an initial knowledge of what is given in our most fundamental intuition of the world.

But in addition to this, there is a second sense in which Pascal used "reasons of the heart," and it is presumably this one that dictated his choice of the phrase. For reasons of the heart are associated with love, and it is in and through love that we reach beyond the grasp of reason. We know this from our personal relations, since no reason can account fully for the way that one person can come to know another through love, friendship, affection. If true of our relations with one another, and even with our animals, how much more true then of our relation with God, of which Pascal wrote: "It is the heart which experiences God, and not the reason. This then is faith: God felt by the heart, not by reason."[60]

With this conclusion we have returned again to knowledge of affective connaturality, or knowing through the emotions, which we found to be an underlying issue in the quarrel between philosophy and poetry. Hence, even though religious faith differs from poetry (and from myth or parable) insofar as it makes cognitive statements about the way things are that can conflict with those of reason and science, nevertheless it shares with poetry the basic conviction that there are more ways of knowing than through conceptual reason alone.

CHAPTER 6: The Quarrel of Ancients and Moderns

The conflict of cultural ideals to which I now turn would seem to be from the very nature of the case a fluctuating and changing one. *Ancient* and *modern* are time-bound words and change their reference with the passing of time. The modern of today is the ancient of tomorrow. Thomas Aquinas was a *modernus* to his Augustinian contemporaries, but to his Nominalist opponents only a few years later he was a proponent of the *via antiqua*. So too, Petrarch has been hailed as the first modern man, yet he ranked himself among the ancients in opposition to the moderns. Although the participants in the quarrel may change sides with the passing of time, there is no doubt that the issue on which it is based is a recurrent one. We have already encountered it in each of the great historical periods that we have considered as well as within each of the corresponding intellectual ideals. Cicero presented his ideal as the reestablishment of an ancient practice that had been destroyed by the rise of philosophical and scientific specialization. The logical, scientifically based theology of the Scholastics was an innovation in its time and marked a break with the historical tradition of biblical theology. Bacon and D'Alembert maintained that the scientific ideal of the modern world demanded the repudiation and destruction of ancient ideals and methods of learning.

The issue may be recurrent, if not perennial, but it also cannot be denied that it has loomed much larger at some times than at others. This was especially true in the seventeenth and eighteenth centuries when, first in France and then in England, the quarrel was argued with unusual intensity. That it should have been so intense at this time is perhaps not surprising. By then the humanists with their emphasis upon the study of ancient Greek and Latin and their classics had captured many of the institutions of higher learning and won the following of the literate public. The new science had achieved its first great physical synthesis in the work of Kepler, Galileo, and Newton. The vernacular literatures had come into their own with a body of writings that challenged comparison with the ancient classics.

Reformation theology had introduced new religious beliefs and practices at the same time that it called for a return to ancient sources. All this, combined with the discovery of new lands and the development of new technologies, had resulted in the overthrow of many traditional forms of social and religious life. Yet traditional thought and practice still retained great power and strength, so much so that, at least in the eyes of the moderns, progress itself was in chains. Such was the situation in which the quarrel of ancients and moderns broke out anew, this time under the form, not of a battle of the arts, but of a "Battel of the Books," as Swift called it.

The Battle of the Books

Swift's own contribution is a slight but significant one in that it highlights important issues at stake in the quarrel. Swift's fable presents the battle as a skirmish in a war that the moderns were waging against the ancients to take the highest part of Mount Parnassus. In asserting that the ancients were in possession of this mountain sacred to Apollo and the Muses, Swift was affirming the superiority of the ancients in literature, yet also recognizing that the moderns were challenging that position. It is significant too that the action is presented as a battle that was fought "between the ancient and the modern books in St. James's Library," for the underlying issue that provided the occasion for Swift's fable was a controversy between his patron, William Temple, and the librarian of St. James's Palace, Richard Bentley, regarding the reading and interpretations of the ancient classics. Temple, in his *Essay upon Ancient and Modern Learning* (1690), which defended the supremacy of the ancients, had praised in particular the literary merits of Aesop's *Fables* and Phalaris's *Epistles*. He had claimed that they dated from the sixth century and were the most ancient Greek writings in prose.[1] Bentley, from a scholarly examination of the history, chronology, and language of the writings, had proved that they could not have been written that early but were forgeries of a later age and, hence, were not the oldest and best books.[2] In Swift's satire, Bentley appears as "a fierce champion for the moderns," who are represented by such men as Tasso, Milton, Dryden, Descartes, Bacon, Hobbes, Harvey, Guicciardini, Aquinas (*sic*), Scotus (*sic*), and Bellarmine.[3] Temple is "general of the allies to the ancients," who are identified as Homer, Pindar, Euclid, Plato, Aristotle, Herodotus, Livy, and Hippocrates. Although the battle itself is presented as inconclusive, Swift's satire clearly favored the cause of Temple and the ancients and ridiculed that of Bentley and the moderns. Thus in his fable of the clash between the spider and the bee, the cause of the latter is identified with the ancients as the source of sweetness and light, while the spider with its dirt and poison is assigned to the moderns.[4]

The outcome of the quarrel appears just the opposite, however, when it is judged from the vantage point of the critical scholar. Bentley's *Dissertation* on Aesop and Phalaris is hailed as marking "an epoch in the history of scholarship . . . an example of critical method, heralding a new era."[5] Two such opposed judgments of the quarrel obviously indicate the use of different criteria. Temple had been primarily concerned with the literary and artistic merit of the writings in question and had praised them for their "race, . . . spirit, . . . force of wit, and genius," whereas Bentley was interested solely in their date of composition and place in the historical development of the Greek language. Between the two, in other words, there is all the difference that there is between a literary and aesthetic judgment on the one side and a historical, even a scientific, judgment on the other.

The quarrel between ancients and moderns did not stop, however, with questions of the interpretation of ancient texts. It extended to a consideration of all the arts and sciences and the relative merits of the ancient and modern achievements in them. D'Alembert in his *Preliminary Discourse to the Encyclopaedia* was drawing upon a long French tradition when he emphatically asserted the superiority of the moderns in all fields. He did so by telling a curious and highly fanciful story of the development of learning from the renaissance of letters to his time in the eighteenth century. He viewed it as a steady progress that had been accomplished by successive steps: "begun with erudition, continued with belles-lettres, and completed with philosophy."[6] The entire Middle Ages is dismissed as a period of unrelieved ignorance and barbarism in which "the principles of the sciences and the arts were lost." Hence, the first step had to consist in the recovery of the achievements of the ancients through the study of languages and history, a work of erudition based upon the cultivation of the memory that was undertaken and accomplished by the humanists.[7] This work itself became an obstacle to further progress when the humanists failed to "realize that the study of words is a kind of passing inconvenience, necessary insofar as it facilitates the study of things," but a waste when it resulted only in Latin imitations of the classics. Progress continued, however, as soon as "men of letters turned their thoughts to perfecting the vulgar tongues, . . . no longer limited themselves to copying the Romans and the Greeks, or even to imitating them; they tried to surpass them." Summing up this development, D'Alembert claimed that in this way "the imagination of the moderns was reborn little by little from that of the ancients; and all the masterpieces of the past century were seen to burst forth almost simultaneously—masterpieces in eloquence, in history, in poetry, and in the different literary genres."[8] In this picture of triumphant progress, the fine arts were also included, inasmuch as "the taste which cultivates one impels men to perfect the other."[9] Philosophy and science were the slowest to find the way to progress, not only because the reading of the ancients contributed more directly to the arts than to the sciences, but also because "as philosophers the ancients did not approach the perfection they achieved as writers." Then too Scholasticism and "theological despotism" are accused of preventing the free use of reason. But with "the immortal Chancellor of England, Francis Bacon," and "the illustrious Descartes," reason broke its bonds and rapidly progressed until it climaxed in the work of Newton, who "gave to philosophy a form which apparently it is to keep," and in that of Locke, who is said to have "created metaphysics almost as Newton had created physics."[10]

In his championing of the moderns, D'Alembert was as intemperate and exaggerated as Temple had been in his claims for the ancients. One tended to the extreme of maintaining that the newest is always the best, whereas the other advanced the same claim for the oldest. Neither writer stopped to consider and analyze the relation of learning to time and to ask whether different forms of learning differ in the way they are related to their own past and future. More sober minds did so, however, and thus raised what is perhaps the most significant issue in the quarrel.

Progress in Learning

For consideration of this question, Pascal has provided a good beginning in the preface to his *Treatise on the Vacuum*. In presenting the results of his scientific investigations, he wrote as a modern, but in his preface he expressly sought to determine the measure of respect that is owed to the ancients. While firm in his belief that some measure is owed, he knew too that it could be excessive and, in fact, noted that in his time it has been "carried so far in matters in which it should have less influence that we treat all its ideas as revelations and even its obscurities as mysteries, . . . and an author's text is enough to destroy the strongest arguments."[11] However, there is no simple rule that will apply to all forms of learning inasmuch as they differ among themselves in the way they advance. To manifest the difference, Pascal distinguished two groups of studies. "One group depend exclusively on memory and are purely historical, having as their only object to know what the authors have written." In this group he located history, geography, jurisprudence, languages, theology, and any work in which in order to know "we must have recourse to books, since all that can be known about such matters is contained there." The other group of studies comprehends those that "depend exclusively on reason and are wholly dogmatic, having as their object to seek and discover hidden truths," among which he enumerated geometry, arithmetic, music, physics, medicine, architecture, and "all the sciences subject to experiment and reason."[12]

The distinction between the two groups is based, on the one hand, upon the different relation they have to authority and reason, and, on the other (the more important for our present purposes), upon the different ways in which they develop and advance through time. The second group of studies grow and develop by "being added to," with the result that "their perfection depends upon time and effort." Merely sketched by the ancients, they will be left "to our successors in a more perfected state than we received them." Previously acquired knowledge serves as the basis from which to make new discoveries, and these in turn provide steps to still further ones, from which it is evident, Pascal wrote, "that even if our effort and time had gained us less than the labor of the ancients, separated from ours, the two together nevertheless must have more effect than either alone."[13] In other words, with this group of studies, to come later is to know more, and in this case more is also better, so that it holds true that the latest is the best.

The other group of studies, in contrast to these, do not grow by being added to. They are then in some sense complete, and Pascal said of them, that "we can have the whole of that knowledge and it is not possible to add anything to it." As instances of such knowledge, he cited history, geography, the dead languages, and, especially, revealed theology.

> If it is a question of knowing who was the first king of France, where the geographers put the first meridian, what words are used in a dead language, and everything of this sort, how could we find it out except from books? And who can add anything new to what they tell us about it, since we desire to know only what they contain?[14]

Of these instances of studies that are noncumulative, the clearest would seem to be the knowledge of dead languages. Indeed, one advantage of a dead over a living language is that it is possible to know *all* the words of the language. In fact, a little handbook of Greek bears

the title, *All the Greek Verbs*.[15] The other examples seem somewhat
forced. Geographical knowledge has grown by being added to as new
explorations of the earth have been made, although we have now
reached the point where all of it has been mapped in some detail. Our
historical knowledge has also grown, for, although the past is over and
done with and not to be added to, our knowledge of the past has grown
with the development of new techniques that provide new and more
knowledge of the past. For example, from archaeology we have obtained evidence of the strucutre of the Parthenon and of Knossos that
enables us to know more about their past in some respects than even
Herodotus and Thucydides knew. Although they remain our major
written evidence for the matters they wrote about, it has been supple-
mented in many, many ways.

But despite the fact that some of his examples may be open to
question, there is no doubt that Pascal's distinction is both sound and
important. Some studies and disciplines are additive or cumulative and
thus progressive, while some are nonprogressive. In fact, if there is any
one conclusion that may be said to have resulted from the quarrel
between ancients and moderns, it is this one, and with it comes the
ensuing realization that value in the nonprogressive disciplines transcends the temporal. Thus, even the most vigorous champions of the
moderns recognized that e.g., in poetry and eloquence, the excellence
of ancient achievements could not be denied and might well be
superior to that of modern works.[16]

This difference in the temporal dimension of learning is crucial for
understanding the difference, and frequently also the conflict, between the humanities and the sciences. The difference is nowhere
more apparent than in the way each regards its own past. Compare, for
example, some of the great figures in the history of mathematical
physics with those of epic poetry: Ptolemy, Copernicus, Newton, and
Einstein on the one hand with Homer, Virgil, Dante, Milton, and
Tolkien on the other. Among the scientists, the knowledge of Einstein
at the end of the list is better than that of his predecessors because,
among other reasons, it has comprehended much, if not all, of their
work; the progress that it marks in the understanding of terrestrial and
celestial motion came about in large part because he could utilize their
results. Yet he had no occasion and no need at all to know at first hand
the actual writings of Newton or Copernicus, let alone that of Ptolemy.
The results that they had achieved had been digested in the body of the
ongoing science and become part of the science that Einstein learned as
a student.

How very different is the relation among the poets. Tolkien's epic is the latest in the group, and he possessed all the others to draw upon in writing his own, yet it is not therefore better just because it comes last. In fact, as epic it has been claimed that Homer's has never been equaled. In poetry, the fact of following upon distinguished predecessors, and even of knowing and utilizing their discoveries and achievements, is no surety at all of a better and superior result. Nor does the earlier work cease to be a potential source of matter, technique, and inspiration for even the latest poet. Ezra Pound, at the age of fifty, and already a master of technique, observed that he could never take up a page of Homer without noting a number of melodic inventions that he had never noted before. Literature he defined as "news that stays news."[17] The fact that it does not date tells much about the way in which literature and the humanities differ from the sciences.

From this, however, it does not follow that poetry does not develop and progress in any sense at all. Literary criticism at its very beginning, in Aristotle's *Poetics*, took note of additions and inventions that various poets had made in the construction of tragedy, and Pound organized his entire *ABC of Reading* according to the inventions and developments in the technique of verse writing. That English prose style has developed greatly since the time of the Tudors is manifest in the parody of that entire history that Joyce inserted in his *Ulysses*.[18] But although development, even progress, occurs in language and in its poetic and literary uses, it is not at all the same kind as in scientific thought. It develops without discarding its past and often progresses in new directions by returning to its past to recover and exploit elements in it that had been slighted or overlooked. Even works that aim at novelty and openly attempt to break with the past, even to overthrow it, do not thereby render obsolete and replace the literary excellence of past achievements. These still remain as capable as ever of fulfilling their poetic purpose, whereas scientific works of the past become obsolete as science and remain a source of interest only for the historian and the philosopher; no one today learns his astronomy by studying Ptolemy.

Although the sciences are cumulative and additive as the humanities are not, it must be noted that they are also eliminative, and they progress by rejecting as well as by adding to their past. Observations, factual data, generalizations may be retained, while the controlling theory is dropped entirely and replaced by another. Thus Copernicus, for the most part, used the same observations as Ptolemy, but he replaced the geocentric theory with his own heliocentric hypothesis. Such a change from one theory to another was once viewed as simply the elimination of a theory proved to be false and the adoption of a true one, with the result that the history of science was viewed as a continuous linear development progressing by the discovery of truth and the elimination of error. We now know that change in science is not so simple and continuous. Whether the change from one controlling theory to another—or the adoption of a new paradigm—constitutes a veritable revolution is still a controversial issue.[19] But there is no doubt that the "discovery" of the heliocentric theory was not at all the same kind as the discovery of America. The latter constituted an addition to geographical knowledge, and although it altered previous views of the world that had allowed no place for America, it did so by the addition of new knowledge about the earth. The Copernican theory was not an addition to existing knowledge, but rather a new way of looking at the heavens and a new way of accounting for their motions. The scientific enterprise includes in its work both kinds of discoveries, but it is the additive one that makes science additive and progressive as the humanities are not. This additive factor lends a quantitative character to the excellence of science: more time, more study, more information means better as well as more knowledge, with the result that, other things being equal, the latest is the best. There is no such quantitative factor in the humanities, and the latest work is not necessarily better. Not that the oldest is best, as Temple held, but rather that time itself provides no criterion for judging excellence in the humanities, so that the ancient may well provide a standard of excellence for the ongoing work. Such, as we saw in discussing the literary ideal, was Mill's claim on behalf of the ancient classics.[20]

So far, in our consideration of the temporal dimension of learning, no mention has been made of philosophy. This omission has been deliberate, since the relation of philosophy to its past and future is still more complex than any we have discussed. On the one hand, its past achievements resemble those of poetry and the fine arts in that they retain contemporary value and utility for the philosophical enterprise. Men learn how to become philosophers and how "to do" philosophy by studying the works of past philosophers, and often very ancient ones, such as Plato and Aristotle, and even the Pre-Socratics. On the other hand, philosophy frequently attempts to ape the sciences and claim that the work of the past can be digested and forgotten once the proper method of philosophizing is discovered. Bacon, Descartes, Kant, Comte, and the logical positivists were all supremely confident that they had found such a method, and all looked to science for their model. Kant spoke for all when he declared that it is an easy matter to tell whether reason is on the right path; you need only look to its results.

> If after repeated preparations it comes to a standstill as soon as its real goal is approached, or is obliged in order to reach it to retrace its steps again and again and strike into fresh paths; again, if it is impossible to produce unanimity among those who are engaged in the same work, as to the manner in which their common object should be obtained, we may be convinced that such a study is far from having attained to the secure method of science, but is groping only in the dark.[21]

Mathematics and natural science had clearly found that path, but, by such criteria, it was no less patent that philosophy had not. Philosophers have been notorious for their disagreements, not only about the conclusions they reached, but even about the methods to be used. Hence, according to Kant, philosophy, unlike science, had made no progress, but was continually coming to a dead end, retracing its steps, and starting over again.

Kant was no less confident than Bacon and Descartes that he had discovered the proper method for philosophy that would set it on a path of progress such as science had discovered. But that his confidence was just as misplaced as theirs is equally clear. Division and disagreement still reign among philosophers, as much about methods as about conclusions. Philosophers still continue to start over again, especially in the sense that they return to Plato and Aristotle as well as to Descartes and Kant in order to learn philosophy. And men continue to express their dismay and discontent with the existence of such division and controversy.

The extent of disagreement and of lack of progress in philosophy appears so great, however, only because it is judged by comparison with science. If it is judged on its own terms, it shows both progress and agreement. Progress is evident from the history of its development. That history is largely the story of the successive unburdening of tasks that it once undertook on its own, but that are now carried out by the special sciences that philosophy helped to bring to birth: First, the separation and distinction of philosophy as abstract thought from myth and poetry; then its distinction from theology; then, more recently, the separation and establishment of the sciences, first of the natural sciences and then, within the past century, of the social sciences. This successive delegating of tasks has gone so far that it is sometimes asserted that nothing remains for philosophy to do and that it will die of inanition. The judgment, however, is premature. As Gilson has observed, philosophy always manages to bury its own grave diggers.[22] That this development has constituted a progress is evident from the fact that philosophy has become clearer about itself and its work—what is amenable to it and what is not.

So too, if we consider philosophy in relation to its past, the disagreement is not as extensive as claimed. Kant's criticism of philosophical disagreement was made from the viewpoint of science as an additive progressive knowledge in which its workers share, as it were, a common frontier. Research physicists, for example, agree for the most part about the results that their science has achieved, about the data and problems that provide the starting point for their own research as well as about the methods to be followed and the kind of result that will count as a solution. Philosophy, however, does not proceed in this fashion, and at any one time philosophers may disagree widely about every one of the points just mentioned. If, however, we shift from a vertical (synchronic) to a horizontal (diachronic) time line and look for agreement and disagreement across the centuries, we obtain a very different picture. When we look at scientists over the centuries, or over just one century, and sometimes over a period of only ten years, we find great disagreement among them. How greatly the physicist or astronomer of today disagrees with Aristotle or Ptolemy. The rate of change has become so rapid in physics that it is claimed there is a new generation of physicists every five years![23] Philosophy refuses to be time-bound in this way. Among contemporary philosophers one can find thinkers who share fundamental positions with their predecessors of centuries ago: some with Kant or with Descartes, but then also others are in basic agreement with Augustine or Thomas, with Aristotle or Plato.

We have thus found three different ways in which learning is related to its past as it continues and carries on its work. These three ways might be compared to three different kinds of metabolism.[24] In the way that characterizes the sciences, the past is digested, its nourishment absorbed and used for its ongoing work, the unusable discarded as waste. In the case of poetry and the fine arts, the past is, as it were, regurgitated, since its masterworks are always capable of providing renewed nourishment and hence are not eliminated. The past for philosophy and theology, however, proves to be indigestible, for although attempts are made repeatedly to digest it, they never succeed. The disagreement that exists among philosophers—in depth and extent so different from that among scientists and poets—is a sign of this indigestible character.

Tradition in Learning

Differences in the temporal dimension show up among the disciplines in their relation to tradition no less than to progress. No established discipline is without some tradition, but disciplines vary in their relation to it according to the ways in which they transmit past accomplishment to present activity. The word *tradition* comes from the Latin *tradere*, meaning *to give over* (*trans* + *dare*).[25] In any act of giving, three elements can be distinguished: the giver, the gift, and the recipient of it. In tradition as an act of transmission, we can accordingly distinguish the subject or agent of transmission, the object that is transmitted—the *traditum* or *transmit*—and the recipient who receives it. The word *tradition* may refer either to the act of transmitting or to the transmit, and it is often important to recognize which of the two senses is foremost.

Philosphers have been known to talk of making a fresh start, a new beginning. Strictly and absolutely speaking, such an act is impossible. Man is a talking animal, and his talk is in a language that is a *traditum* that he has received from his forebears which carries with it not only a vocabulary and a syntax, but a whole set of cultural values. Hence, to make a completely new start would call for a completely new language. This point was tellingly made in Orwell's *1984*, in which the new society sets out to destroy the values of the past by imposing the use of its "Newspeak" in place of the native language, the "Oldspeak."

An intellectual discipline has in addition to its language, which is often a highly specialized one, a tradition of achievements and results, of methods and practices, of questions and problems, as well as goals and agreed-upon standards for its answers and solutions. This manner of describing a discipline is obviously weighted in favor of the sciences, since we would not ordinarily speak in this way about writing a poem, painting a picture, or composing a piece of music. Yet no harm will be done if we restrict our attention to the product or result rather than to the disciplinary activity as such, i.e., to the poem, the painting, the philosophical discourse, or the scientific monograph. With regard to tradition then, we can ask: To what extent does the achieved product become a *traditum* for the ongoing disciplinary activity?

The answer varies, of course, with the discipline. As I have already had occasion to note, poets still can learn about poetry and how to write it by studying Homer, whereas no astronomer turns to Ptolemy to learn astronomy. In general, it seems to be the case that, in the special sense in which I am now speaking, the sciences are the least traditional, the humanities the most. But before seeking reasons for this fact, I should consider in more detail specific cases of this difference.

If we take scientists, or spokesmen for science, at their word, the science in which conceptual change is most rapid and so presumably least traditional, in our sense of the term, is mathematical physics. Thus, according to one estimate, "a mean period of some five years is a

realistic interval for measuring significant historical changes whether
professional or disciplinary."[26] Another study showed that of the references to past work cited in research papers published in the *Physical
Review*, eighty-two percent were to recent articles in scientific journals,
fifty percent of which were less than three years old, and only twenty
percent of all the references were to any work more than seven years
old.[27] Indeed, scientists have been known to assert that they read
nothing more than five years old. Such figures seem incredible. Even
though it is well to remember that these figures indicate only something about the sociology of science and how some science is now done
by some scientists, they remain symptomatic of how this science looks
upon itself. It works only with, upon, and from the most recent
achievements, results, and problems, and it is almost completely obliv-
ious of the writings of the past, which are forgotten and regarded as
over and done with and obsolete.

If in this respect physics is the least traditional of disciplines, there is
no doubt that the most traditional is theology—the revealed theology
of the Catholic church. The reason is simple: its *traditum* is regarded as
a revelation given by God to man at one time in the past that is to last for
all time. In the words of Fr. Yves Congar, it consists of

> a belief that certain facts once occurred that offered a definitive covenant
> destined for all men. There was *one* Abraham, *one* exodus from Egypt, *one*
> Moses, *one* covenant on Sinai, *one* history of the Jewish people with its
> prophets and psalms. There was *one* John the Baptist, *one* Mary of
> Nazareth, *one* Jesus Christ, God-with-us. There was *one* confession of
> Peter, *one* Last Supper, *one* Resurrection, *one* Pentecost. All this, along with
> other facts and words, constitutes "the faith which has been once and for
> all entrusted to the saints," of which the *Letter of Jude* speaks.[28]

The meaning and function of tradition in theology is highly complex,
but for our purposes here there is no need to go further into the
question. It is well known that for the theologian as for the humblest
Christian, the words and events accepted as God's revelation are treasured as old, yet ever new, and never obsolete.

In this respect, the humanities resemble theology more than they
do physics. Poetry and the fine arts, history, and philosophy not only
preserve and respect, but they also continually return to the study of
the great works of the past. The reason for this is not only that the past
in these cases still continues to speak to the present as it does not in the
sciences, but also, as the text just cited emphasizes, because there is a
concern for the unique individual that is entirely absent from scientific
investigation. In fact, this difference with regard to individual unique-

ness has been taken as a fundamental criterion for distinguishing various kinds of disciplines.[29] One kind is characterized by the fact that its whole enterprise is a collective or communal one: goals, ideals of explanation, problems and questions to be faced, as well as criteria for judging the explanations that are proposed have the more or less complete agreement of all working within the discipline. The so-called hard sciences provide the best example of this type of discipline. Poetry and the fine arts and, to a lesser extent philosophy, share no such widespread agreement, and although there may be a commonly shared technique, still the problems and goals as well as the means of solving and achieving them remain matters of individual choice. The work itself, both as activity and as result, is individual and not teamwork. *The Wasteland* was a uniquely individual and personal achievement in a way that cracking the genetic code was not, even though its final shape owed something to Pound's editing.

The two types of discipline thus differ with respect to the *traditum* that they transmit. In the sciences it is primarily the ongoing process of formulating the questions to be answered and devising methods for finding answers to them that then become the basis for new questions, all of which is a collective possession of the discipline. Thus it was possible for Newton to lay down a program for physics that was, in a sense, to occupy the whole of physics down until, say, 1900, by which time it had been completed.[30] But no such claim could be made for poetry or philosophy. They just are not that kind of discipline. Individual poets and philosophers may lay down programs for themselves and achieve them in their works; they may even attract disciples and followers to participate in their program. But they do not establish programs for their disciplines as such. In fact, it has been observed that in the case of the arts the establishment of a tradition in the form of a school is usually a regressive rather than a progressive factor.[31] But this is only another way of noting that more and later usually means better in the sciences, but not in the humanities.

Another aspect of this difference with regard to tradition appears in the place and function of the classic or great book. As we have seen, the idea of the classic arose as a result of ranking authors according to their merit as writers, the classic comprising those held to be worthy of imitation and emulation as standards of excellence; although in principle recent works were not ruled out, in practice the lists seldom included any writer less than a century old.[32] If it is true that physicists seldom bother to read anything more than seven years old, it would appear that the very possibility of a classic in physics is eliminated by definition, and it has been claimed that there are no classics in the progressive modern sciences.[33] It does seem to be true that in the advanced sciences the normal mode of communication tends to become the monograph rather than the book, thereby rendering obsolete the idea of a great book. Of course, there are recognized classics of science, such as those that are included in Comte's *Positivist Library* as well as in contemporary set of *Great Books of the Western World*.[34] Admittedly, the works of Ptolemy, Copernicus, Kepler, Newton, Harvey, and Faraday are great books, great achievements of reason and understanding, eminently deserving of study and admiration as monuments of the human spirit. It remains true, nonetheless, that they belong to the history of science, not to science-in-process, and no scientist turns to them for his questions and problems or the methods and procedures of solving them. Nor does he turn to them to learn of the results that they record.

Of course, in any discipline the questions, methods and results consist of those with which the current practitioners of the discipline are concerned. Theology no less than physics in its actual practice as an ongoing activity is constantly undergoing change. Even though the *traditum* that it treasures and hands on remains the same, its reception is subject to the historical and cultural conditions of its recipients. Its message has to be addressed to the new problems arising from the changes in conditions that result from, among other things, the new knowledge and understanding that has been gained. Hence, even in the case of a *traditum* that remains one, there is a development and progress in the understanding of it.[35] However, for theology as for the humanities generally, the works and results of past achievement constitute a *traditum* that continues to remain an integral and living part of the disciplinary activity as such, not just of its history.

The Outcome of the Quarrel

What then can be said in conclusion about the quarrel of ancients and moderns? Is it no more than an unimportant argument of interest only to old-fashioned scholars, as it was described in a recent novel?[36] Is it the result of men venting their different temperaments and casts of mind in their worship of Francis Bacon's idols of the cave? Some minds, he observed, are "given to an extreme admiration of antiquity, others to an extreme love and appetite for novelty," but both are extremes to be avoided since they work "to the great injury of the sciences and philosophy, since these affectations of antiquity and novelty are the humors of partisans rather than judgments."[37] But then again it has also been suggested that the quarrel is grounded on permanent needs of the human spirit. Thus an early historian of the quarrel began his account with the claim: "Two spirits divide the world, the ancient spirit and the modern spirit, both justifiable, for they correspond to two real needs of humanity, tradition and progress."[38]

In fact, the quarrel has usually broken out when something new has arisen in the world of learning and begun to win power and influence. Thus we saw there is reason for believing that the quarrel in the Platonic dialogues discloses the opposition between the new conceptual literate scientific culture and the older, preliterate, oral poetic culture. In Quintilian it was the emergence of the new poets, the *neoteroi*, that posed the issue, whereas in the mediaeval battle of the arts it was the new logic and the new philosophy that resulted from the rediscovery of the Aristotelian corpus that precipitated the quarrel. Here it is worth noting that the *moderni* were still the proponents of very ancient authors and books. The same was true of the Renaissance humanists as well as of the educational reformers of a generation ago who based their teaching on the "great books." Thus, the moderns sometimes espouse the cause of the ancients, but read in a new way according to new methods, for new purposes. But whether the cause of the moderns is identified with new ways of reading old books or with the discovery of new sciences and new learning, the quarrel of ancients and moderns has served to mark major steps in the development of our intellectual culture.[39]

More than providing landmarks, the quarrel has also served to focus attention upon the temporal dimension of learning and the different ways in which the various disciplines are related to past and future and, accordingly, to tradition and progress. This feature provides a "powerful discriminant" for distinguishing between the sciences and the humanities, and C.P. Snow, reviewing the decade of controversy generated by his essay, *The Two Cultures*, concluded that perhaps its greatest contribution lay in providing a clearer understanding of this discriminant.

> So we seem to have reached a clear divide between two cultures or traditions. One is cumulative, incorporative, collective, consensual, so designed that it must progress through time. The other is non-cumulative, non-incorporative, unable to abandon its past but also unable to embody it. This second culture has to be represented by negatives, because it is not a collectivity but is inherent in individual human beings. That means it possesses qualities which the scientific culture does not and never can: and, on the other hand, since there is a principle of mutual exclusion, it loses by

its nature the diachronic progress which is science's greatest gift to the mind of man.[40]

Snow, in restricting his attention to science and literature, did not have occasion to inquire whether philosophy and theology may not differ from both in the way that they are related to their past, as has been argued here. His text and his original essay, however, do raise the question whether there is good reason for thinking that there are fundamentally only two intellectual cultures. To that controversy I now turn.

CHAPTER 7: The Two Cultures

The Snow-Leavis Controversy

The contemporary instance of the conflict of cultural ideals that has received the most publicity is without doubt the controversy over the so-called two cultures. It began with a lecture that the English novelist and civil servant, C. P. Snow, delivered at the University of Cambridge and published in book form in 1959 under the title *The Two Cultures and the Scientific Revolution*. Although neither original nor profound, it was featured in the popular press and given an importance out of all proportion to its merit. The literary critic and professor of English at Cambridge, F.R. Leavis, outraged at this instance of the portentous power possessed by the press of "creating publicity values," then undertook to deflate the reputation of Snow and his work in a lecture also given at Cambridge in 1962 and published with the title, *Two Cultures? The Significance of C.P. Snow*. But this effort, far from diminishing the force of the discussion, gave it still greater momentum, until the bibliography of writings on the topic must by now run easily to more than one hundred separate items.[1] In fact, the principals themselves have continued the controversy. In 1963 Snow issued another edition of his essay, to which he appended his further reflections, called "A Second Look," in which he took note of Leavis's attack. Then, in 1970, Leavis returned to the subject in a lecture entitled " 'Literarism' versus 'Scientism': The Misconception and the Menace,"[2] to which Snow, in turn, responded with "The Case of Leavis and the Serious Case."[3]

The original essay confused several issues, as Snow himself later acknowledged.[4] One was social and political, especially the gap between the rich and poor nations and the dangers that might result if nothing were done to close it. The other was theoretical and philosophical in that it concerned the two cultures from which the essay derived its title. One of these cultures was identified with science, especially with mathematical physics, in which Snow had been trained at Cambridge. The second culture was described in numer-

114

ous ways. At first, Snow referred to it as the culture of the "literary intellectuals,"[5] then that of the "non-scientists."[6] Later he spoke of "the whole 'traditional' culture",[7] and most recently he has settled upon "the 'humanist' culture," although he notes that "there should be a more acceptable term, but it has not yet emerged."[8]

It is of interest to note that the Rede lectureship which was the sponsor of Snow's original address was the same one for which Matthew Arnold in 1882 had read his essay, "Literature and Science," as a reply to T.H. Huxley's "Science and Culture" of the year before.[9] In many respects, the Snow-Leavis controversy was a resumption of this earlier one. It began on a narrower basis in being concerned at first only with literature and science. Thus the examples first cited by Snow as representatives of the traditional culture were all modern men of letters, and the same was true of Leavis's first essay. The earlier controversy was considerably broader inasmuch as Arnold was defending the value of a classical education in Greek and Latin that included a knowledge of history and philosophy as well as of literature. Yet in both cases the same ideals are clearly in conflict: the literary on one side and the scientific on the other. Yet in the seventy-seven years intervening between Snow and Arnold, a significant change had occurred; it was nothing less, in fact, than a complete reversal of roles. Arnold, in his exposition, spoke with confidence of an ideal that was predominant not only in the control that it exercised over intellectual and educational life, but also in the respect it enjoyed with the wider public. Despite the great achievements that science already had to its credit by 1882, it still remained in many respects an "up-start," seeking public approval and acclaim. Snow, in his lecture, spoke, if anything, with still greater confidence and self-assurance, but it was based on the ideal of science, not literature, a science that has already remade the world and has "the future in its bones."[10]

Snow originally made three main points about the contemporary intellectual situation: first, that there are the two cultures, one scientific, the other literary; second, that they exist as two polarized groups that have ceased to communicate and between which there is mutual incomprehension, if not dislike and outright hostility; and third, that this division constitutes a serious danger, not only to individuals, but to the entire human race. Snow spoke as one who was equally at home in both cultures, and, although he was pleading for bridges across the two cultures, he also left no doubt that his own sympathies were almost wholly with science. He wrote, as though it were self-evident, that "the scientific edifice of the physical world . . . in its intellectual depth, complexity, and articulation [is] the most beautiful and wonderful collective work of the mind of man."[11] He accused the proponents of the nonscientific culture of being "natural Luddites," resolutely looking toward the past and away from the future, and still opposing the industrial revolution.[12] His criticism of the "moderns," represented by such men as Yeats, Pound, and Eliot, was thus almost exclusively social and political. His position was well indicated by a question he posed near the conclusion of his "Second Look," in which he asked: "How far is it possible to share the hopes of the scientific revolution, the modest difficult hopes for other human lives, and at the same time participate without qualification in the kind of literature, which has just been defined [the moderns]."[13] By such political criteria, the scientific culture, according to Snow, was clearly superior.

In the philosophical order, which is the center of our concern, two questions in the controversy stand out. One is the question of the two cultures, whether there are basically two different kinds of intellectual culture. The other question concerns the possibility and desirability of communication and exchange between the two cultures. Consideration of this latter question will be postponed until the final chapter.

After more than ten years of the controversy, Snow remarked: "Perhaps we have been feeling our way towards a clearer concept of the distinction between the scientific and the nonscientific cultures."[14] Snow was evidently speaking for himself. In his original essay he had made many facile comparisons between the two, not only calling Rutherford another Shakespeare, but asserting that a question about the second law of thermodynamics was "about the scientific equivalent of: Have you read a work of Shakespeare's?"[15] Leavis was certainly right to ridicule the comparison and declare: "There *is* no scientific equivalent of that question; equations between orders so disparate are meaningless."[16] In the end Snow himself was saying that there are "two ways of knowing," "two kinds of understanding," and "a clear divide between two cultures or traditions."[17] He located the difference primarily in the temporal dimension of learning, as we saw from the text quoted at the close of the preceding chapter. But considerably greater illumination upon the nature of these differences can be derived from earlier discussions of the topic, and especially from those regarding the distinction between the *Naturwissenschaften* and the *Geisteswissenschaften*.

Vico, Dilthey, and the Geisteswissenschaften

For the theory of the humanities as well as for understanding the conflict of cultural ideals, the work of Giambattista Vico is especially valuable. His *Discourse on the Study Methods of Our Times* (as his *De nostri temporis studiorum ratione* of 1709 has been translated) not only made a sound contribution to the quarrel of ancients and moderns, but also provided a strong defense of poetry against philosophy and of rhetoric and eloquence against logic and mathematics. Then his masterpiece, *The New Science*, the very title of which challenged comparison with the *Two New Sciences* of Galileo as well as the *New Organon* of Bacon, laid the foundations for a general theory of the humanities as a unified field of study.

In his *ratio studiorum* Vico compared and evaluated the methods of study and education of the moderns as compared with those of the ancients. That of the moderns is identified with the rationalistic critical method of Descartes as popularized by Arnauld in *The Port Royal Logic (La logique ou l'art du penser)*, while that of the ancients is substantially that of Cicero and Quintilian. The two methods, according to Vico, differed in both their basis and their aim. The one concentrated upon reason and the critical faculties, spurning imagination and memory in favor of a mathematical method that aimed at rigorous and demonstrative certitude. The other method aimed at the cultivation of the judgment through exercise of imagination and memory and of the faculty of invention in order to make arguments that would be effective in matters where probability is the most that can be achieved. Vico was not opposed to mathematical and scientific reasoning as such, but he thought that they were highly detrimental to the mind if they were developed too early to the exclusion of the other powers. For this reason he claimed that the methods of the ancients were superior to those of the moderns. He did not stop with his recommendation, however, but went on to attack the moderns at the very point at which they claimed the most for their method, namely, that it achieved absolutely certain knowledge. While he did not deny that the method is capable of reaching demonstrative certitude, he argued that it could do so only within the very restricted and limited area of mathematical abstraction. Applied outside of mathematics itself, as it is in physics to the natural world, it can never achieve more than a measure of probability. This is so, Vico asserted, because the mind can be certain only of what it has itself made, and mathematical objects yield such certainty just because they are made by the mind itself. Physics, however, has for its object the natural world, and since it has not made this world, its knowledge can never attain demonstrative certitude.[18] In other words, there is always a gap between our mathematics and the natural world to which we apply it, with the result that we can never be absolutely sure of the fit of the one upon the other. While it is certain that $2+2=4$, two quarts of mercury added to two quarts of mercury does not yield four quarts, but something less.

Vico's principle here, that we know best what we make ourselves, is not dependent upon this philosophy of mathematics. One might hold with the nineteenth-century German mathematician that God and not man made the natural numbers, and yet still allow with Vico that the *verum* in the fullest sense is literally the *factum*, i.e., "what has been made," and not merely in the ordinary sense that a fact is something that is true. It was upon this as its "first indubitable principle," that Vico founded his new science, namely,

> that the world of civil society has certainly been made by men, and that its principles are therefore to be found within the modifications of our own human mind. Whoever reflects on this cannot but marvel that the philosophers should have bent all their energies to the study of the world of nature, which since God made it, He alone knows; and that they should have neglected the study of the world of nations, or civil world, which, since men had made it, men could come to know.[19]

There are two points worth emphasizing here. First, Vico, in effect, was drawing a line between nature and culture, taking the latter now in a broad sense to comprehend all that man himself has made, as distinguished from that which he has not made but which has been given in nature. Accordingly, there is knowledge of culture as distinguished from knowledge of nature. Second, he implicitly raised the question as to which of the two—nature or man—we can know best, and he answered it in favor of the latter, thereby asserting that the humanities as the knowledge of culture should constitute our best knowledge.

For a fuller understanding of the importance of this distinction and a development of its implications, it is useful to consider the work of Wilhelm Dilthey (1833–1911) who devoted much of his life to elaborating a theory of the humanities. Dilthey himself expressed some hesitation over the name to be given to the disciplines that as a group he wanted to distinguish from the natural sciences, *Naturwissenschaften*. He considered calling them the social sciences, or the moral, or historical, or cultural sciences before he finally chose the term *Geisteswissenschaften*.[20] The word *Geist* roughly translates as *spirit* or *mind*, but it would be completely misleading in English to speak of the *sciences of spirit* or of *mental sciences*. Hence, recourse is usually had to *human sciences* or *humane studies*. However, there is good reason for taking *humanities* as the most satisfactory translation.

Yet, at first sight, it appears that many of the disciplines that Dilthey included among the *Geisteswissenschaften* would be grouped today with the social sciences rather than with the humanities. Thus he put together in one group "history, economics, law, political science, the science of religion, the study of literature and poetry, architecture, and music, and finally psychology."[21] This may seem an odd collection, but Dilthey had good reason for it in maintaining that all these studies have as their objects things that are the results of man's making and doing and, furthermore, all of them are known and studied in a way that uniquely distinguishes them from the natural sciences.

Thus it can be argued that it is the idea of the social sciences that is ambiguous, and not the *Geisteswissenschaften*, as Dilthey conceived of them. In fact, the social sciences today, in both theory and practice, divide into two schools according as one is modeled upon the natural sciences and the other upon the humanities. Psychology offers a telling example of this division. The behaviorist psychology of B.F. Skinner, for example, claims to be based upon the methods of physics, whereas the analytical psychology of C. G. Jung draws heavily instead upon art, poetry, philosophy, and religion. This division betwen a *scientific* and a *humanistic* conception of a discipline is widespread among the social sciences and runs as deep as that between Snow's two cultures. Hence it is hard to believe that there is any ground to his hope that the social sciences might provide a third culture that would bridge the gap between the two.[22]

According to Dilthey, the distinguishing feature of the *Geisteswissenschaften*, or of the humanities as we will henceforth say, is that "all these studies refer to the same great fact: mankind, which they describe, recount, and judge, and about which they form concepts and theories." They may concern men as individuals or as groups, families, nations, even humanity itself, their institutions or works or customs, rituals, poems, paintings, but in any case they always refer to "one and the same fact: humanity or human-social-historical reality."[23]

However, the same statement can be made about the sciences, natural as well as social. They too turn their attention to man and the things of man. The fact then that man provides the subject matter is not sufficient to distinguish the humanities from the sciences. A poem constitutes a structure of sounds that can be analyzed as a physical pattern manifesting certain physical laws. Or it can be studied for what it expresses and reveals about the poet's mind and the psychology of creativity. But studied in either of these ways, Dilthey claimed, it is not read as a poem nor is taken as the object that is the primary concern of literature as a discipline. As a poem and a literary object, it is before all "a meaningful structure of words, through which it receives expression," and hence more than physical sounds alone or a mental process in the mind of the poet and his reader. "It is a whole objectively realized mental structure [*ein geistiger Zusammenhang realisiert*] that enters the world of the senses, but that is only to be understood by going behind it," so as to understand it as an expression of human life.[24]

Understanding (Verstehen), expression (Ausdruck), and *life (Leben)* are key words in Dilthey's writing, and although they are common and ordinary, the weight that he placed upon them and the way he related them were sufficient to distinguish the humanities definitely from the sciences. For the intimate union of the three defines the object as well as the method of the humanities. They have their basis in the life that men live as men and that we understand from our own lives as men what it is to be human and to express ourselves. We understand from within, from living as men, what it is to be man in a way that we cannot possibly know anything else, and it is this fact, Dilthey maintained, that underlies and pervades the humanities and separates them from the sciences. The results and achievements of the sciences he called "esoteric" in the sense that they are "separated from our connection with the world" insofar as they are abstract and specialized. The humanities, however, "keep the relation between life and knowledge inasmuch as the foundation of their knowing remains the thought arising from life itself."[25] In maintaining relation to the lived experience of men, to his *Lebenswelt* as phenomenology calls it, the humanities remain rooted in the fundamental experience available to every man—the experience of being human and having emotions, likes and dislikes, goals and purposes, of knowing success and failure, birth and death, loneliness and friendship, and all the difficulties of communicating. The sciences are esoteric from the fact, not that they are not related to this life, but that in expressing their results they abstract entirely from it. Perhaps the most extreme example of this kind of abstracting and separating is offered by mathematical logic, which prefers not only to have nothing to do with life, but aims to do away with the need of assuming the existence of anything at all.[26]

To note and characterize the way of knowing proper to the humanities, Dilthey used the term *Verstehen* (understanding) as distinguished from *Kennen* ("scientific knowing").[27] It is by understanding that we know other persons as well as ourselves, and so too the products of man's making and doing. A linguistic utterance, a gesture, a smile, a painting, a poem, a scientific experiment, an institution, are all "expressions" of meanings in human life in addition to being physical or material entities, and it is by understanding that we grasp the meanings of expresssions. Since man is understood only in and through his lived experience, it is ultimately the individual person and not the abstract mankind in general that is of special concern for understanding. Because they proceed by means of understanding, the humanities have a much greater interest then the sciences in the singular individual and in history. For science the individual entity is mainly of interest only for what it can tell about its general type so as to lead to the formulation of a general law. It is not that the humanities are not also interested in arriving at generalizations. In fact, some are so much interested that Dilthey considered it useful to distinguish the systematic humanities from those that are historical. But both classes of humanities stand out and apart from the sciences by their greater interest in the individual, whether person, event, or work.

Among the disciplines, it is history that has the greatest concern for the individual in all his individuating circumstances. For this reason Dilthey attributed unique importance to history, and especially to biography and autobiography. He even went so far as to assert that "the only complete, self-contained, and clearly defined event . . . [is] the course of a human life . . . circumscribed by birth and death."[28] The life of a man, however, cannot be fully understood except with reference to the time, place, and society in which he lived. Dilthey came to attach such great importance to the historical dependence of man's life, work, and thought, that he finally espoused the relativistic skepticism of historicism with its claim that all our knowledge is entirely timebound, an extreme to which there is no good reason for following him.

Two Minds or Two Logics?

We seem to be fast approaching the conclusion that a great and decisive gulf separates the sciences from the humanities. Our analysis of the previous conflicts seemed to lead in that direction. The two-cultures controversy and the background to it provided by the work of Vico and Dilthey still further strengthens that conclusion, if it does not confirm it. But granting that such a gulf or division does exist, how is it to be explained? Among recent theories of the humanities, two of the most comprehensive have been addressed to this very question. One of them, the work of A. W. Levi, attributes it to the existence within man of two faculties so distinct and different as to amount, in effect, to the existence of two minds. The other theory, that put forward by H. B. Veatch, locates the source of the difference in the employment of two different logics.

According to Levi, the two cultures dramatized by Snow have roots that go much deeper than he suspected. The mutual incomprehension and hostility between them derives not so much from "human obstinacy and willfulness" as it does from "that basic schism of the mind upon which this obstinacy is founded."[29] As a sign of this split, Levi points to the fact that the sciences and the humanities operate with significantly different and even opposed sets of terms and concepts. In "the scientific chain of meanings," we find such terms as *true and false propositions, error, scientific law, causality, chance, prediction, fact, change, equilibrium, stasis*, whereas in the humanistic complex" there are such terms as *appearance and reality, illusion, destiny, free will, fortune, fate, drama, tragedy, happiness, peace*.[30] The contrast between these two language sets recalls the table of contraries (supra) drawn to characterize the scientific and poetic uses of language, and Levi in the course of his analysis used many of the same terms.[31] For Levi, however, the difference is not merely a matter of language use, but is based on the fact that the two sets stem from two different faculties of mind: the understanding and the imagination.

It must be noted at once that Levi takes *understanding* in the sense that Kant gave to it, and not that of Dilthey. It is the faculty by which we know things as presented in time and space and organized by the scientific chain of meaning. Although he does occasionally qualify it by using such adjectives as *cognitive* or *scientific*, he does not intend, as far as I can tell, to distinguish different kinds of understanding. He means by it, as Kant did, the faculty of mind that is specifically manifested in Newtonian physics.[32] *Imagination* is used by Levi in the positive and creative sense that Coleridge gave to the term, but including also Kant's notion of aesthetic judgment, in which the note of purposiveness is supreme. Imagination thus becomes for him the faculty for knowing and dealing with all that escapes and transcends space, time, and sense experience and, hence, is as much at home in metaphysics as in poetry.[33]

Levi's position is "frankly dualistic," as he acknowledges, in that it "sees the age-old quarrel between the sciences and the humanities as deeply motivated, as grounded not merely in the accidents of temperament, but in basic commitments founded upon the structure of the human mind."[34] He traces the development of this dualism, especially in its theory of imagination, from its source in Kant in the division between pure reason and judgment—not in the division between the pure and practical reason that we met in our discussion of reason and faith—then through Kant's immediate successors, Vaihinger, Nietzsche, and Lange, reappearing in the work of Bergson and Spengler, but "finding its best expression," he claims, in the thought of Santayana. The work of Kant, however, is admitted to be the "origin and central focus" of Levi's endeavor, and he asserts that in providing a philosophical justification of the humanities based on an analysis of the imagination, he is attempting a work comparable to Kant's justification of science based on a theory of the understanding.[35]

By his exposition of the "humanistic complex," Levi intends to show that the humanities are concerned with questions and problems that have been of perennial and frequently of tragic interest in ways that the sciences shun, when they do not in fact repudiate them. As expressed in works of literature, philosophy, and religion, they are ineradicably anthropomorphic and teleological: they struggle with problems of fortune, fate, destiny, tragedy, and peace; they appeal to intuition, imagination, emotion, and subjectivity by means of metaphor, legend, myth, drama, and fiction; they seek, demand, and assert the existence of more than is given by a science that limits itself to what is phenomenally given in space-time and to theories and speculations about that given. In sharing such concerns as these, the humanities, according to Levi, are radically more "human" than the sciences because such are the concerns of every man and always have been.

The humanities and sciences speak different languages and employ separate categories because they have their source in different faculties, Levi claims, and for that reason they also look to different objects, one devoting itself to the study of nature, the other to the study of man. Nor does he hesitate to assert that "in a most important sense, they *think* differently."[36] Even more, he maintains that "when you push the superficial intent of science and the humanities back far enough, you come upon fundamentally discordant approaches to life—to a conflict of basic philosophies."[37] Thus, according to Levi, the two cultures are two and opposed, not only because they have different languages and ways and objects of thought, but still more fundamentally because they express and represent two different minds with two different views of the world.

Professor Veatch would agree with Levi that the conflict is one of basic philosophies, but he would also claim that it is far deeper and wider than Levi allows. For, according to Levi, there is at least one philosopher whose teaching provides the basis for understanding both the sciences and the humanities, namely, Kant in the *Critique of Pure*

Reason and the *Critique of Aesthetic Judgment* respectively. But, in the judgment of Veatch, Kant is perhaps more responsible than any other philosopher for the widespread confusion about the humanities and their consequent depreciation inasmuch as Kant's is a preeminent example of the kind of thinking that Veatch calls a "relating-logic," which is sharply different from the "what-logic" that is characteristic of the humanities.

The term *logic*, as Veatch uses it here, refers not to formal logic, but, as he notes, to the discipline that the Scholastics called "material logic" and that Kant called "transcendental logic," a logic, that is to say, that is concerned with the nature of knowledge, and not just with the formal laws of validity.[38] What he means by the two logics is most readily gathered from an example, one that he himself uses: the experience of perceiving an apple, and how this would be accounted for by the two logics. A relating-logic would account for it as the American philosopher, C. I. Lewis, did in the following passage:

> At the moment, a certain 'that' which I can only describe [in terms of concepts] as a round, ruddy, tangy-smelling some-what, means to me an 'edible apple'. . . . An object such as an apple is never given; between the real apple in all its complexity and this fragmentary presentation lies that interval which only interpretation can bridge.

For Lewis, as for Kant, our experience is a construction ultimately based upon a we-know-not-what. But the what-logic maintains, on the contrary, that we know very well what we perceive. In Veatch's words: "Normally, and apart from the sophistications of modern epistemologies, we all suppose that the real apple, the actual substance, is there before us, and that it is this that we see and are presented with."[39] The concept *apple* for the one logic has a purely relational function, whereas for the other it presents a real substance, a *what*.

Veatch, like Levi, acknowledges that the sciences and humanities employ different sets of concepts and of languages, and that they do so because they are for the most part concerned with different objects. But the underlying reason for all these differences, according to Veatch, is that they constitute different knowledges: one is a knowledge of real substances apprehended directly in the everyday world of our common experience, whereas the other is a knowledge of a relational network of the mind's own constructing, a "substantive knowledge" in the one case, a "calculative knowledge" in the other.[40] To contrast the two knowledges Veatch, in the introduction of his book, entitled "The Battle of the Books Renewed," adapts to his own purposes Swift's parable of the bee and the spider. The bee represents the what-logic of the traditional humanities in that it ranges widely over the world of our ordinary experience, whereas the spider, since it spins all out of itself, represents the relating-logic of modern science.[41] Like Swift and Vico before him, Veatch is here passing judgment on the relative merits of science and the humanities as knowledge. The issue, in short, is what knowledge is most worth having, to paraphrase a title from a work by Herbert Spencer.[42] This issue, which was lurking in the background throughout the controversy over the two cultures, deserves to be considered for its own sake.

The Conflict of Science and Philosophy

A surprising, if not startling, omission in the original formulation of the Snow-Leavis controversy over the two cultures was the lack of any reference to philosophy. Yet certainly the most fundamental of all the issues on which they were divided was a philosophical one, namely that regarding our best and most fundamental knowledge. Neither writer left any doubt of his own position. Snow, as we have seen, hailed science as "the most beautiful and wonderful collective work of the mind of man." To this Leavis responded with the assertion that there is "a more basic work of the mind of man (and more than the mind), one without which the triumphant erection of the scientific edifice would not have been possible: that is, the creation of the human world, including language."[43] Sharing the same position as Leavis on this issue are Veatch, Levi, Dilthey, and Vico, as would, generally, any proponent of either the literary or the theological ideals of culture. Taking the position enunciated by Snow would be Francis Bacon as well as Descartes, Kant, D'Alembert, Comte and the followers of the positivist tradition, and, generally, anyone holding that science constitutes our best if not our only genuine knowledge. It is scarcely an exaggeration to claim that this issue is perhaps the most basic one in the modern conflict of cultural ideals.

Yet to make sense, the issue obviously needs further specification. How can we hope to determine which knowledge is best and most worth having until we have settled the question: best for what? Chesterton, once asked in a journalistic survey what books he would want if he were stranded on a desert island, replied, "books on ship-building." So too, one can imagine readily any number of situations in which the best knowledge for a given purpose would be provided by one science or another. Yet if religious faith can provide knowledge of the way to eternal life in union with God, that would be not only the best knowledge, but could be likened to the *unum necessarium* of the Gospel.[44] Nor is the question to be understood as Aristotle took it when he argued that metaphysics is the first science since it considers the highest and most knowable object, although something of this doctrine is pertinent to our consideration of the issue. But I construe the question as Veatch would in speaking of the knowledge that is fundamental, basic, indispensable, logically prior, and deserving more than any other to be considered the paradigm of the very idea of knowledge.[45]

Exactness, precision, clarity, and demonstrability are often taken as distinguishing virtues of science, and, in their places, excellencies they are. Yet too frequently they demand more than their share of respect, especially when the "exact sciences" and the "hard sciences" are hailed not only as the epitome of all science, but the standard and model of all knowledge. The ideal of exactness pursued so unthinkingly can only too readily become a Baconian idol. Exactness deserves thinking about. Aristotle observed, in beginning his consideration of ethics, certainly an "inexact" subject, that an educated man does not look for more certitude than the matter is capable of.[46] Wittgenstein has also provided an amusing example of the way in which the demand for clarity and exactness can result in a bad case of intellectual cramps, if it is supposed that in order to be clear we must be exact. Our ordinary speech is seldom exact, a fact that is substantiated by the very word *exact*, which has no exact meaning. "We understand what it means to set a pocket watch to the exact time or to regulate it to be exact", yet, as Wittgenstein pointed out, this meaning is not ideally exact.

> We can speak of measurements of time in which there is a different . . . a greater exactness than in the measurement of time by a pocket-watch. . . . Now, if I tell someone: "You should come to dinner more punctually; you know it begins at one o'clock exactly"—is there really no question of exactness here? Because it is impossible to say: "Think of the determination of time in the laboratory or the observatory: *there* you see what "exactness" means?" "Inexact" is really a reproach, and "exact" is praise. . . . Am I inexact when I do not give our distance from the sun to the nearest foot, or tell a joiner the width of a table to the nearest thousandth of an inch. No *single* ideal of exactness has been laid down; we do not know what we should be supposed to imagine under this head.[47]

Science and scientists are well aware of this fact, it may be said, and take it into account in recognizing the limits of measurement. It is sometimes overlooked or forgotten, however, how very rough, inexact, and "unscientific" the conditions of measurement itself are. Research on subatomic particles calls for measurement of a very high order. Yet as microphysicist G. Chew has observed, the possibility of measurement rests upon three propositions, the truth of which the scientist shares with the common man: (1) that there is a three-dimensional space, a time flowing in one direction, and an associated cause-effect relationship between events; (2) that there is such a thing as an "isolated object" that remains recognizably the same from one day to another so that the physicist can identify his laboratory and equipment; and (3) that however much his probing may disturb the atom whose interior he is investigating, it must remain weak enough not to destroy the object of his research.[48] If such are the conditions for the possibility of measurement, even the most exact science depends upon and supposes an experience so little "scientific" that it is one all men would recognize once their attention was drawn to it.

Then too, as Leavis emphasized, science itself would not be possible without ordinary language. This is true even of mathematical logic, which in its pursuit of clarity, precision, and rigor, has constructed a highly elaborate and artificial language for expressing its results without recourse to ordinary "natural" language. It cannot do so completely, however, for it is only by the use of ordinary language that it can get going at all.[49] But even though it can continue once it gets started, as Veatch points out, it cannot *say* anything in the ordinary sense of the word, since it abstracts completely from what is.[50]

Yet despite such dependence, human experience. of the lived-world, especially in the sense of *Verstehen*, is sometimes violently repudiated as having nothing at all to do with science. The idea of *Geisteswissenschaften* is dismissed as a contradiction in terms on the ground that *Geist* is all subjectivity and, therefore, cannot qualify as a *Wissenschaft*.[51] Perhaps the most flagrant representatives of this position are the behaviorist psychologists, who refuse to accept as a matter of principle any reference to ideas, motives, feelings, or any "inner phenomenon," and attempt to confine their science entirely to overt behavior. To the objection that to do so is to leave out much that is most characteristically human, the behaviorist responds: "So much the better." Thus B.F. Skinner expressly welcomes the "abolition of man" as an event that "has long been over-due," since he maintains as a good behaviorist that "what is being abolished is autonomous man—the inner man, the homunculus, the possessing demon, the man defended by the literatures of freedom and dignity." From Hamlet's "how like a god" to Pavlov's "how like a dog" is seen by Skinner as a marked advance in the scientific understanding of man. For Pavlov's salivating dog displays a conditioned response, whereas "a god is the archetypal pattern of an explanatory fiction, of a miracle-working mind, of the metaphysical."[52] Yet as Brand Blanshard, the American philosopher, pointed out in debate with Skinner, no behaviorist can ever behave as though his theory were true, nor can he carry on his science without assuming the truth of the very thing he denies. The behaviorist would explain our conscious experience, such as rage for example, by referring only to physical responses. But in order to correlate a physical response with the emotion of rage, he must first know what is meant by the emotion of rage. Thus the behaviorist, Blanshard noted, "must resort to the conscious state as our only reliable index to the behavior that is supposed to supplant it." Again, it is a question of what we know best. Seeing matter in motion, i.e., physical behavior, is not the only kind of awareness that we have. As Blanshard said, "We may be vividly aware not only of shapes and sizes, but also of our activity of thinking, of our being hot, of being in doubt what should be done about Viet Nam, of the last time we saw Paris, of the funniness of a joke, or of 2-and-2's making 4." Although such experiences are admittedly difficult to analyze, "no argument by which people have sought to analyze them is half so certain as their own disclosures to us."[53]

The point of these arguments, examples, and quotations, or, rather, the fact to which they point, is that there is a fundamental and basic human experience that cannot be avoided, that refuses to be talked or thought away, and that underlies and is taken for granted by science itself. Not only all our science, but all our thinking, starts from it. It goes by many different names among philosophers: common experience, general experience, macroscopic experience, naive experience, public experience, primary objectivity, originary evidence, and elementary experience.[54] Since our purpose here is to emphasize that it underlies all our thinking, it may be best to call it our "underlying experience."

This underlying experience has many aspects. In one aspect it is so primordial that all men everwhere for as long as we have any record have shared the same experience: the rhythms of day and night, the motions of sun, moon, and stars, and so of time, space, and motion, the diversity of things in the world; and the life of man as a mortal being who is born and dies and whose life depends on satisfying such needs as for food, air, shelter, and human association with all its joys and sorrows. In these respects, this experience is of what is given in the world in which man finds himself as the kind of being that he is, a world that is not of his making as such. Yet, in another aspect, the experience of even the naturally given comes into being only in and through, as mediated by, the culture that man has made for himself. Man everywhere and at all times has needed food to live, but that his diet should be mainly meat rather than cereal is a fact of culture, subject, of course, to some extent to the geographical situation in which he lives. So too is it that he speaks English rather than Chinese, that he adopts one mode of dress rather than another, and that one type of activity is valued more highly than another and that its participants enjoy a status of privilege. All this constitutes the lived-world of man's making, in, through, and from which man has everywhere and always begun and carried on his thinking, yet that often differs in many very important respects from one culture to another.

This underlying experience is thus of both the natural phenomenal world and the cultural world of man's making. Both are integral to our knowledge and understanding, since they are mutually inter-dependent in our experience. No experience is every purely cultural, since all of man's creations, as Auden liked to emphasize, are never more than "sub-creations" inasmuch as man does not create *ex nihilo*. Hence, if we accept Vico's claim that the humanities can provide a better knowledge than the sciences, it is not entirely for the reason he gave, namely, that they study the cultural objects of man's making. More significant, more decisive, it seems to me, is the fact that they address objects that for the most part, fall within our underlying experience and discuss and analyze them in terms of that experience.

The great and overwhelming difference between the humanities and the sciences lies in the kind and character of the experience with which they are respectively concerned. The famous example of the two tables with which Eddington began his lectures on the nature of the physical world remains an illuminating statement of the difference. One table, he said, is "a commonplace object of that environment which I call the world." The other, the scientific table, "is a more recent acquaintance, and I do not feel so familiar with it. . . . It is part of a world which in more devious ways has forced itself on my attention. . . . [It] is mostly emptiness. Sparsely scattered in that empti-ness are numerous electric charges rushing about with great speed; but their combined bulk amounts to less than a billionth of the bulk of the table itself."[55] Eddington went on to argue for the superiority of the scientific conception. Yet he did not deny, nor could he truthfully deny, which table we know best from our experience. As he noted, one belongs to our commonplace world, whereas the other is an object of experience only in a most special and recondite sense as an abstraction and construction based upon highly rarified physical experiments and measurements. The scientific table may be a highly efficient one for advancing scientific research and its technological extensions and applications. But it is of no use at all in the ordinary world of human experience, which is the world, incidentally, in which Eddington wrote and delivered his lectures on the unreality of this world.

A word of warning is perhaps in order about the meaning of the word *experience* as it is here being used. It should not be identified with opinion or judgment, as though our underlying experience were always a true judgment of the way things are. This experience is common as available to all men, but it is not the same as common opinion. We experience the earth's landscape as more or less flat and at rest, and at one time many also thought and judged that the world was indeed flat and stationary. This judgment, however, is not the same as the experience, and we now know from other experiences that this judgment is false. But the fact that this judgment is false does not deny or invalidate our experience, for in our position on the surface of the earth, it continues to present itself to us as flat and stationary. The experience in any given case may or may not suffice by itself to support and validate a true judgment. More than it by itself may be needed. Yet of itself it remains fundamental and indispensable.

Although underlying experience cannot be eliminated, one has to admit that it can be neglected, overlooked, depreciated, and even denied. The denial of it, however, is intellectually self-destructive, since no knowledge is possible without referring to it in one way or another, if only by the employment of ordinary languages. There is something dubious, not to say suspicious, about a position that denies the very basis on which it rests and by which it is supported.

What we know best is this world of our underlying experience. Yet this knowledge, fundamental as it is, is not without its shortcomings. As Veatch said a propos of our knowledge of *whats*,[56] we may know very well what a thing is and yet be hard pressed to say much or anything very precise about what it is. Even when we can say something more, it very well may not take us very far along. We know very well what an apple is, we know the accidental properties that distinguish one variety from another, and we have no trouble in differentiating it from an ape or an aphid; yet we cannot go far in assigning specific differences or in determining what it is that makes the apple to be what and as it is. Thus our what-knowledge of things is severely limited. Nor is there any necessary infallibility about it. We know very well that we can, and frequently do, make mistakes, get confused, and are unclear about our experiences, but just because we may be mistaken sometimes, it does not follow that we never apprehend things for what and as they are. As I am writing here and now, I notice through the window birds eating at the feeding station. What are they? The big ones are blue jays; the little ones redpolls. And that, in truth, is what they are.

If the experience that we have been discussing is so fundamental, indispensable, and factually undeniable, why is it not everywhere admitted to constitute our best knowledge? Among the many answers, certainly one of the most far-reaching is the one that traces the failure to the different evaluations that men put upon what is fundamental in import and significance, of what there is to wonder at, and, in short, of what it is that carries most weight. If it is the power to predict and control, to reshape the face of the world and alter the course of events, to make things work as men direct, then it is not this fundamental experience that we have been talking of, but the sciences, that will be judged to constitute our best knowledge. And so the scientific ideal has been loudly proclaiming since the time of Francis Bacon. This, however, is not our only choice. "The wonder of all wonders is the pure ego and pure subjectivity," Husserl declared.[57] This conviction, as it has been developed in phenomenology and existentialism, has resulted in a reaffirmation of the value and importance of man's underlying experience and of the worth of the humanities. In fact, it has also sometimes been accompanied by a criticism of science—even a repudiation of it—for its objectivity which is seen as a betrayal and falsification of man. Such a conclusion goes too far and thereby exposes the weakness of this whole position. It too readily goes to extremes and lands in excesses of subjectivity, to the extent even of denying the data of our human condition. Thus Sartre has expressly declared that man has no nature, but makes his own.[58] Read literally, the statement is obviously exaggerated. Any individual man is not only genetically determined in many important respects (certainly a fact of nature), but he is also subject to all the conditions of life as an animal on the planet earth, which is part of the solar system, whereas in his "second nature," he is in many ways a product of his culture. Sartre himself is both a twentieth-century Frenchman and a member of the human race, neither of which is the result of his own making.

There is yet a third position that locates what is of greatest import in the mere fact that there is something rather than nothing. "The wonder of all wonders" as Heidegger declared: "that what-is *is*."[59] Not just human subjectivity, as for Husserl, but things in the world, neither of which, in regard to their being, are of our own making. That there should be something rather than nothing is certainly a most ordinary, commonplace experience. Yet the knowledge is fundamental; in fact, it is even more fundamental than any of our what-knowledge, since we may know *that* something is without knowing *what* it is. Yet that is a fact of greatest weight. As Thomas wrote in the introduction to his study of being, "Man cannot attain complete knowledge of it, but the little {*modicum*} that he can achieve is of far more weight {*praeponderat*} than everything known by the other sciences."[60]

With this position we have entered within the reach of metaphysics and ontology. Of course, to ask what is our best knowledge? is to ask a metaphysical question. But we have now come to the point where the question is becoming, what is most real? And with this we have gone further than we need in order to locate the basic distinction between the sciences and the humanities. For that, our argument has needed only the assertion of the priority of our underlying experience over the specialized constructions of science, and that assertion, as we have just seen, is not the exclusive property of any one metaphysics.

PART III: *The City of the Muses*

In Part One we considered the great historical paradigms of intellectual culture and then, in Part Two, analyzed the major battles and quarrels in which the followers of these ideals came into conflict. In principle, since we have been dealing with three ideals, the conflict should have been a three-sided one. Yet, in actuality, the controversy has tended to polarize about two positions, until in the two-cultures debate only two protagonists are recognized. At the start, in the original papers of Snow and Leavis, the only cultures in question were literature and science, and no cognizance was taken of any other ideal. Yet the issue, in fact, was much broader; it was nothing less than a confrontation between the sciences and the humanities. Indeed, it has begun to appear that this is perhaps the basic division and is so deep and broad that there is no meeting between the two. So far, however, our attention has been directed primarily upon conflict and the issues and differences, disagreements, and oppositions that generate it. But before concluding that the differences are so great that conflict is inevitable, I ought first to investigate the similarities between the various disciplines and ways of knowing and note the things they share in common. Although conflict does not arise unless there is some disagreement or some difference, it nevertheless supposes that there is some common meeting and agreement. To locate and consider such similarities and agreements is one of the major aims of Part Three.

CHAPTER 8: Maps of the World of Learning

We have had occasion in the course of our investigation to notice several of the schemes for organizing the world of knowledge: from Plato's divided line, the trivium and quadrivium of mediaeval fame, Bacon's elaborate globe of the intellectual world, Comte's evolutionary line of positive science, down to Dilthey's division of *Natur-und-Geisteswissenschaften*. However, I have yet to consider any of these schemes in detail so as to see the result as well as the work that such a task entails. The problem of organizing and mapping the world of learning is a large one, and many solutions have been offered.[1] Here I shall consider only a few of the major ones, primarily those that can contribute most directly to the work of constructing a theory of the humanities.

Of the various maps of learning, the most widely used today, and hence the most familiar, are those embodied in the encyclopedia on the one hand and in the university on the other. The general reference encyclopedia, in the form that it has now come to assume, is an organization for the storage and retrieval of information and knowledge, and thus it represents, in microcosm, the principle of the library as an information system. The university is an organization of knowledge for the purpose of learning and teaching, for the achievement of which it also has to have available the knowledge previously acquired. Universities as well as encyclopedias are organized according to different principles, but it would not be to the point here to analyze these principles in detail. One example of each will suffice to indicate the type of organization of knowledge that is embodied in these structures.

The Encyclopedia

As representative of the encyclopedic organization of knowledge, I shall consider the new, fifteenth edition of the *Encyclopaedia Britannica*. Not only is it the most recent large reference encyclopedia, but it also has in its initial volume, called *Propaedia,* an outline of knowledge that is a systematically organized, topical presentation of the contents of the articles contained in the major corpus of the encyclopedia. Since in aim and scope the *Britannica* is comprehensive, the outline constitutes an organization or map of the world of learning as it now exists. The whole, which is described as a "circle of learning," is divided into ten parts. Each of these parts has several major divisions, totaling forty-two in all. Each of these major divisions is broken down, in turn, into a number of sections, for a total of 189, and these sections contain the outlines of the topics and subjects treated in the articles contained in the main body of the set. Thus the overall structure is determined by the ten parts, the titles of which are as follows: Matter and Energy, The Earth, Life on Earth, Human Life, Human Society, Art, Technology, Religion, The History of Mankind, and The Branches of Knowledge.

One might ask by what principle this order was established. Dr. M. J. Adler, the architect of the plan, emphasizes in his introduction that the choice was based primarily upon ease of reference. He further recommends that the ten parts be pictured rather as segments of a circle, no one of which provides a privileged entry, since any one of the ten segments can serve as such. The ten parts of knowledge are thus to be viewed as coordinate with one another, not in the sense that they are all of equal value and importance, but rather that a reader can begin the exploration of the world of knowledge as it is represented in the outline from wherever his interest may lead him to begin.[2] The one organizing principle that is explicitly noted is that which distinguishes the tenth part from the rest. This part is devoted to "what we know about the branches of learning or departments of scholarship—the various academic disciplines themselves," and is thus a second-order consideration, whereas the other nine parts are concerned with the first-order consideration of "what we know about the world of nature, of man and society, and of human institutions *by means of* the various branches of learning or departments of scholarship."[3] This distinction reflects the twofold sense of "teaching-and-learning" according to whether the reference is to the aim and result—in this case what is known about the knowable world—or to the process and method of acquiring and communicating that knowledge. Thus this distinction corresponds to the ancient one between *doctrina* and *disciplina.* The disciplines or branches of knowledge can themselves be taken as objects of inquiry, and thus the knowledge, or doctrine, about them is one part of the whole circle of knowledge.

Part ten then constitutes a map of the disciplines. It consists of five major divisions, broken down as follows:

1. Logic
    History and philosophy of logic
    Formal logic, metalogic, and applied logic
2. Mathematics
    History and foundations of mathematics
    Branches of mathematics
    Applications of mathematics
3. Science
    History and philosophy of science
    The physical sciences
    The earth sciences
    The biological sciences
    Medicine and affiliated disciplines
    The social sciences and psychology
    The technological sciences
4. History and the humanities
    Historiography and the study of history
    The humanities and humanistic scholarship
5. Philosophy
    The nature and divisions of philosophy
    History of philosophy
    Philosophical schools and doctrines

Here in the middle we find the sciences and humanities, but they are preceded by logic and mathematics, both of them sciences, and followed by philosophy, some kinds or parts of which would be grouped with the humanities. Evidently, several different principles are at work. One reason for this is the fact that the first, second and fifth divisions include in their outlines the first-order consideration of their content as well as the second-order treatment of them as disciplines, whereas the third and fourth divisions are restricted to the latter alone. By implication, the former divisions stand apart from the others. They do so, of course, in their high degree of generality and extensive applicability. Logic and mathematics are instruments and methods for almost all forms of inquiry, while philosophy ranges so widely that it is sometimes doubted whether it has any subject matter of its own and must perforce think only about the knowledge supplied by the other disciplines.

In his introduction to the tenth part, Adler lists three questions as the most challenging ones regarding the organization of knowledge, and they bear directly upon our own inquiry. The first is whether the disciplines can and should be ordered in a hierarchy. The second concerns the unity of truth and whether the results achieved by the various disciplines form a coherent and consistent whole. The third, noting the rift between the sciences and the humanities, concerns whether the sciences and humanities form one world or two, whether they are so opposed to each other that no communication is possible.

By its conception of the circle of learning that one may enter from any segment, the *Encyclopaedia* has avoided any attempt to establish a hierarchy among the disciplines. Although he foregoes any answer to the second and third question, Adler does note that the encyclopedia as an organized whole would by that very fact favor the view that the world of learning constitutes one world, coherent and consistent. With regard to the sciences and the humanities, he notes that the differences between them are "not entirely clear," since there are no methods or criteria of validity that are uniquely characteristic of either.[4]

The University

The university embodies an organization of knowledge, but it does so as an institution established for carrying on the tasks of teaching and learning. At first sight, it appears that the basic organizational principle is provided by the academic department, since it is in classes organized according to departments that most of the teaching is done. An academic department, however, is a highly anomalous entity and more characteristic of higher learning in the United States than elsewhere. It is primarily an administrative device for bringing teachers and students together in a more or less orderly fashion. In some cases a department represents an established, well-organized discipline, such as mathematics. But then again it may be an organization in which various disciplines are brought together to study one definite area, as mediaeval studies or urban affairs. Or it may constitute a training program to prepare and qualify one for a definite career, such as accounting. It may even constitute an entire program of studies in all major disciplines, as in a department of integrated studies. With such great diversity among departments, based often only on principles of administrative, if not of personal, convenience, it is obvious that the departmental structure cannot represent a well-articulated division of the world of knowledge.

However, the higher level at which academic departments are organized into divisions presents a clearer and more coherent structure. The college and the graduate school of arts and sciences, which traditionally have claimed responsibility for the world of learning as such, are frequently organized in three divisions: natural sciences, social sciences, and humanities. Verbally, at least, the division is in fact a two-fold one into science—either natural or social—and humanities. In many cases, of course, we find that *arts* is used instead of *humanities,* but the result is the same. Of this latter term the most summary and capacious one is that given in the law establishing the National Endowment for the Humanities, which reads as follows:

> The term "humanities" includes but is not limited to, the study of the following: language, both modern and classical; linguistics; literature; history, ethics; the history, theory, and practice of the arts; and those aspects of the social sciences which have humanistic content and employ humanistic methods.[5]

As indicated by the last phrase, the humanities are characterized by method as well as content. One might well question whether the enumeration is not too broad, whether the practice of the fine arts, for example, should be included, and whether linguistics, as frequently practiced, is not a science.

This twofold division into the sciences and the humanities reflects more closely than any other we have seen the division that Dilthey made. For that reason alone his map of the world of learning deserves more attention than has been given to it.

Dilthey's Subject Matters and Methods

Dilthey was not a systematic thinker, and, so far as I know, he did not attempt to construct a scheme of all the main kinds of knowledge. Yet, as we have already seen, he devoted much attention to the differences between the sciences and the humanities, and from his remarks about them it is possible to draw up a broad outline of the world of knowledge as he conceived it.

Natural Sciences *(Naturwissenschaften)*
    nonhuman natural phenomena not made by man (the natural sciences)
    man's mental processes and behavior as natural phenomena (the behavioral sciences)
Humanities *(Geisteswissenschaften)*
    Historical
      history, biography, autobiography

    economics, law, politics
    moral and social life
    religion
    poetry, architecture, music
    philosophical world views
    psychology
Systematic
    grammar, rhetoric, literary criticism
    ethics, political philosophy
    economics, sociology, psychology[6]

There was much discussion in Dilthey's time regarding the relative importance of subject matter and method as the decisive principle of division.[7] Yet for Dilthey there is little doubt that it was the subject matter that dictated the method. He maintained, as we have seen, that the study of man and his work as human is unique in that we can understand it from within from the very life that we live as men, and thus he used *Verstehen* as a technical term denoting a unique method.[8]

Dilthey's scheme, it should be noted, can accommodate several overlaps. Since man in some of his behavior as well as some of his psychological processes is a natural phenomenon and not only a cultural product, he can be studied as such by the methods of the empirical sciences. Dilthey's scheme can thus include the behavioral and social sciences in addition to the natural sciences as commonly understood. He would insist, however, that such scientific study is neither the only nor the best knowledge that man can have of man. That of the humanities is superior inasmuch as it is based on a privileged understanding of what it is to be human. The broad distinction within the humanities corresponds to still further ways in which man and his work can be studied. It is either historical or systematic according as it looks primarily to the singular, unique individual (whether as person, action, or event) or to recurrent patterns that provide the basis for generalization. Thus, for example, man's moral and social life can be investigated both historically and philosophically. This investigation can achieve a kind of knowledge that belongs to the humanities as it is grounded in *Verstehen*, distinct from an investigation of the same subject that restricts itself to empirical and mathematical methods. With respect to metaphysics, i.e., to philosophical world views, Dilthey would not allow such a distinction, since he maintained that metaphysics is impossible except as a historical study of what men have believed—a position it might be noted, that reveals the shortcomings of historicism.[9]

Bacon's Methods and Faculties

The "small globe of the intellectual world" that Francis Bacon constructed in *The Advancement of Learning* is a vast one, containing many details, all carefully articulated, and all of considerable interest. But to enter into all its many details would lead us far astray. We need consider only the basic principles of his division of learning, which can be tabulated as follows:

Human learning
  History
      literary, natural, civil, ecclesiastical
  Poesy
  Philosophy
    Philosophia prima
    Natural theology
    Natural philosophy
      physics, metaphysics, mathematics
      experimental, magical operative-prudence
    Human philosophy or humanity·
      medicine, cosmetics, athletics, arts voluptuary
      invention, judgment, memory, tradition
      morals
      conversation, negotiation, government
Divine learning

The first division distinguishes human and divine learning according as it "is grounded" upon the light of nature or upon the revealed word of God.[10] The source of knowledge thus provides the first and most basic principle of division. This is the only major respect, it might be noted, in which the French *Encyclopédie* departed from the Baconian scheme; revealed theology is there included within philosophy.[11]

The next division is the partition of learning according to "the three parts of man's understanding, which is the seat of learning: history to his memory, poesy to his imagination, and philosophy to his reason," a division which is applied to divine as well as human learning.[12] Hence, this principle of division is not only the largest in scope, but also the controlling one. Yet Bacon said little in explanation or defense of it, and left it to speak for itself. The first and immediate consequence of it is that the world of learning is viewed and approached from the way that man knows rather than from the being that he knows, and from the means and method of his knowing rather than from its aim and purpose. This division according to faculties must also ultimately be more one of emphasis than of exclusive designation. For none of our knowledge is exclusively the work of any one faculty; history is no more solely and exclusively the work of memory than poetry is of imagination or philosophy of reason. The basis for the distinction must then lie elsewhere. Presumably, it is because history is like memory in being concerned with the past; poetry is like imagination in "feigning" and, "not being tied to the laws of matter [, it] may at pleasure join that which nature hath severed, and sever that which nature hath joined; and so make unlawful matches and divorces of thing."[13] Philosophy, like the intellectual arts and sciences, is primarily the work of reason. While there is something to be said for the distinction, it tends to throw history and poetry into special prominence as somehow not as much the work of reason as the other disciplines.

Philosophy is much the most comprehensive division within Bacon's scheme. It includes not only both theoretical and practical philosophy, but also all the linguistic arts, all mathematics, all the knowledge that would now be the concern of the physical, biological, and social sciences, as well as engineering, medicine, the fine arts, and even athletics and cosmetics. Such comprehensiveness is not entirely accounted for by the fact that in Bacon's time *philosophy* still referred to many disciplines that are no longer so called. For he included many arts under philosophy that others before him had expressly excluded; even in antiquity Aristotelians had argued that logic was propaedeutic to philosophy, not a part of it.

For the many subdivisions of philosophy, Bacon appealed to different principles. The first, grounded on the degree of generality, yields the "one universal science, by the name of *philosophia prima*, primitive or summary philosophy," which considers those common adjuncts of things and those common principles and axioms "as fall not within the compass of any of the special parts of philosophy or sciences, but are more common and of a higher stage."[14] The special sciences are distinguished by their object, and, according as they look to God, nature, or man, constitute divine philosophy or natural theology, natural philosophy, and human philosophy, or "humanity."[15] According to the end pursued, whether knowledge of causes or production of effects, natural philosophy divides into speculative, natural science, or theory on the one side and operative or natural prudence on the other. In the first of these, Bacon placed metaphysics as well as mathematics and all the arts of the quadrivium. The second includes "natural" magic," or all that we would now call engineering and technology.[16]

Human philosophy is divided first insofar as man is considered "segregate and distributively," i.e., individually, and second insofar as he is seen as "congregate and in society."[17] Knowledge of man individually is divided according to body and mind. Knowledge of the human body consists of medicine, cosmetics, athletics, and the voluptuary arts, while philosophy of mind, after a general consideration of its nature, is divided according to the faculties of reason and will, yielding rational philosophy or the arts intellectual on the one hand and moral philosophy on the other.

Bacon's bent toward rhetoric is revealed in his treatment of the intellectual arts. These arts, which include all the linguistic arts, are brought together in a scheme which derives from the traditional art of rhetoric. Four arts are distinguished according to the end or purpose to which they are referred. "For man's labor is to invent that which is sought or propounded; or to judge that which is invented; or to retain that which is judged; or to deliver over that which is retained." Accordingly, there are four arts: "Art of inquiry or invention; art of examination, or judgment; art of custody or memory; and art of elocution or tradition."[18] As is made clear from his comments upon them, these arts are an adaptation of the traditional parts of rhetoric.[19] Invention, or heuristic, as the art of discovery, is of two kinds, according as it seeks to find things or words. The former is the method expounded for science in the *Novum Organum,* while the latter consists of the rhetorical topics as sources of argument. The whole of logic, or all of it considered to be of any use, is brought under the art of judgment, whereas grammar is made a part of tradition as its organon. Under tradition, which is the particular home of rhetoric, Bacon also included the consideration of method and argued expressly against the position that there is one best method for all subject matters. There should be "diversity of methods . . . according to the subject or matter which is handled. For there is a great difference in delivery of the mathematics, which are the most abstracted of knowledges, and policy, which is the most immersed." He charged that the practice of "uniformity of method in multiformity of matter . . . taketh the way to reduce learning to certain empty and barren generalities."[20]

Civil knowledge, or the study of "man congregate," is the last division of human philosophy and consists of conversation, negotiation, and government according as its object is the behavior of man, of business, or of government. In other words, it is the place for the social sciences as well as business management, the latter of which, incidentally, Bacon reported to be deficient in his time.[21]

The Arts of Hugh of St. Victor

The humanities, as we have seen, have a long history of association with the arts, especially with the liberal arts. In the Middle Ages, at least up until the return of Aristotle, the arts themselves provided the basic and preferred partition of the world of learning. Of this kind of division one of the most fully worked out is that of Hugh of St. Victor.[22]

For Hugh, all of human learning consisted of arts, but all the arts themselves are placed under philosophy. Even such arts as commerce, agriculture, and medicine are considered to be parts of philosophy, although he emphasized that this holds true only of the theory, not the practice, of them.[23] Philosophy, however, in Hugh's understanding of it, consisted in the love of that wisdom which is God, and its whole purpose, in all the arts, is to restore within man the likeness to the divine which has been lost.[24] That learning is like healing is a comparison that goes back to antiquity, but Hugh took it to be literally true: all of learning is therapeutic to provide remedies for man's diseases and disabilities. The three main evils of human life are ignorance, vice, and want, the remedies of which are wisdom, virtue, and the satisfaction of our wants respectively. To supply these remedies the arts have been discovered: the theoretical arts for wisdom, the practical arts for virtue, and the mechanical arts for satisfying our wants. The linguistic-logical arts, which comprise a fourth group, were invented after these at first for the sake of eloquence, but then to be propaedeutic to all the rest.[25]

The whole of learning is divided according to these four groups of arts, as follows:

Linguistic-logical arts
  Grammar
  Logic or theory of argument
    Probable argument
      Dialectic
      Rhetoric
    Necessary argument
    Sophistical argument
Practical or moral arts
  Ethics
  Economics
  Politics
Theoretical arts
  Theology
  Physics

Mathematics
  Arithmetic
  Music
  Geometry
  Astronomy
Mechanical arts
  Fabric making
  Armament
  Commerce
  Agriculture
  Hunting
  Medicine
  Theatrics

The sequence is based on the order of learning. The linguistic-logical arts should be learned first since they provide the means of learning all the others. The practical or moral arts are placed second, and before the theoretical arts, because "the eye of the heart must be cleansed by the study of virtue, so that it may thereafter see clearly for the investigation of truth." The mechanical arts come last, not because they are the highest, but because they need to be informed and directed by the preceding arts.[27]

The subdivisions within these four sets, constituting the individual arts, correspond to the diversity of objects that they study. Thus there are ultimately as many arts as there are diversities of things *(tot partes quot rerum diversitates)*.[28]

In order of importance and dignity, the linguistic arts, especially grammar and logic, are the most fundamental in that they provide the basis and means for acquiring all the rest. Theology is the highest as having the highest object in its study of God.

Aristotle's Aims, Subject Matters, and Methods

The Aristotelian organization of knowledge is the most complicated and difficult of any that we have considered and, for that reason, calls for more detailed consideration. Part of the difficulty is caused by the fact that there is no systematic treatment of the topic to be found in any one place within the Aristotelian corpus. Not that Aristotle was not interested in the question; in fact, he was particularly interested in methods of knowing and elaborated much more fully than Plato ever did a map of the world of learning. But his remarks on this topic are

scattered throughout his various works, and to obtain a full and anything approaching a systematic account, one has to collect them and
relate them to one another. This makes interpretation a necessity and,
at the same time, leaves room for much disagreement. It may be well
then at the start to present his scheme as I understand it.

Theoretic knowledge
  Theology or first philosophy (metaphysics)
  Mathematics
    Universal mathematics
    Special
      arithmetic, geometry,
      astronomy, optics, harmonics
  Natural philosophy (physics)
    General physics
    Special
      inorganic world, plants, animals,
      man (psychology)
Practical knowledge
  Politics
  Household management (economics)
  Ethics
Productive knowledge
  Liberal arts
    Grammar, music, graphics, gymnastic
    Logic, rhetoric, poetics
  Nonliberal arts
Poetry
History

The first and broadest division to be made among these is that
which separates and distinguishes poetry and history from all the
others inasmuch as the latter have as their object the singular individual and not the universal or general. Poetry treats of individual
persons, actions, and events by representing and imitating them in
words and music, such as Odysseus, Circe, Oedipus, the Trojan War,
and the wanderings of Odysseus and his men. History too considers the
singular, but as actually happening in the past, as in the war between
the Greeks and the Persians, or the Peloponnesian War between
Athens and Sparta in the fifth century B.C., and the political and
military leadership of Pericles, Alcibiades, and Nicias. Although both
poetry and history deal with singulars, poetry enjoys a greater freedom
in that its concern is with what might have been, whereas history is

limited to what actually happened. In this sense, poetry is more universal than history and, accordingly, more philosophical.[29]

The other three kinds of knowledge comprise knowledge of the universal and consider the singular only as leading to such knowledge. The first broad division, corresponding to the triad of theoretical, practical, and productive knowledge, is based on the difference between knowing, doing, and making. These constitute three different activities, and knowledge differs with respect to them both in aim and in subject matter. Thus one kind of knowledge is concerned solely with knowing what and how such-and-such a thing is and perhaps how it came to be that way, as is exemplified most clearly in the case of things such as the stars, whose courses lie beyond the reach of our doing and making. Knowledge that is concerned with the realm of human action as based upon deliberation and decision is of another kind, since it can aim beyond knowing to the actual determination of action through the choice of means and ends. Knowledge of making is of yet a third kind inasmuch as it looks beyond both knowing and doing to the actual producing of a product that can then exist by itself independent of its maker.[30] Aim and subject matter thus suffice to distinguish three principal kinds of knowledge: the theoretical, the practical or moral, and the productive or "poietic."

The division of theoretical knowledge depends upon a difference in method and our ability to consider only one aspect of an object and to study that while leaving out of account its other aspects or components.[31] Mathematics offers the clearest example, as is evident from even the simplest procedure of counting. One may have occasion to count seven wives with seven cats and each with seven kittens or to handle such circular objects as coins, plates, and rings. These instances represent different embodiments or realizations of the number seven and of the circle as a figure. Although neither sevenness or circularity exist in their purity, apart from their material embodiment, it is perfectly possible to consider them as so separated and to investigate the properties that they possess, as is done in arithmetic and geometry. This feature led Aristotle to describe mathematics as the inquiry into objects that in existence are inseparable from matter but that are separable from it in thought. The great advantage of doing so is that the object is thereby removed from the effect of change. Whereas such things as wives, cats, and kittens, coins, plates, and rings can very well change not only in number, shape, but even in existence, the arithmetical seven and the geometrical circle remain forever just what they are.

With these two notes—of being either separable or inseparable in either existence or thought—Aristotle distinguished three kinds of theoretical knowledge. Objects of inquiry that are inseparable from matter in both existence and thought, and which are therefore necessarily subject to change, constitute the field of natural philosophy, or physics, or the science of change and motion. Objects that are separable from matter in thought, and so unchangeable, but inseparable from matter in existence, constitute the mathematicals, and thereby identify mathematical knowledge. Objects that are separable from matter in both existence and thought belong uniquely to first philosophy, (later known as metaphysics) or theology, so called because God is the principal being of this kind. Each of these three kinds of theoretical science has further subdivisions, some of which are listed in the outline. But for these, still further principles of discrimination are needed. The only feature that I would note here is that there is place in both physics and mathematics for a more general science that is prior to and more fundamental than its particular or specialized sciences.[32]

Practical or moral knowledge, as we have seen, is distinguished from both theoretical and productive knowledge. It has as the field of its investigation the realm of the deliberative, i.e., the world of human action as it is determined by men deciding upon means and ends in striving to achieve the human good. It is subdivided according to whether the good that it considers and aims to achieve is the good life of the individual person, of the household, or of the political community.[33] Two remarks concerning these sciences are particularly worth noting. One is that there is a hierarchy among them, since politics is architectonic in being able to direct the others and to make use of them for its own ends. The other is that the degree of certitude that can be achieved in these sciences is not as great as that in the theoretical sciences, and an educated man, therefore, would not expect any greater certitude from them than their subject matter allows.[34]

The field of productive knowledge is the realm of objects produced by the transitive actions of men that result in a product capable of existing by itself apart from the action of the men who produce it. Thus it consists of shoes and ships and sealing wax, but not of cabbages, except in a secondary way, and not of kings at all, unless the clothes make the king. It also includes houses, paintings, poems, even speeches and arguments, as well as ordinary talk. These are things that are distinct, on the one hand, from human activities that do not result in a product, but terminate with the action itself (such as walking, thinking, loving, and being angry), and, on the other hand, from those entities that are not of man's making or doing (such as the stars, trees, the earth, and man himself as a natural being).

Productive knowledge is the realm of the arts. Among the arts the basic distinction, according to Aristotle, is that which divides the liberal arts from those that are illiberal or vulgar *(banausic)*[35] The illiberal arts are those that are not fit for a free man, since they make a life of leisure and citizenship impossible; hence, they should be left to slaves. From this it might appear that the distinction owes more to the fact that Aristotle lived in a slave-owning society than to a difference grounded in the arts. Yet there do seem to be some arts and occupations that make difficult, if not impossible, the practice of virtue and a worthy leisure. Activities such as mining, ditch digging, earth moving, and some of the drudgery of farming, especially if it is unrelieved for long hours every day of the week, would seem to qualify, and the same would seem to hold true of the monotonous work of a factory assembly line. But there are still other and even better reaons for drawing a distinction between arts that are liberal and those that are not. One comes from the end for whose sake the art is pursued: Is it pursued for itself as an end that is intrinsically good, or is it wanted only as it is a means to a further end? Shoemaking and automobile-making are pursued for the sake of their products, but reading, writing, and playing tennis can be their own excuse for being, even though they may also have extrinsic benefits. Still another basis for the distinction is provided by the nature of the object: whether or not it is primarily one that involves language and meanings, their use and adventures. The liberal arts then appear primarily as arts of signs and meanings, and so arts of the mind. From these considerations it would appear that the distinction between liberal arts and those that are not has better grounds than the historical fact that Aristotle lived in a slave-owning society. It is useful and important to distinguish the arts of leisure from arts of work, especially from the drudgery that is replaceable by a machine, and the linguistic or semiotic arts from those that are not.

Three works within the Aristotelian corpus deal explicitly with the linguistic arts: the *Poetics*, the *Rhetoric*, and the six separate treatises that comprise logic. Each of these three pertains particularly to one of the main parts of philosophy rather than to the others: poetics to productive knowledge and making (which in Greek is *poietiké*); rhetoric to persuasion, which is important for political deliberation in the realm of practical knowledge; and logic to those functions which serve as the organon of theoretical knowledge. Yet for all this it has always remained something of a puzzle to find a place for these linguistic arts within the overall Aristotelian organization of knowledge. The fact that logic was considered an organon (and accordingly the books were so entitled) would indicate that the linguistic arts should be looked upon as propaedeutic to other knowledge. A further reason for thinking so can be found in the distinction that Aristotle drew between *paideia* and *epistéme*. There are, he wrote, two ways of grasping a subject and method and, accordingly, two different kinds of proficiency with respect to it: one is by *epistéme* and characterizes the scientist; the other is by *paedeia* and characterizes the man of general and liberal education, who is "able to form a fair offhand judgment of the goodness or badness of the specialist's presentation . . . and who in his own person is able to judge critically in all or nearly all branches of knowledge and not merely in some special subject."[36] The use of the word *paideia* here is significant. For in his discussion of the best education, in the eighth book of the *Politics,* he expressly enumerated as subjects included as *paideia* grammar, gymnastics, music, and graphics.[37] From this it seems clear that the learning in question is the same as that *puerilis institutio* of Quintilian, which included not only grammar, but also *mousiké*, understood as the study of poetry and literature. Since these studies are arts, there would seem to be good reason for including poetics, rhetoric, and logic under the liberal arts.

Such in its general lines is Aristotle's map of the world of learning. It includes many kinds of knowledge, many subject matters and methods, each with its own aim and purpose. Hence there is no one royal road to knowledge, but many roads, all needed for knowing one's way about this world. Yet there is also a definite hierarchy. The linguistic and liberal arts are basic as propaedeutic to all other learning. Theoretic knowledge is the highest because it is purest, not looking beyond itself to action and production. Among the various kinds of theoretic knowledge, metaphysics is the first philosophy, since it deals with the highest and best object.

Principles of Organization

Although we have considered only a few of the many maps that have been made of the world of learning, we have now seen enough for our purpose. The ones that have been exhibited and analyzed are representative and typical in that they serve to indicate the kind of problem that is posed by attempting to map the world of knowledge. They also provide the principles that we will need for our own much less ambitious task of constructing a theory of the humanities and distinguishing them from the sciences.

In long-range influence, the maps made by Aristotle and Bacon are perhaps the most important of any that have ever been made. The differences between the two are perhaps also the most fundamental. In

Bacon's organization the controlling principle lies in the mind according to which faculty is primary in the knowing, whereas in Aristotle's plan greater importance is placed upon subject matters and aims. Yet it is also certainly no less significant that neither Aristotle nor Bacon attempted to accomplish the entire task by employing only one principle of organization. Indeed, perhaps the most striking fact to emerge from a review of the various maps or schemes is the diversity of principles that have been employed. Not just differences and distinctions according to objects and faculties are employed. There are also diversities of subject matters based on different ways of determining them; diversities of methods—empirical, historical, mathematical, or that grounded upon *Verstehen;* different degrees of generality or abstractness; differences in aims, purposes, and ends—as theoretic, practical, or productive; arts of words and arts of things; and various hierarchies according to the order of learning, the organization of teaching, the convenience of retrieval, or the dignity of the object. Not only are there as many parts of knowledge as there are differences of things; there are also as many parts as there are different principles of organization.

CHAPTER 9: The Liberal Arts and the Humanities

From the start of our undertaking we have been noting, identifying, and describing the features and ways in which man's intellectual disciplines differ from one another. In particular we have gathered a variety of evidence tending to show that there is one group of disciplines, commonly referred to as the humanities, that differ in marked and perhaps fundamental ways from those known as the sciences. So far, however, I have not addressed directly the question of the nature of the humanities and the grounds on which they can be grouped together so as to constitute a unified field of study. To this task I now turn.

The word *humanities*, as we saw from our study of the classical literary ideal, derives from the Ciceronian concept of *humanitas*. The term expressed not only an ideal of learning, but also a program of studies designed to achieve it. Within this program two parts were distinguished: a more elementary part consisting of certain basic arts of learning, such as the liberal arts that later came to be divided into trivium and quadrivium; and more advanced studies, the *politior humanitas*, identified for the most part with history, law, and philosophy. The prominent place given to law indicates that the composition of this latter part was determined by the professional orientation of the program toward the training and preparation of the lawyer-orator. The program itself, however, was not necessarily restricted to this one profession. It was readily taken over and adapted to form the basis of the mediaeval theological ideal in which law was replaced by religion and theology.

In this first formulation of the humanities, language and the arts of words enjoyed a special place. However, they were not the sole concern to the exclusion of all else. The ideal envisioned the union of word and reason, of eloquence and philosophy, and the basic program comprised mathematical as well as linguistic arts. This distinction was sometimes viewed as one dividing the arts of the real from arts of words (*artes reales et sermocinales*). It then contained the seeds of a wider and deeper division as scientists like Galileo came to be convinced that the book of nature was written mostly in the language of mathematics.[1] The arts of the real could then conceivably be sought for their own sake, to the exclusion, if not outright repudiation, of the others as obstacles to the understanding of nature. With this the ground was prepared for a conflict between the sciences and the humanities.

A further development in the formulation of the humanities came with the distinction that the Renaissance humanists drew between *studia humanitatis* and *studia divinitatis*. The former were identified primarily with grammar, rhetoric, poetry, history, and moral philosophy.[2] As a program of studies, this enumeration is a shorter and truncated version of the earlier one, less philosophical and scientific in that it omitted logic and the mathematical arts. The limit in the progressive narrowing of the idea of the humanities was reached when the term came to be used to refer exclusively to the study of Latin and a little Greek, as it was, for example, in the eighteenth-century *Encyclopédie*.[3]

The principle of division according to difference in object was further generalized when the basic distinction was made, not between the human and the divine, but rather between culture and nature, i.e., between man and his productions on one side and the natural world not of man's making on the other. When this principle was conjoined with the additional one that knowledge of man from within, based on our fundamental experience of what it is to be man, provides a privileged form of understanding, the ground was laid for a comprehensive division between the humanities and the sciences—the *Geisteswissenschaften* and the *Naturwissenshaften*. Difference between the two is not limited to ways of knowing or kinds of experience. It appears also in differences in linguistic usage and in preference for forms of expression that tend, on the one side, toward the poetic, and, on the other, toward the logical, Perhaps the most striking evidence of the division, however, appears in differences in the temporal dimension of knowledge, i.e., in the way that a discipline is related to its past and future. Knowledge that develops cumulatively, consuming the achievements of its past or leaving them behind in a progressive advance, tends to hold that its latest achievements provide the best and fullest account. But for knowledge that is noncumulative, the achievements of the past remain not only as monuments, but as continuing sources of learning and standards of excellence.

Such, in summary form, is the evidence that we have gathered so far. Is it sufficient and solid enough to support the claim that the humanities constitute a unified and coherent form of learning? In justification of this claim, two items or aspects of the evidence would appear to be of special and extraordinary importance. One is the emphasis given to language and the arts of their use; the other concerns the stress placed upon the uniquely human, both as an object and a method of inquiry. The two, of course, are intimately related inasmuch as language itself appears to be a uniquely human achievement, if not, in fact, as Cicero emphasized, the feature that makes man distinctively human. Certainly, any theory of the humanities could not be adequate unless it provided an account of the importance of language as well as of the uniqueness of human experience, thereby revealing the bond that joins the humanities to *humanitas*. In fact, these two aspects correspond to the two parts of the Ciceronian ideal of *litterae et doctrinae*, to the first of which the *artes* correspond as supplying the arts of language, while the second concerns the *magnae res* or great concerns fundamental to human experience. These two, I shall argue, suitably interpreted and developed, can provide the basis for a comprehensive theory of the humanities.

The Fundamental Arts of Language

In the ancient program of the liberal arts, the arts of language consisted of the trivium of grammar, rhetoric, and logic. They were understood as the arts needed for reading, writing, and thinking, each with its own task and even its own vocabulary and rules for achieving that task. In fact, they were thought to be so distinct that they could do battle with one another for the position of primacy, as we have seen from the mediaeval account of the battle between grammar and logic. Today, however, this conception of the arts of language might be dismissed as of little more than antiquarian interest, a curiosity of the history of learning, and at best picturesque. Yet it has haso been argued that the three arts constitute the fundamental arts of language today as truly as they ever did in the past. Thus I. A. Richards has written, for example, that "the three traditional modes of the study of language keep or renew their importance. They meet and mingle incessantly; they cannot . . . be separated without frustration." While acknowledging that "each is for us today cumbered with much deadfall and much obsolete technical tackle which we must shift from the path," he claimed that we neglect them only to our own great loss.[4]

There is much to be said for thus interpreting the liberal arts as fundamentally arts of learning and identifying them with the arts of language. Language certainly constitutes our basic resource for learning, if it is not in fact our greatest intellectual achievement. It reaches and applies to all subject matters, ranging as widely as the mind itself, and being no less indispensable to the sciences than it is to the humanities. Although it has many functions and works in various ways to diverse ends, it is the undeniable medium of all communicated knowledge.

This position, as it is expressed in the text from Richards, makes two claims: (1) that there are three distinct arts of language, and (2) that the three in actual use form an inseparable unity. The basis for both claims lies in the structure and function characteristic of any linguistic utterance. Any instance of it that is of sufficient complexity displays three distinct elements or aspects. It is, in the first place, a linguistic structure consisting of sounds or letters arranged in a pattern that conforms to the rules and practices of the language group to which it belongs. Second, these sounds or letters are something more than mere material entities since, as signs, they indicate, present, or refer to objects other than themselves. Third, as an utterance, language is an expression of a speaker or writer addressed to another as hearer or reader and designed to cause a certain effect upon that hearer or reader. Thus, as an example, consider the statement, "There are three hundred words on the preceding page." It is an expression in the English language, conforming to its usage in such matters as word order, the formation of the plural, and the use of a linking verb whose number is governed by its grammatical subject. But the letters so grouped and arranged make a statement about something outside themselves, namely the number of words on the page preceding this one. Further, the statement so made is an expression designed by the writer to illustrate, and so clarify for the reader the point that a linguistic utterance has at least three distinct aspects.

Without pressing further—for to do so would quickly involve us in many thorny, difficult, and controversial problems of the meaning of meaning—it is clear that there are not only these three distinguishable aspects, but each one makes a significant contribution to the linguistic utterance as a meaningful structure. The first aspect is the most obvious, since to know a language at all is to know a minimum of vocabulary and syntax sufficient to be able to operate with it. Yet the two other aspects are no less essential. In fact, the extralinguistic object is often the most important determinant, since our talk for the most part is about nonlinguistic objects. Even though our example concerned the number of words on a page, these linguistic entities are something other than the statement expressing their number and the determinative of it. The third element is no less essential, since no utterance is without some function or purpose.

After this brief sally into the theory of meaning, we are in a position to see how three distinct arts are at work in the use of language. Just as there are three distinct factors that contribute to determine a linguistic utterance as a meaningful structure, so too three arts are needed to confer skill in their respective use. To know a language is to possess these skills which constitute the know-how needed (1) to use the vocabulary and syntax of a language, (2) to construct a coherently meaningful structure, and (3) to achieve the purpose intended. To learn a language consists in acquiring these arts or skills, and, since all men (almost without exception) do learn how to talk, these three arts are the most common and, in this sense, the most human of all arts. Yet, although these arts are present and at work wherever language is in use, they are not all possessed equally or to the same extent, so that a person may excel more in one than another. One person may speak more fluently and gracefully than others, another be better at persuading his listeners to adopt a course of action, and a third excel in the analysis and construction of argument. Such differences presumably would be observable even within a preliterate society that had given no thought to the formal arts of grammar, rhetoric, and logic. These arts, then, are natural in the sense that they develop in the course of using language to achieve its multifarious purposes. Yet the fact that not all uses of languages are equally successful, that some are better and some are worse than others, would indicate that art can improve upon nature and thus make highly valuable the formal study of the arts of language.

The need for grammar, in the wide sense as skill in arranging words in accordance with the genius of the language, is most obvious from the babbling of a beginner, who frequently fails entirely to make himself understood. The difference between greater and lesser skill, i.e., in command of the art, shows up with respect to such qualities as correctness, precision, appropriateness, grace, and beauty. The art of grammar so understood consists not in knowledge of the rules that professional grammarians have drawn up, but rather in the know-how, the actual skill of composing with words.

Rhetoric, in the broad sense that we are considering, is the art of using linguistic means to achieve a non- or extra-linguistic end. Grammar's aim is strictly verbal—for example, to compose an expression that makes sense in English. Rhetoric looks beyond the act of expressing to the purpose that is to be achieved. Any use of language fulfills some purpose, even when its only purpose is idling. Rhetoric then should not be restricted to a concern only for persuasion aiming at action. It is at work in a mathematical demonstration, in a scientific exposition, as well as in a political speech, for in all three instances linguistic materials and means are organized and used to achieve a certain end. The changing forms of scientific exposition reveal the presence and work of rhetoric. Galileo presented his science in the form of a dialogue; Newton organized the results of his investigations into an axiomatized system; Einstein and contemporary physicists write monographs that only the experts at the frontiers of the science can understand. Einstein may preface his work with the remark that he will not bother about rhetoric,[5] but this in itself is a rhetorical device —the same one, incidentally, that Socrates used in his defense.[6] Such protestations cannot hide the fact that Einstein's paper, no less than Socrates' speech (at least in the form in which it is presented by Plato), is a carefully constructed work of rhetorical art. If the scientific monograph devotes little attention to the preparation of the audience, it does so because it can count on its audience being already prepared by the tradition of the science itself. Science does not do without rhetoric; rhetoric only works differently in science from the way it works in other disciplines.

The third element or aspect of the linguistic utterance concerns the object that it presents, e.g., the above cited case of the number of words on a page. Since this is usually a nonliguistic entity, or at least something different from the utterance itself, there would seem to be no place here for a formal linguistic art. In the case of our example, one needs to know how to recognize and count the words on a page, which is a matter of information outside the statement that expresses it. But if we add to the example in order to connect it to another statement, the need for still a third art appears clearly enough. Thus, e.g., if there are three hundred words on a page, and if there are over three hundred pages in the book, then there are more than ninety thousand words in the book as a whole (other things remaining the same, such as there being three hundred words per page). We now have a new statement, one not contained in the previous one, that provides knowledge about the world (i.e., about the words and pages in this book), and not about the statement itself. Furthermore, this knowledge has been obtained without counting any more words or pages. Although dependent upon a property of numbers, the knowledge so obtained is a consequence of the relations established between the various statements by the connectives "if . . . and if . . . then . . . ." Although these are prepositions of the English language, their force is not peculiar to this language or, indeed, to any language. it is grounded in the relations that they establish as an objective fact. The connectives join statements, each of which concerns a state of affairs in the world (albeit a hypothetical one), to produce a third one concluding with new information.

The art of using such connectives as "if . . . then," "and," "or," and "not" is one that is distinct from both grammar and rhetoric. It concerns neither the arrangement and construction of words to conform to the patterns of a particular language nor the organizing of them in a particular way so as to achieve a certain kind of effect upon a listener or reader. Instead of these, it is the function of this art to assure that such connectives do the work that they are capable of doing and as they should. This art of logic is particularly interested in the truth and validity of consequence, in order to secure the path of inference and keep it from passing wrongly from a true to a false statement. Inferring, reasoning, arguing, and so pushing beyond the immediately evident are thus its great delight. For this reason logic is especially important in all conceptual and scientific knowledge. But it is by no means limited to these realms. All human discourse is studded with "ifs," "ands," "ors" and "nots." Hence logic is at work wherever there is language.

We thus have located and identified three arts corresponding to three distinct aspects of a linguistic utterance. They are distinct arts inasmuch as they have different interests and functions. Yet all three are necessary, indeed, indispensable. Since each of them concerns an integral part of linguistic utterance, these arts of grammar, rhetoric, and logic are to be found wherever man is present using language. In practice and use they are inseparable. Everyone who speaks possesses them to some extent, although it is evident from their products that not all men possess them to the same degree. But if all three arts are necessary, why should there ever be any battle between them? Indeed, how can there be?

There should not be any conflict. Each art is not only distinct with its own proper task to do, but none is independent and able to function on its own in complete separation from the others. The linguistic arts form a continuum no less than the various language functions do.[7] Although there should be no conflict, it is not difficult to see how and why conflict does occur. Since the arts are distinct from one another, each one may be studied and valued for itself. A person may find greater interest in one than in another and have greater talent for it. But even more important is the fact that for some purposes and uses of language one art is more valuable than another. Science in its search for truth about the way things are places greater dependence upon logic than upon the other arts. Poetry from its devotion to the beauty of verbal structure has a greater attachment to the grammatical art and the way in which words can compose patterns with intrinsic value. As a consequence, the various ideals of intellectual culture, each with its own privileged discipline, differ about the importance and value of the three linguistic arts. Thus there is nothing surprising in the fact that the literary ideal of Cicero and Quintilian attributed special importance to rhetoric or that the scientific ideal often expresses unconcern about the "merely" verbal arts compared with the arts of discovering truth about things or that the theological ideal in one form emphasized grammar and rhetoric while in another it gave precedence to logic among the linguistic arts.

These arts are tools and means that are indispensable for the work of the mind. So considered and employed, they are ordered to ends beyond themselves, and for this reason they appear in the allegories of the liberal arts as handmaids in the service of another. Yet the linguistic arts can also be studied for themselves, and they then supply the subject matters for distinct sciences—the sciences of linguistics, of communication, and of logic. As sciences, they possess their own special and restricted subject matters, their own methods of inquiry, even their own specialized vocabularies, any one of which can be pursued independently of the other two. The knowledge that they acquire can make important contributions to the work of the linguistic arts. Yet it is essential to note that as they are being considered here the linguistic arts are not identical with the linguistic sciences, and command of the science does not necessarily entail equal command of the corresponding art. One may be an expert in linguistics and yet show little skill in the grammatical art of composing with words. Logic as a science goes far beyond the concern of the art of logic. Aristotle's logic, with its emphasis upon the syllogism and its interest in the informal arguments of the *Topics*, remains much closer to the needs of ordinary language than much mathematical logic, yet it too has strictly scientific interests, as is evident from the way the valid moods of the syllogism are organized into an axiomatic system.[8] The liberal arts are the skills of using language for any purpose and in any situation; hence they are general arts that transcend any subject matter and can be applied to all. The corresponding sciences, however, remain special and specialized in that they are restricted to the definite subject matters marked off for their inquiry.

Human Experience

The humanities have long been closely associated with the linguistic arts. They should not, however, be identified with them. To do so would be, in effect, to deprive them of content. Cicero was certainly right in emphasizing that verbal art by itself does not suffice to make a man eloquent. Language may serve to distinguish man as *human* and set him apart from the rest of the animal creation, but by itself this does not make him *humane*. There is more than an accidental verbal connection between such words as *human, humane, human or humane studies,* and *humanities*. They serve to determine an area of concern, interest, and inquiry that centers upon man and all that is most distinctive and characteristic about him, his common humanity that is shared by all men. The question to ask now, however, is whether or not this concern and interest is the exclusive preserve only of certain disciplines; in other words, the question is whether or not the humanities can be identified with certain disciplines as such.

Dilthey tried harder perhaps than anyone else to identify the humanities with a specific subject matter, reserving for them "the great fact of humanity," and assigning to the sciences the natural world. Yet Dilthey had to go beyond subject matter and appeal also to a distinctive method to obtain the discriminations that are needed.[9] From this it would appear that a subject matter discipline cannot be identified as one of the humanities merely because it takes man for its subject. The fact that social scientists who favor empirical methods so often strongly insist that their discipline is a science indicates that they do not want it counted among the humanities. Nevertheless, it is also true that some subject-matter disciplines are considered to belong more properly and more intimately to the humanities than some others. This is especially true of literature, history, and philosophy[10] It is time to consider the basis of this claim to see how good and sound it is.

We already have found solid ground for it in our consideration of the two cultures in chapter seven, regarding what constitutes our best knowledge. As Dilthey emphasized in his discussion of *Verstehen*, we possess a privileged mode of knowing in the understanding that we have of ourselves as men from our lived-experience, and this fact establishes our human experience as the most fundamental of all the knowledge that we have. It is also a fact that literature, history, and philosophy have throughout their long history dealt primarily with the great concerns of human life—with Cicero's *res magnae*—such as the problems of life, death, pleasure, pain, our duties and their conflicts, misery and happiness, and human destiny. As found in such concerns as these, the underlying fundamental human experience has always provided a common subject that has been open and available to all.

The distinguishing feature of the humanities in both method and subject matter, especially in comparison with the sciences, is the centrality, generality, or commonness of their concern in that they are open to all human experience through all the ways of awareness available to man. Compared with this openness, the sciences are ineradicably specialized—esoteric, as Dilthey called them. They are closed within the confines set up by their methods. They are empirically bound by what is observable in sense experience, either by way of beginning or of ultimate confirmation; and they are rationally bound by the abstracness of their conceptual and often mathematical reasoning. Moreover they are specialized in the abstractness of their object insofar as the concrete individual of experience is valued only as an instance of a type or a generalization. Therefore, they are specialized in excluding large segments of experience. In sum, they are specialized in the knowledge that is achieved and that is represented in the sciences.

We tend to think of the specialization of the sciences as a recent development, a feature characteristic of the modern world. It is well to recall, however, that in the thinking about the humanities, scientific specialization has long been singled out as a discriminating feature. Cicero saw in the scientific and philosophical speculation of the Greeks the beginning of the divorce between eloquence and wisdom.[11] The "scientific" theology of the Scholastics was criticized in effect by the Augustian theologians as well as the humanists for the specialization that separated it from the common concern of Christians.[12] Vico criticized the mathematical method of science for warping and dehumanizing the mind by its exccessive specialization when practiced too early and too exclusively.[13] And from Vico it is only a short way to Dilthey and more recent theories of the humanities, such as those of Crane, Jones, Levi, McKeon, and Veatch.

The centrality of fundamental human experience for the humanities also helps to explain the position of the humanities in the many conflicts in which they have joined issue with the specialization of science. On issues involving the place and function of feeling in relation to thought, of faith to reason, of tradition to progress, of ancients to moderns, of arts of words to arts of things, as well as of general understanding and experience to the specialized knowledge of the expert, the cause of the humanities has rested in an appeal to common and fundamental human experience, in a reaffirmation of the relevance and value of that experience, and in its right to be judged for itself and not only by comparison with the achievements of science.

This basic concern for the human also helps to explain the interest the humanities have always had with questions and judgments of value. In fact, this interest has sometimes been taken as the identifying characteristic of the humanities. There is scarcely an aspect of human life in which men are not concerned with values, not only in constantly expressing judgments about the good and bad, but responding to them through emotions, beliefs, and all the nonconceptual parts of their being. The commitment to the wholeness of human experience has been an insistent and permanent feature of the humanities and a constant theme in their exposition and defense. Matthew Arnold, for example, made it the basic and central point in his defense of them when he emphasized that, in sharp contrast to the partiality of the sciences, they refuse to omit, and abstract from, the moral, aesthetic, and emotional dimensions in their intellectual work, and that they constantly aim at a whole and connected view of human life.[14]

The same feature also explains why the humanities continue to find inspiration, insight, and understanding in the great achievements of the past. They not only express the human condition, but they also address it in the problems that they confront and the solutions that they offer since the human experience that is their subject remains fundamental. How very different science is in this respect is strikingly illustrated by the length of time that it has taken for the history of science to win recognition as a valid discipline, and it is still a discipline honored more by historians than by scientists. The attitude of many scientists is still the same as that of Auguste Comte, who held that the history of science would lose all significance once the era of positive science became fully established, since all that was true in the past would be absorbed by the ongoing science, and all else was false and to be discarded and forgotten. In this view, the history of science could be no more than a history of errors.[15] Few men still retain such confidence in the ability to distinguish so sharply between truth and falsity in science. There is also much to be learned even from mistakes and errors not only about man and his behavior, but about science itself.

It may seem odd and exaggerated, if not actually misleading, to attach such great importance to the common and fundamental experience of mankind. Yet the fact is decisive for understanding how the humanities stand with regard to the sciences. Indeed, one of the great services rendered by the modern phenomenological movement in philosophy is the way it has directed attention to the presence and importance of the lived-world of human experience for all our knowing and activity. Nothing is more characteristic of science than the way in which it immediately departs from this *lebenswelt* and not only leaves it behind, but also ceases to take it into account. The physicist, in his analysis of light, ignores the difference between sight and blindness, considering it only as a ray or wave of a certain frequence and length. Thus he leaves out the most striking feature of light in our experience of it.

In this respect Descartes's famous method is typical of science. According to the first rule, which is that of evidence, we must accept only what is clear and distinct to the mind; the second, the rule of division, directs us to divide a problem into as many parts as possible and thereby make it easier to solve.[16] Thus the very heart of the method consists in separating, abstracting and simplifying so as to isolate and make a problem stand out apart from the complex pattern in which it is merged, when not actually confused, with the many thing of the world in which it occurs. This method would lead to practical as well as theoretical discoveries, as Descartes showed. It would lead not just to the solution of the Pappus problem, a geometrical problem dating from classical antiquity that no one had been able to solve before, not only to the invention of analytical geometry, but also to a better understanding of light and vision, and, finally, to a machine for grinding and polishing lenses.[17] Indeed, the step is a short one from Descartes's method to Adam Smith's pin factory, organized according to a division of labor which allotted a separate man to each separate operation in the manufacture of a pin.[18] The method resulted in the very fruitful marriage of science and technology that has altered the shape of the world, but that has also generated a host of new problems that in many cases derive directly from the method of isolating and solving piecemeal without regard to the effects upon the surrounding environment.

If dependence upon fundamental human experience and relevance to it are their essential features, it also becomes clear that the humanities cannot be completely identified with any subject-matter discipline as such. Literature, history, and philosophy, like the various linguistic arts, can also become the objects of specialized study and can be pursued as narrowly as any of the specialized sciences. Their end then becomes the advancement of a profession through the posing and solving of problems that are of direct concern only to the members of that profession. In fact, it is useful, as Stephen Toulmin has shown, to distinguish rational enterprises according to the degree of their professional organization and the extent to which they share commonly agreed-upon problems, techniques, and solutions. By this criterion Toulmin distinguishes disciplines, quasi-disciplines, and nondisciplines, represented by physical science at one end and philosophy at the other.[19] *Discipline* is too good and important a word to hand over to the sciences and has a long history of referring to the humanities. But Toulmin's criterion does serve to draw a line between the sciences and the humanities. By his "quasi disciplines," I would understand those studies, such as history and the social sciences in particular, that readily lend themselves to either kind of pursuit. I would also argue that the same holds true of both literature and philosophy, although it must be admitted that the professionalization of these disciplines has not occurred without certain ironies. Thus the professionalization and specialization of philosophy in the contemporary American and English universities has been promoted most strenuously in many cases by disciples of Wittgenstein, whereas the master himself was firmly opposed to it, as Toulmin has shown.[20]

The humanities, then, like the linguistic arts, should not be identified exclusively with any subject-matter discipline. Nonetheless, it must also be admitted that some disciplines are more closely associated with the humanities than others. This is especially true of philosophy, history, and language study, which are unique in the universality of their application. This feature is evident from the fact that it makes good sense to inquire into the philosophy of _____, the history of _____, or the language of _____, any study or discipline whatsoever. Such questions can be addressed, it should be noted, to science itself and its various branches. Science then can be of interest to the humanities and enter within the field of their concern. In considering some of the ways in which this comes about, I shall also have occasion to look for the respects in which the two are similar and share a common life.

The Sciences as Humanities

This somewhat queer subtitle is needed because there is no adjective to do for the humanities what *scientific* does for the sciences. For this purpose *humanistic* is sometimes employed, but the choice is not a happy one, since it has too many connotations that are wrong and misleading. The humanities cannot be identified with the activity of the Renaissance humanists or with the secular religion that goes by the name of *humanism*. Nor can religion and much of theology be denied to the humanities on the ground that they concern God and not man, for this concern remains too one that is centrally and fundamentally human. Now, however, my purpose is to consider the way in which the sciences too can enter into the humanities.

Science is a great human achievement, a work of the mind, and a product of culture. Its practical effects are present everywhere about us, and are so overwhelming that we sometimes tend to forget that science is first of all a great theoretical achievement of knowing. More than any other kind of knowledge, it is cumulative and progressive, as we have seen. One discovery constitutes a truth achieved that then serves as a starting point on the way to new discoveries in a process that continues seemingly without end. Science as a work of mind and of culture is eminently worth studying in and for itself, quite apart from its practical results. Its history is the story of one of the greatest adventures of ideas—a laboratory for the study of many ideas and a source and record of the development of the mind. It shows perhaps more clearly and dramatically than anywhere else the revolutionary changes that occur with the appearance of new world views, such as the shifts in the conception of man and the universe that are associated with the work of Copernicus, Darwin, and Freud. If we would understand what man has made of man, we must take science into account. Indeed, it provides many privileged cases of the effect of theory upon the way in which we approach the world and attempt to order and understand our experience of it. The history of science is thus obviously of great interest and concern to the humanities.

The history of science, it can be objected, is not science, but history; and so it is. But science as science is itself a work of art, and it is in this respect that science has close similarities with the humanities. Yet the artistic aspect of science is frequently overlooked and neglected, when it is not entirely denied. Freedom and creativity are thought of as belonging to the poet, painter, and musician, and contrasted with the patient, meticulous, and often tedious observation and experimentation of the scientist. Scientists frequently express complete disdain for expression and composition and much of their writing too frequently lacks verbal nicety and grace. It remains a fact, nonetheless, that science is a structure of words and reasons and, hence, a work of liberal art. As such, it has many similarities with the work of the humanities.

To appreciate this fact, it is useful to distinguish between science as an ongoing inquiry, i.e., science in process, and science as an achieved result and finished product, or between S_1 and S_2, as Gerald Holton has called them.[21] These two sides of science are strikingly different. That of S_2, or the achieved result, which up to now has been almost our sole concern in considering science, exhibits all the differences that have been noted and emphasized as setting it apart as distinct and different from and even opposed to, the humanities. When we consider S_1, however, and look at the scientist actually at work, we find many of the same features and qualities that are associated with the humanities.

Science as inquiry does not consist merely in the accumulation of facts and strict adherence to empirical observation and mathematical reasoning. A fact in the sense of a mere occurrence or event has little meaning until it is brought together with other facts and caught up and interpreted by a theory or hypothesis. Indeed, it is often the theory that initiates the search for facts. The theory, at first often only a vague hunch or even a suggestion from a dream, poses the questions for which answers are sought by ascertaining the facts through observation and experimentation. But as a discovery, the theory is a work of creative imagination and has behind it all the mysterious powers and feelings that motivate and impel the activity of discovery. There is no logic of discovery, no heuristic, as there is a logic of deduction. Creative inspiration, as Shelly pointed out, is not at the beck and call of conscious reason and will.[22] Science, as a creative achievement, is thus in its source no different from any of the most creative works of the humanities and the arts.

The difference between science as S_1 and S_2 is an important one. Yet it should not be allowed to obscure the fact that in both respects science as a structure of words and meanings, of reasons and arguments, is a work of liberal art. In achieving this work, science employs all the ways of knowing that we possess: experience, ideas, imagination, memory, reasoning, insight, as well as all the arts of signs and of learning. Even the most formal sciences—such as those represented in the work of Euclid and of Russell and Whitehead—need grammar and rhetoric as well as logic. Logic alone is unable to determine unequivocally or uniquely either beginning, middle, or end, i.e., the propositions with which to begin, the order in which the theorems should be presented, or the conclusion at which to aim. Thus even a deductive system, where logical sequence exercises its greatest power, still requires the help of the other liberal arts.

Science enters into the humanities when it is considered for its historical development or its achievement as a work of liberal and linguistic art. Its presence is perhaps even more evident within philosophy, where it has manifested itself in a variety of ways. The most obvious is the direct influence that it has exerted upon philosophical inquiry, at the very beginning of its career in the work of the pre-Socratics, Plato, and Aristotle, continuing thereafter from Descartes and Leibniz, through Locke, Berkeley, Hume, Kant, Mill, Bergson, James, Whitehead, and Dewey down to Wittgenstein, Husserl, and even Sartre. In the course of this career, science has influenced philosophy by providing new approaches, problems, and methods, but especially by unburdening and taking upon itself tasks previously borne by philosophy, aiding it thereby to become clearer about its own mission.[23]

Within scientific inquiry proper, there are problems of great philosophical import that lie beyond solution within the science itself. Among the most interesting are those concerning the fundamental preconceptions of science that cannot be decided by observation and rational analysis alone and that are often assumed more or less unconsciously. Scientists are beginning to take cognizance of these principles, especially as they become increasingly aware of their importance in scientific discovery. Holton, for example, calls them "themata" or "thematic presuppositions," since he views them as "general themes that have guided the process of scientific discovery." as examples of such themata, he lists the following:

> the thematic dyad of Constancy and Change; . . . the efficacy of mathematical forms *versus* the efficacy of materialistic or mechanistic models; . . . simplicity, order, and symmetry; the primacy of experience *versus* that of symbolic formalism; reductionism *versus* holism; discontinuity *versus* the continuum; hierarchical structure *versus* unity; the animate *versus* the inanimate; the use of mechanisms *versus* teleological or anthropomorphic modes of approach.[24]

This is rather a mixed bag, but it is significant that so many of the themata appear as alternatives and rivals for a position of privilege. From this it seems clear that the efficacy of *Verstehen* versus empirical methods could count as still another thema. With this we are brought back to the question of the relation between the specialized experience of science and the fundamental human experience of the humanities; in short, we are brought back to what constitutes our best knowledge.

Nothing shows as directly and immediately the impact of science upon the humanities, the extent to which it demands their attention and concern, as the fact that it is impossible to develop a philosophy of the humanities without constantly addressing the question of their relation to one another and of their differences even more than their similarities. Although some may feel, as Karl Popper does, that "laboring the difference . . . has become a bore,"[25] it is only by becoming clear about their differences as well as their similarities that understanding can be achieved.

Cum Humanitate et Doctrina

Cicero is a hero of the humanities; yet he was blind to the value of science, including any rigorous philosophy, and even its detractor. In fact, it has been claimed on good authority that his work and influence were instrumental in bringing on the Dark Ages in science that can be dated as beginning with the end of Hellenistic science during the

Roman Republic and lasting until the twelfth century.[26] A telling instance that illustrates both features of his character occurs in the *Tusculan Disputations,* where he told of seeking out the tomb of Archimedes, while he was in Sicily as *quaestor* in 75 B.C. Archimedes, one of the greatest mathematicians of all time, is acknowledged to have had "a most acute mind," but is then described as "an obscure insignificant person" (*humilis homunculus*). However, if Archimedes is compared with a tyrant, such as Dionysius of Syracuse, then, Cicero went on to remark, "who is there in all the world who has any association with the Muses [*cum Musis*], that is, *cum humanitate et doctrina* [literally: with humanity and learning], who would not choose to be the mathematician rather than the tyrant."[27]

In this text there are two points worth noting. One is the implication that the life of a mathematician represents an extreme of undesirability comparable with that of a tyrant: Archimedes was so insignificant that even his fellow citizens had ceased to remember the location of his tomb. The other is the fact that Cicero not only knew who Archimedes was and that his tombstone was surmounted by a figure of a sphere and a cylinder (commemorating his favorite discovery of the ratio between a sphere and its circumscribed cylinder), but he was also enough concerned to want to restore the tomb to memory and rescue it from oblivion. In so doing, Cicero demonstrated that he was one who was friendly with the Muses, that is, he went on to say in a phrase that is definitive, *cum humanitate et cum doctrina.*

Perhaps for more than any other reason Cicero is a hero of the humanities because of the felicity of his phrases. The phrase just emphasized captures the very essence of the humanities. But to see how it does so, we must interpret it in light of the whole Ciceronian cultural ideal. That, as we have seen, consisted of two distinguishable parts: *litterae* and *doctrinae,* or the *artes* and the *magnae res* with which the *politior humanitas* was concerned. The phrase under consideration, I suggest, can be correlated with the same two parts. In fact, we already have *humanitas* as the first term, which is prior to and presupposed by *politior humanitas.* Accordingly, Cicero can be understood to be defining friendship with the Muses as consisting in the possession of the basic linguistic arts (*artes*) that certify the humanity of man and knowledge (*doctrina*) of the fundamental human concerns (*magnae res*) that make a more perfect, more polished humanity (*politior humanitas*).

This understanding of the humanities explains why they have the name they do by rooting it in the learning closest to the humanity of man—his basic arts and most fundamental concerns. The arts of language are the basic arts of learning that enter into every work of man, practical as well as theoretical, and they are the indispensable means of intellectual activity. But the learning, the subject-matter content, of the second part is equally indispensable and equally universal. What would go if the humanities were to disappear? For one thing, sources of delight would go, as well as understanding of what it is to be man, gained through the lived-experience of what it is to be man and reflection upon it. But also, among other things, reference books, dictionaries, and encyclopedias would also disappear. For the humanities, unlike the sciences, take all knowledge, all experience, all that is, for their field.[28]

The humanities are based upon the general understanding at the same time that they are perfective of it. Generality, however, must not be confused with superficiality and inaccuracy, as it sometimes is.[29] Accuracy and exactness, and the degree to which it is obtainable, vary from one subject matter to another, as has already been emphasized.[30] So too, understanding and knowledge should not be identified exclusively with the specialized knowledge of the expert. This point was well made by J. S. Mill in his defense of liberal education, when he wrote:

> To have a general knowledge of a subject is to know only its leading truths, but to know these not superficially, but thoroughly, so as to have a true conception of the subject in its great features, leaving the minor details to those who require them for the purposes of their special pursuit.[31]

To conceive of the humanities as having as their field the basic liberal and linguistic arts as exercised upon man's most fundamental experience also explains the characteristics ordinarily attributed to them and that have been emphasized here time and again. It becomes clear, for example, why some disciplines and subject matters are more closely allied with the humanities than others. For some are more immediately dependent upon the linguistic arts and more centrally located in their concern for the great human problems, the great matters that have supplied the perennial subjects of literature, history, philosophy, and religion. Yet it is also clear that no subject-matter discipline as such can be identified exclusively with the humanities. For every discipline is capable of marking off a part of its subject matter and making it the object of specialized study for which it develops its own tools and methods for achieving particular and professional aims. The study of language and literature thus has linguistics, prosody, textual criticism; history has auxiliary sciences, such as epigraphy, paleography, archeology; philosophy has the science of logic and those parts that it endeavors to treat professionally and scientifically; and a specialized theology makes use of any or all of these sciences. So too, the fine arts, as special arts of making and performing, do not fall among the humanities. On the one hand, they are not products of the linguistic arts as such, and, on the other hand, their concern for making and performing is a special one calling for the development of special talent and experience. Yet the appreciation and understanding of the fine arts, through art history, criticism, and theory, with whatever practice is needed for their accomplishment, do belong to the humanities. The same holds true of the sciences. In fact, any subject-matter discipline can become allied with the humanities insofar as it can be studied and developed by means of the general arts of the understanding with reference to our fundamental human experience. Evidence of this possibility is supplied by the fact that of any discipline we can always inquire into its history, its philosophy, and the special features of its use of language.

From this conception of them it is also clear why the great achievements of man in any order, but especially in the intellectual life, are of continuing use and importance to the humanities. The classics, great books, and master works are monuments and models of the liberal arts. As human achievements, they belong to the general experience of mankind as a permanent record of the possibilities of human accomplishment and at once embody and exhibit standards of excellence. For the same reason they are less time bound than the special sciences. In addressing the great concerns of men that remain of perennial urgency and import, they merit the title of disciplines that are permanent in contrast from those that are progressive.[32]

It might still appear that the grounds for claiming that the humanities constitute a unified field of studies are much too vague, tenuous, and "general" to support it. After all, literature, history, philosophy, and religion employ quite different methods, appeal to different sources, and possess different criteria of validity and excellence. But while this statement is true, it is scarcely telling as an objection. The same charge can be made about the sciences; geography, chemistry, and astronomy differ from one another in all the same respects, and yet all are counted as sciences. In other words, the criteria for bringing the sciences together in a group are no less vague, tenuous, and general than is the case with the humanities. Yet they suffice. The same is true of the criteria for the humanities, and the clearest evidence of this is the fact that they serve to distinguish them as a group from the sciences.

CHAPTER 10: The Dream of the Academy

The Academy and the Muses

Learning and the humanities have long been identified with the Muses. In fact, Cicero, as we have just seen, went so far as to identify them. Plato's school in the grove of Academos was dedicated to the cult of the Muses, as were many other schools.[1] The center of learning at Alexandria with its great library by its very name of *Mouseion*, "Museum," "Place of the Muses," gave witness to the same devotion. Very few particulars now remain of what life was like at the Platonic Academy. We know neither the identity of the Muses that were honored nor the kind of cult paid to them. Yet in Plato's day there was already a long tradition about the nine Muses. Their history is of interest and worth considering in some detail, especially since it serves to express an issue, if not in fact a principle, that is central to the idea as well as the ideal of the academy.

In Cicero's reference to them, the Muses represent and manifest the triumph of a literary ideal of culture. With two exceptions—and these are more apparent than real—all the traditional nine Muses are readily identifiable with literary arts and achievements. Calliope is the Muse of epic, Erato of lyric, Thalia of comedy, and Melpomene of tragedy, while a fifth, Polymnia, is identified with rhetoric. Terpsichore and Euterpe, the Muses of dance and music respectively, are obviously closely associated with poetry as its accompaniment. Only Clio and Urania, the Muses of history and astronomy, would appear to fall outside the literary ideal. However, if they are seen as representing the deeds of great men, on the one hand and of the gods on the other, then they too cease to be exceptions, since they then stand for the main subject matter of epic poetry.[2]

On the exclusively literary interpretation of them, the Muses declare the triumph of the literary ideal of culture and of one kind of learning as distinct from others. By Cicero's time, however, many

173

other arts and sciences had not only been discovered, but had reached a high level of development. One need only recall the logic of the Stoics and the mathematics and science of Archimedes. The fact that the *Mouseion* was so called and yet also included all learning—mathematics and science as well as the literary arts—indicates that the Muses could stand for all learning and not just for one ideal of it. And such, it has been recently claimed, was their original function.

The record of this tradition is to be found in Hesiod's *Theogony*, the beginning of which constitutes a hymn to the Muses. There they are presented as the daughters of Mnemosyne, or memory. Since all our learning is an acquired achievement, and not an inheritance that is transmitted through the genes, such an ancestry is especially appropriate. This fact would stand out even more prominently in a preliterate society in which all knowledge and culture depended on an oral tradition and so, literally, on memorization. In such a situation, epic poetry "functioned as a record of culture," and the Muses accordingly can be understood as representing nine different aspects of the epic poet's art, a learning that was at once "encyclopaedic and magisterial" in preserving and transmitting man's cultural achievement.[3] The Muses thus symbolize "the bard's command of professional secrets," and, since poetry in that early age was the repository as well as the privileged means of communication of the entire cultural tradition, the Muses in effect would represent all learning.[4]

In these two different conceptions of the Muses we have uncovered another issue that has been a perennial one in the world of learning. In Hesiod's poem they represent all of learning as constituting a unity, and this same conception is embodied and enshrined in the *Mouseion* at Alexandria, where many diverse kinds of learning were represented. In the work of Cicero, however, they symbolize only one ideal of intellectual culture, an exclusively literary one that is prepared to challenge and do battle with other ideals of learning. Which of these two conceptions, we may now ask, is better and more adequate, not so much to the way things are or have been, but to the way they should be in the world of learning? With its many disciplines and varied arts and sciences, is it one world capable of peace in unity or many worlds inevitably in conflict with one another? Are the issues and differences that we have been considering so deeply rooted that conflict is unavoidable, or is there an underlying basis for unity and peace?

One World or Many Worlds?

One of the most determined efforts ever made to affirm, if not to demonstrate, the unity of learning was that of the late English philosopher, R.B. Collingwood, in the book entitled *Speculum Mentis*. This work deserves our attention for several reasons. Not only does it coincide at many points with the course of our investigation, but it also raises sharply and decisively the question of the unity of knowledge. In order to reaffirm and reestablish this principle of unity, Collingwood first undertook to construct a map of the world of knowledge. For this purpose he distinguished five provinces within human experience: art, religion, science, history, and philosophy. He emphasized, however, that the exact number was not as important as the fact that each of these forms "makes for itself the unequivocal claim to be knowledge."[5] This is a proposition, of course, with which we can concur and one that has been asserted at least implicitly from the very beginning of our work. But Collingwood then went on to make the stronger assertion that each of the five types claims "not only to give truth, but to give the absolute or ultimate truth concerning the nature of the universe."[6] Because of this claim, he declared that "the different forms of experience seem to be competitors for one prize, the prize of truth."[7]

From this description it may appear that Collingwood was addressing the same problem that we have been dealing with in the conflict of cultural ideals, but that he has distinguished five compared to our three. While it must be admitted that Collingwood did deal in his fashion with many of the problems that we have been considering, I must confess that I find his treatment eccentric, erratic, and often baffling. A good example is the way he handled the problem of awarding the "prize of truth" among his five competitors. As he pointed out, there are three ways of dealing with a prize: (1) it can be awarded to one of the competitors and denied to the others; (2) it can be shared among two or more competitors; or (3) it need not be awarded at all. Collingwood eliminated the last two possibilities, from which it would seem to follow that the first alternative must hold and the prize be given to one of the five contenders. Yet he rufused to draw his conclusion in so many words. Thus he argued that it would be contradictory and stultifying not to award the prize at all, since that would imply that the judge himself possessed the very truth that he declared was lacking in the five.[8] The same sort of argument is employed to rule out the alternative of sharing the prize among two or more of the five contenders: To consider art, religion, science, history, and philosophy as five coordinate species of knowledge, each with its own kind of truth, is declared equivalent to subjecting all to logic as the science of genus and species, and thus to introducing a sixth form superior to all the others. Collingwood not only denied this form of superiority, but denied that there is any "single reality" to take the place of genus for the five forms.[9] Having taken away two of the three possibilities, Collingwood might have been expected to posit the third one. Yet he did not, at least not explicitly. Implicitly, however, there is a sense in which it may be said that the prize is awarded to philosophy.

Collingwood's puzzling inclusiveness on this matter becomes clearer from his final conclusion regarding the construction of a map of knowledge. In working toward that end, he had many illuminating observations to make about the five provinces of experience. His conclusion, however, obviated the need for any discussion of the criteria he proposed for distinguishing them. For in the end he reached the position that the task of making such a map is an impossible one on the ground that "there are no autonomous and mutually exclusive forms of experience, and, what is more, it is in no one's interest to assume that there are."[10] There can be no map of the world of knowledge, according to Collingwood, because each of the forms of experience in actual practice claims the whole territory for itself: "The artist does not want a map of knowledge: he only wants a map of art, and this map is art itself." The same thing is said to be true of all the other forms of experience: "Every person who is actually absorbed in any given form of experience is by this very absorption committed to the opinion that no other form is valid, that his form is the only one adequate to the comprehension of reality." As a result, conflict is said to be inevitable.

> The "ancient quarrel between poetry and philosophy" is only one of a whole series of such quarrels in a ceaseless international war . . . complete even down to the existence of pacifists of the mind, getting between the legs of the combatants and kindly offering to explain to "religion and science," or whatever the combatants may be, that they are fighting about nothing.[11]

Collingwood did not offer to serve as peacemaker and was apparently pessimistic about even the possibility of peace, since he declared: "Artists and scientists must fight; it is their nature to." Yet he did go on to claim that the fight is based on "the error of regarding art and science as independent things."[12] Art, science, and the other forms are charged with committing a twofold error: each claims to be independent when in fact no one of them is, and each also lays claim to the whole of truth, when none of them actually possesses it. All of them, according to Collingwood, are only "Variously distorted versions of one and the same country." This one country is the country of the mind, of which he wrote:

> To explore that country is the endless task of the mind; and it only exists in being explored. Of such a country there is no map, for it is itself its own map. The explorer, the country explored, and the map are one and the same thing.[13]

Such in brief is Collingwood's vision of the world of learning. It is one world because it is constituted a world by the mind. But it is a world in which conflict is inevitable because any expression of it is a distortion and yet also an imperialistic claim to sovereignty. But unity at such a price, it may be objected, is just too expensive. It would also seem to rest on a very shaky basis. All our knowledge may indeed be knowledge of mind, but this does not entail that mind is the only object that we know. Even though mind may make a difference to everything known, with the result that what is known is not in every respect exactly the same as that which is known, it does not at all follow from this that the mind is the only thing that is known. So too, although all the disciplines are works of mind, they are not for that reason all the same work. The differences that we have found between the sciences and the humanities are genuine and real differences, not merely errors of thinking. In fact, Collingwood's notion of error, as well as the claim based upon it that each of the basic disciplines is necessarily erroneous, is itself highly questionable.

Any view or knowledge that is partial and abstract, according to Collingwood, is necessarily false and erroneous; there is no true knowledge of anything unless it is known in all its relations to everything else.[14] Yet such an extreme assertion as this is by no means born out in actual practice. One may know and know truly that one has a fever without knowing that it is malaria, or know that quinine will help to cure the fever without knowing how it does so, or know that it is transmitted by the anopheles mosquito without knowing anything about the ecological niche occupied by that insect. To the same effect it can be urged that the understanding and knowledge achieved by any one discipline is not necessarily erroneous just because it is partial and something less than knowledge of everything. Error necessarily enters in only when the further claim is made that it possesses the whole truth. Collingwood assumed that any basic discipline would necessarily put forward such a claim. Yet such an assumption can certainly be challenged. In fact, it can be argued with better justification that advancing such a claim constitutes the very imperialism that is responsible for the worst forms of cultural conflict. Collingwood deserves our gratitude for having located and identified a major cause of the conflict, but we do not have to accept his conclusion that the conflict is inevitable and unavoidable.

Intellectual Imperialism

The various conflicts that have come under our investigation have all been based upon some form of intellectual imperialism. Every one of them has involved an attempt by one type of knowledge to assert its supremacy over all others, either by claiming to dictate and judge their actions and achievements, or to seize for itself fields already occupied, and in some cases even to deny others the right to exist by arrogating to itself the whole world of knowledge. In the modern world the most flagrant case of such imperialism has been the claim staked out by the exponents of the positivist ideal, which in effect appropriates the title not only to all of science, but to knowledge and truth as well.[15] Yet it should not be forgotten or overlooked that claims scarcely less extensive have also been made for the theological as well as for the literary ideals of intellectual culture.

The establishment of these various ideals and the ensuing conflicts have all involved intellectual imperialism through acts of aggression in which one discipline attempts to enforce its rights and power over others. In so doing, that discipline necessarily overreaches itself and becomes, as Collingwood pointed out, a philosophy, and a false philosophy. Thus, for example, the claim made for science, understood as the kind of knowledge that is constituted by empirical methods and abstract, mathematical reasoning, to be the only genuine and valid knowledge is not itself a claim that can be validated by science. It is a philosophical, not a scientific, claim, since it takes more than empirical methods and mathematical reasoning to show that there is nothing more. In fact, as we have seen, it takes more than these to account for science itself. Consequently, the claim is made not by science as such, but by a certain philosophy of science, namely, by the positivist ideal. But, according to Collingwood, not only science, but every major discipline, is guilty of laying claim to the whole of knowledge. Thus he held that art, religion, science, and history each constitute an erroneous philosophy.[16] To make such a claim for any one of these disciplines is to make a philosophical statement, and one too that is false. Yet despite Collingwood's assertion, there certainly is no necessary connection between the two. Science does not have to maintain that it is the *only* valid knowledge. If it did, positivism would provide the only possible philosophy of science. Yet, as is well known, there are many philosophies of science.

Positivism, however, is not the only philosophy that has committed imperialism in the name of science. Although it has provided the most flagrant instance, perhaps an even more pernicious influence has been exerted by the scientific imperialism of Descartes and Kant inasmuch as their philosophies are so much more powerful than that of any positivist thinker. Descartes's concentration upon mathematical reasoning based upon clear and distinct ideas led to a neglect of other ways of knowing and the denigration of the humanities, of which Vico complained.[17] Kant, by taking Newton's mathematical physics as the paradigm of all objective knowledge, removed the moral and aesthetic dimensions of experience from the realm of the true and produced a veritable schism in the mind of man.[18] In both cases the result was the attribution to science of paradigmatic importance as knowledge and the attenuation and diminution of that of the humanities.

Intellectual imperialism does not always assume such totalitarian proportions. It also occurs when one discipline moves over into a field already occupied by another and then proceeds to lay exclusive claim to it. It is the latter feature, of course, that is imperialistic; there is no a priori reason why two disciplines may not both have the same field of concern. That imperialistic moves of this sort do occur appears clearly from the list of complaints that literary criticism once brought against certain sciences, charging them with launching "a destructive invasion of the humanities." The bill was drawn up by I.A. Richards as a *jeu d'esprit*, but it was one that had a serious point. In it, literary criticism accuses linguistic science of attempting "to usurp authority" with regard to the choice of words "on the ground that how men actually do speak and write is sufficient to determine how men *should* speak and write," with the result that linguistics can assume responsibility that was once held by criticism.[19] History and certain social sciences are charged with attempting to infiltrate its forces and subvert the critical analysis and evaluation of literature by replacing it with "factual administrations on the model of sundry Sciences commonly known as Social."[20] Psychology of the behavioristic variety is singled out for attempting to destroy the foundations of criticism by denying the very possibility of free choice and reducing the liberal art of choice in words and meanings to a matter of conditioning. A somewhat similar charge is directed against anthropology for "aiming to reshape the definition of *culture* and thereby reduce Literary Criticism to the role of apologist for the passing fashion."[21]

The complaints are justified, it can be argued, because the actions as described would deprive literary criticism of its proper function. Yet it should be noted that, as is so frequently the case in such matters, the complaint itself is not entirely free from imperialistic pretensions. For literary criticism claimed to be in itself "the guardian study most widely responsible for maintaining the art of choice—that exercise of personal freedom."[22] While such a claim might be allowed by the humanities in a protest directed in the name of all against usurpation by the sciences, it would not, taken by itself, go unchallenged. Moral philosophy as well as religion claim a right to have some say over the exercise of freedom, and with these claims and counterclaims, we would once again be involved in conflict. Yet Richards drew up the complaint in the first place as part of an effort to bring an end to conflict and to achieve peace. He held that there would be a basis for peace if the disciplines would agree upon the following six points:

> 1. That none of them has or can have any clear, precise, or consistent view of any of the others.
> 2. That what information each possesses about the others is based on hearsay reports which have undergone incalculable transformations through intellectual translation.
> 3. That intermediaries are to be suspected of distorting their reports through self-interest: since they are for the most part agents employed by the Studies—sometimes by several at once—and are naturally anxious to please their employers.
> 4. That the overall philosophies hitherto developed to prevent or ease conflicts between the Studies have been associations concerned to promote the interests of one party or another among the Studies and have thus tended rather to increase than to diminish tension and suspicion.
> 5. That courtesy, decorum, and good manners are a chief means whereby improved relations between the Studies may be forwarded and that abusive language used in complaints is an indication that the guilt is not wholly where it is alleged to be.
> 6. That complaints be drawn up—so far as is possible—in neutral language.[23]

The complaints of literary criticism, as we have seen, are scarcely neutral when it claims to be the most important art of choice. It may be that, psychologically, the expert cannot avoid having an inflated judgment of the value of his speciality, as Collingwood suggested. Such an exaggeration does not assume dangerous proportions, however, until it reaches out to limit and restrain, if not actually to silence and destroy, other disciplines. An imperialistic move of this sort is most often made, of course, in the name of disciplines that belong to an intellectual ideal that has become a paradigm. Thus, all of the attacks of which literary criticism complained came from disciplines that boast of being sciences and of upholding the scientific ideal of culture.

The cost of intellectual imperialism is unquestionably high. A paradigm ideal by its power and influence frequently slows down and stunts the development of disciplines that do not serve that ideal. It does so not only by attracting to its own ranks the best brains and the greatest resources, but also by inspiring imitation of its practices and methods in disciplines where they are not at all suitable. The scientific ideal has already had extremely deleterious effects upon the humanities. Of these, specialization provides a striking example. Specialization is at home among the sciences, where it is a necessity, but it is disastrous among the humanities, which by their very nature address the whole gamut of human concerns.[24] Equally bad and harmful is the adoption of methods that constrict and methodically blind the eyes of the investigator to wide ranges of experience that are perfectly well known by other means. Of this the most extreme example is that of behavioristic psychology in its pretense that overt behavior is the only human behavior worth noting. Because of this much social science is pathetically thin in the results it obtains compared with the wealth of human experience that is available.[25]

That this kind of harm is the effect of an ideal that has been made a paradigm, and not of science as such, is evident from the fact that something analogous has occurred under the influence of other paradigms of intellectual culture. There is good reason to believe, as we have seen, that the predominance of the exclusively literary ideal in Roman antiquity was largely responsible for the aborting and decay of Greek science.[26] It also seems to be true that the free and bold theological and philosophical speculation characteristic of the West in the twelfth and thirteenth centuries was seriously dampened by the condemnation of 1277 in which the Bishop of Paris attempted to kill any opposition to the Augustinian ideal of theological culture.[27] Indeed, history would seem to show that a paradigm tends to establish an orthodoxy that becomes repressive to those outside of it.

Intellectual imperialism is not only harmful to those disciplines that suffer under its power, but it is also harmful to the imperialistic power itself. Any discipline is a work of mind. Hence any diminution in the power, activity, and reach of the mind is likely to affect ultimately the particular activity that produces a discipline. Such an effect will be strongest among the disciplines that are closely interdependent and highly sensitive to one another. If all our knowledge forms a unified whole and constitutes, as it were, one organic body, then weakness, injury, or atrophy in any one part would also affect the other parts through its effect upon the whole. The health and strength of a part would thus be dependent upon the health of the whole. This principle was taken by Newman to be the foundation and controlling element of the idea of the university as an intellectual community. His use of it was largely restricted to arguing for the inclusion of theology within the university, yet the principle is so general that it readily applies also to the relation between the sciences and the humanities. To use it for this purpose will help to show still more clearly the danger of intellectual imperialism and at the same time indicate the conditions that must be satisfied to achieve a healthy intellectual community.

Not all our kinds and ways of knowing are equally sensitive to mutual influence. Mathematics, as Newman pointed out, is influenced little, if at all, by theology; chemistry is affected less than biology, biology less than politics, and politics less than history, ethics or metaphysics.[28] In fact, history, ethics, and metaphysics tell vastly different stories according as they accept or refuse what theology has to say. This difference in degree regarding the extent to which a discipline can be affected from without—its sensitivity to others—reveals a significant way in which disciplines differ from one another. They differ, that is to say, according to the extent to which they can simplify and restrict their concern so as not to depend upon anything outside themselves to accomplish their purpose.[29] Mathematics in this sense is the most restricted. Physics comes next and is less restricted than mathematics in that it has to put up with the vagaries of things in motion. Biology is still less restricted inasmuch as it has to contend with the even further complexities of life. The social sciences are even less restricted since they have to take into account human deliberation as a factor in the acts of men and society. The humanities are the most unrestricted of all inasmuch as they not only address the most complex object, but they do not limit their work to the empirical and mathematical methods of science. The move here from simple to complex and from restricted to unrestricted is from the uniquely disciplinary to the interdisciplinary investigation. There are more ways of knowing about man, for example, than of knowing anything else, for every science and discipline is a work of man and to that extent has something to tell about man himself.

Interconnectedness and sensitivity to one another is greatest at the level of unrestricted knowledge. It is here that the principle of the unity of knowledge is most evident, along with its corollary that the weakness or atrophy of one part will thereby harmfully affect the others. Thus, as Newman pointed out, if moral philosophy and theology are denied and no attention given to their results, the questions they consider will be left dangling. But they will not disappear, since they are questions that men cannot avoid facing sometime or another. Hence when that time comes, some other discipline will attempt to provide an answer that will tie them down. Disciplines not at all prepared to address such questions and without practice in investigating them will then endeavor to decide matters regarding the supreme being, the supreme value, and how men ought to act to achieve a good life. Since the answers so offered are frequently based on the unquestioned assumptions of the disciplines making them, with inadequate criticism and understanding of the principles needed for their solution, it should not be surprising if the results redound to the injury and disadvantage of those making them.

A striking example of this phenomenon can be seen from the way in which a positivist interpretation of science can beget a spirit of irrationalism that turns upon science itself and attacks it as the principal cause of the dehumanization of man. On this view, the development of science has resulted in a progressive diminution and degradation in the status of man: from man created in the image of God, to man the autonomous, then to man descended from the ape, becoming next the creature of instinct and the unconscious, and winding up most recently as man the computer. This view of man rests on a conception of science that is one of the most extreme forms of intellectual imperialism. It has arrogated for positive science the exclusive right to reason, knowledge, and truth. Nothing except what has been obtained by empirical methods and mathematical reasoning deserves to be considered a work of reason, knowledge, or truth. Values, however, cannot be reached by such methods. They are not then objects of knowledge. But if this is the case, science itself ceases to have any rational basis in the nature of things; it is not something *known* to be good. Why then should one accept it as something good? Because one wants to? But what then if one does not want to accept it? If there is no rational ojective basis for an answer, the way is open to the wildest irrationalism, including the repudiation of science.

Exactly this line of thinking has been taken in the book by the Nobel prise-winning biologist, Jacques Monod, entitled *Chance and Necessity*. He asserts unequivocally that "knowledge is the supreme value."[30] The knowledge referred to is the "objective knowledge" such as is reached by positive science. The best test of objectivity is said to lie in computerizability, i.e., in the possibility of programming the knowledge so that it can be put to use in a computer.[31] This objective knowledge, which is the only one that can claim to be true, is declared to be radically distinct from any judgment of value, since objectivity "prohibits any confusion of value judgments with judgments arrived at through knowledge."[32] It is claimed that values and all of ethics are "in essence *nonobjective* [and] forever barred from the sphere of knowledge.[33]

Although science is supposed to be no judge of values and can make no statement about them, Monod acknowledges that it continually "outrages values," especially the traditional ones, inasmuch as values are always associated with knowledge, in action no less than in our discourse about them.[34] But objectivity is itself a value, and hence so too is objective knowledge. But this is to say that the first commandment, never to confuse knowledge and values, is itself nonobjective, as Monod freely admits. What then is its basis? It is 'axiomatic . . . an ethical choice," which man makes himself: this "ethic of knowledge," as Monod calls it, is said to be one that "does not obtrude itself upon man; on the contrary, it is he who prescribes it to himself." But if the principle of objectivity is the basis of all true knowledge, it follows that truth itself is ultimately only a postulate, a free choice on the part of man. Nor does Monod hesitate to accept this conclusion: "There cannot have been any 'true' knowledge," he writes, "prior to this arbitral choice."[35] But if the values that underlie our action and discourse, as well as our search for knowledge, are ultimately grounded on only a free and voluntary postulation or choice, what is there to prevent the irrationalist from exercising the same privilege and demanding the repudiation and destruction of the whole scientific enterprise?

The value of "objective knowledge" deserves a better defense than Monod provides, which is to say that it calls for more than "objectivity" so understood can deliver. Science, in attempting to claim the whole of knowledge for itself, proves unable to defend its own value. No more striking example could be asked for of the truth of Newman's principle. For Monod's "science" pretends to answer philosophical and even theological questions, delivering dogmatic opinions about objectivity and values with very little attempt to analyze them and, from all that is said, in complete ignorance of the long, hard, and intensive thinking that has been given to them by the intellectual community. Science, which is only a part of this community, needs it as much as, if not more than, any other discipline.

The Intellectual Community

The ideal of intellectual community remains today much the same, in principle, as it was for Plato's Academy. It is summed up in the words describing the final stage of the ideal curriculum as that at which "the arts and sciences constituting the *paideia* are put into connection in a comprehensive synoptic view of their relations with one another and with what truly is."[36] To avoid getting bogged down in questions about the Platonic ontology, suffice it to say that the disciplines are to be related not only to one another, but also to our fundamental human experience. If this is the ideal, it is clear at once that the provisions suggested by Richards as the basis for intellectual cooperation are by themselves insufficient. They may be enough to ensure peaceful co-existence, but they do nothing to promote positively "a comprehensive synoptic view." Richards himself admitted as much when, in an essay entitled "Toward a More Synoptic View," he called for a "truly Universal Study" that would have "more than police-functions [and] be advisor-general and therapist as well."[37]

It should be noted that the intellectual community as it is now being considered consists of the disciplines themselves, and not of their practitioners. The ideal of a synoptic view supposes that the world of learning can be grasped in one view, i.e., that the various disciplines can be related to one another and brought together in a coherent whole. Yet the very possibility of such an achievement has come into question and has even been denied. The question has been one of the issues in the controversy over the two cultures. Snow, as we have seen, did not hesitate to draw comparisons between the accomplishments of the sciences and the humanities, and he lamented the polarization between the representatives of the two and their lack of communication.[38] Leavis, however, ridiculed such a comparison, claiming that the two are so diverse as to defy comparison, and, in publishing his lecture, he included an essay by a biologist that maintained that no communication is possible between the two cultures. He based the denial on the claim that science has achieved such a high degree of specialization that it can only be understood in a specialized way by the specialist.[39] Perhaps also implicit is the assumption that all knowledge is specialized with the denial that there is any general knowledge that is not superficial and hence not worth bothering about. The controversy involves, as already noted, the conflict of science and philosophy and the issue of what knowledge is best.[40]

The emphasis upon specialization, as is to be expected, comes mostly from the side of science. Yet it is certainly excessive when it goes to the extreme of denying the possibility of comparison and communication. To communicate at the frontiers of contemporary science admittedly demands a high degree of specialization. But there are other ways of understanding science then by working at the frontiers. It is possible to obtain an understanding of formal science, and especially of an axiomatic system, through the study of Euclidian geometry and of the logic of propositions and of the syllogism. Much can be learned about experimental science from the works of the founders of modern physics, such as those of Galileo. An easy and interesting entry into taxonomic and observational science can be made through botany and ecology. All of these studies can be pursued in an elementary way that is still scientific, i.e., that involves the actual *doing* of science, and so results in much more than mere knowledge *about* science, as is often charged. Knowledge of the frontiers of science may indeed be too specialized to communicate to the nonspecialist except in the form of information *about* science. Yet it is not too much to aspire to an understanding of how the world now appears in its main lines to the basic sciences: the structure of the universe as it is seen by the astronomer, the physicist, and the chemist; the earth as it is now understood by the geologist; the basic patterns of life as it appears to the biologist; and man and human society as discussed by the social scientist. Indeed, scientists themselves have begun to appreciate the danger of being cut off from the general public and to emphasize the need for expositions that relate scientific achievements to common human experience and the world in which all of us, scientists included, live each day of our lives.[41]

Granted that communication is possible, and that the specialization of science is not a windowless prison, is there anything more that might be done to promote a more synoptic view? In our society the university is presumably better suited than any other institution to pursue that end as a goal. The various arts and sciences that reside within the university, however, are more a collection of specialist departments than a center of human consciousness, as Leavis has noted.[42] Hence, from time to time, voicing a recurrent hope, the proposal has been made that there should be a central organ responsible for the intellectual community as a community and engaged in developing comprehension and pursuing a more synoptic view.

The dream of such a center has been a constituent element of the positivist ideal from the time of Comte down to that of the Movement for Unified Science. Its conception of such a center, however, has attracted only those who subscribe to the positivist doctrine. To others their proposal has appeared as an imperialistic attempt to impose doctrinal unity based on acceptance of a narrow criterion of positive knowledge that dismisses as without worth much human achievement.[43] In itself, however, the idea of a center for intellectual community is not necessarily an expression of intellectual imperialism.

Another proposal that embodies the same dream, but does not suffer from such a doctrinal disadvantage, emerged from the renewal of interest in general education after the Second World War. This interest in general education was, in part, a response to the need for a more synoptic view than the specialized disciplines are capable of achieving. To achieve this aim, H. M. Jones proposed the establishment of an autonomous Graduate College, separate and distinct from all research specialities, which would have as its members a small number of men from all the major disciplines, "whose professional history perhaps began with research work, but who have since come to reflect philosophically upon science, the arts, and the social sciences in relation to human culture, notably in relation to education as a social and intellectual process. This faculty would have as its principal task to reflect upon and to discuss such topics as "the philosophy of language and the meaning of literature, the social, metaphysical, and pedagogical problems arising from mathematics, theories of science and their application, and the uses of history and the other social sciences for modern man."[44] Such a work, Jones claimed, would be an ideal preparation for those entering the profession of undergraduate college teaching inasmuch as it would provide a better and fuller understanding of the arts and sciences in their relation to one another and to the intellectual community as a whole.

There is still a third proposal that falls, as it were, in between those of Comte on the one hand and of Jones on the other. It aims at no such doctrinal or dogmatic unity as the one proposes, yet at more than the other seems to envisage. It is based on the fact that the intellectual community can have different degrees of unity. The maximum degree of unity consists in agreement regarding the true and false, the good and bad, and thus is a unity of doctrine. The minimum degree of unity consists in agreement upon the end that the community is pursuing together, and is thus a unity of purpose. An example of doctrinal unity is provided by the positivist ideal. The minimal unity of purpose is found in some universities, which provide a common place in which many diverse disciplines as well as different and even opposed philosophies and theologies can work toward the one end of knowledge. In between these two there is a degree of unity that can be called dialectical, since it consists in agreement about controversy or discussion.

While acknowledging that men disagree not only about conclusions, but also about principles and the methods by which conclusions can be reached, this proposal maintains that it is possible to obtain some measure of agreement about the controversial situation as such: the questions that pose issues and give rise to different and conflicting answers that establish positions related in various ways to one another, involving different points of agreement and disagreement. To establish the basis for such dialectical unity, Mortimer Adler proposed, in 1927, the construction of a *summa dialectica* to make manifest and illuminate the pattern of agreement and disagreement in the philosophical controversies over basic ideas.[45] Although it was originally intended as an instrument for promoting unity only within the philosophical community, the suggestion itself could be broadened in scope to envision a project that would include the whole intellectual community. The conflict of cultural ideals, as we have seen especially in the case of the controversy over the two cultures, reaches into many disciplines as it involves all the sciences and humanities.

The need for a center or an agency charged with responsibility for the intellectual community as such, i.e., with protecting and promoting it as a community, is more urgent today than ever before. Specialization in learning is rampant and is ever continuing to advance. Yet the university, in becoming a multiversity, has relinquished even the tenuous hold that it once had upon the ideal of intellectual unity. With the financial retrenchment now forced upon it which is being accompanied by a regressive emphasis upon departmental specialization, even the very modest efforts that had been made toward a more general and integrated education are fast acquiring the status of an endangered species. In this situation, despite the fact that the need may be greater, the prospect of establishing any kind of organ for intellectual community would seem to remain as much a dream as ever.

Yet, on the positive side, there are a few optimistic signs, although they may turn out to be gestures of desperation. The ecological crisis demands for its solution a collaboration of disciplines as well as of men. Not only is ecology an unrestricted and interdisciplinary science, but any action at the ecological level depends upon decisions regarding values that are not only political and social, but aesthetic, moral, and even religious. The ecumenical movement within the churches of Christendom also marks a concern for community and, with regard to matters of doctrine, is even an attempt to discover the foundations for dialectical unity. Even more, on a worldwide scale, the increasing contacts between diverse national cultures, with its promise of a world community, put an ever-greater urgency upon successful communication. But it is difficult, to say the least, to see what chance there is of establishing communication and community between East and West if at home we cannot achieve even a minimum degree of intellectual community. Yet, as we have seen from our investigation, the conflict of cultural ideals within the Western tradition has exhibited at the extremes of intellectual imperialism not even the minimum degree of intellectual community.

From this, however, it would not be true to conclude that disunity, incomprehension, and conflict are inevitable. Our investigation, however inadequate and wanting it may be, has demonstrated that the conflicts that have divided this community can be studied, analyzed, and made comprehensible. Not only have questions and issues been identified, as well as the differing positions to which they give rise, but in many cases we have seen that these differences are based upon differences in methods and aims which are not in themselves incompatible—that are *diversa, non adversa*. If, in addition, it is true that perhaps the major cause of conflict has been a form of imperialism, that is not something that need be eternal and unavoidable. In fact, we have reason for confidence, if not consolation, in the discovery that a basis already exists for more than a minimum degree of unity within the intellectual community.

AN IRENIC EPILOGUE

I began my investigation by striking a polemical note. Throughout I have been concerned with quarrels, battles, conflicts, and controversies. It is also true that the place of concern has not always been a neutral one above and apart from the battle. I have frequently been actively engaged in opposing those who attack the humanities and attempt to belittle or deny the value and importance of the humanities. In our time these attacks have come most frequently from those within the world of learning who uphold the scientific ideal as paradigm. Consequently, my counterattack has been directed most against the claims of science, and at times, perhaps, without the courtesy, decorum, good manners, and mildness of language that, as Richards emphasized, are conducive to peace.

Yet, at the close, it is worth affirming again that, just as war is for the sake of peace, so from the start, my intent and purpose has been irenic. Conflict has been my object, not to perpetuate it, but to see how it has come about in the hope of lessening it. I have located the main cause of it in greatness and *hybris*. Each of the three ideals of intellectual culture represents, in both thought and expression, a truly great achievement of the human spirit. Yet none of the ideals in coming to greatness has succeeded in avoiding the *hybris* that results in intellectual imperialism, with its denial of the rights of others and eventual conflict.

The best hope of peace, then, would seem to lie in the eschewing of imperialism. But this calls for acknowledgment and recognition that there exist different ideals of intellectual culture, each with its own preferred ways of thought and expression, each responding in its own way to different needs and aiming at different purposes, and all of them equally the work of mind. To recognize the rights of these different ideals, however, is not sufficient by itself. It must also be recognized that there is an overarching ideal of all, namely, the intellectual community as the place within which the various ideals with their disciplines are so many different provinces.

Yet, it must also be recognized that these provinces have no definite boundaries fixed for all time. The world of learning is continually developing, losing as well as gaining. It is perhaps useful to picture it as a continually growing cylinder described by an ascending spiral. All that man has ever learned and known is represented by the cylinder as a whole, which has been growing larger as knowledge has increased. Yet at no time is the whole of that cylinder actually known, since no one knows all that has been forgotten and lost. The actual knowledge at any time is rather a section through the cylinder. These circles of knowledge are divided up differently at different times, reflecting the existence of different arts and sciences as well as different ways of mapping.

The cultural ideals with which we have been concerned represent different ways of viewing the world of knowledge, preferences for one part over another, with different purposes to serve. Yet all have their locus and their life within that one world. If in the course of this work, I have been insisting upon difference, division, and conflict, it was not to separate so as to rend apart and destroy, but rather to distinguish in order to unite (*distinguer pour unir*).

NOTES

Chapter 1

1. *Studia humanitatis*, or humane studies, in the Renaissance were often contrasted with *studia divinitatis*, or divine studies. See Trinkaus, *In Our Image or Likeness*, vol. 2, p. 560.

2. Homer *Iliad* 9. 443, quoted in Cicero *De Oratore* 3. 15. 57.

3. Cic. *De orat*. 3. 15-16. 60-61, where I have quoted with some alteration the translation of J. S. Watson in the Bohn Library.

4. Ibid., 3. 17. 63-64.

5. Ibid., 1. 17. 75.

6. Ibid., 3. 35. 142-43.

7. Ibid., 1. 8. 33.

8. Ibid., 1. 9. 35.

9. Aulus Gellius *Noctes Atticue* 13. 16.

10. Jaeger, *Paideia*, vol. 1, p. 283.

11. Aristotle *Parts of Animals* 1. 1. 639a1-12.

12. For the origin of *enkuklios paideia*, see Marrou, "Lex Arts libéraux dans l'antiquité," in *Arts Libéraux et Philosophie au Moyen Âge* (hereafter cited as *ALPMA*), pp. 16-18.

13. Cic. *De orat*. 2. 1. 1; 3. 31. 125.

14. Ibid., 2. 17. 72.

15. Quintilian *Institutio oratoria* 1. 10. 1: "Having spoken about Grammatica, . . . I will now consider the other arts that the boys need to be instructed in before being handed over to the teacher of Rhetoric, in order to complete the circle of learning that the Greeks call *enkuklios paideia*."

16. Kennedy, *The Art of Rhetoric in the Roman World, 300 B.C.–A.D. 300*, p. 496.

17. Quint. *Inst. orat*. 2. 1. 4.

18. Ibid., 1. 4. 1-4; 10. 3-5; and 10. 35.

19. Ibid., 2. 1. 4: "Nos suum cuique professioni modum demus."

20. Perelman and Olbrechts-Tyteca, *The New Rhetoric*, and for a summary statement, see Perelman's essay of the same title in *The Great Ideas Today 1970*, pp. 273-312.

21. See Sr. Miriam Joseph, *Shakespeare's Use of the Arts of Language*, for an excellent analysis of the rhetorical tradition on the figures of speech, with abundant illustrations from Shakespeare.

22. Quint. *Inst. orat*. 10. 1. 5-7, trans. by J. S. Watson, Bohn Library.

23. Ibid., 1. 4. 3.

24. Ibid., 1. 6. 45, quoted in *The American Heritage Dictionary* (1969), p. xxiia, but attributed solely to Ben Jonson.

25. *American Heritage Dictionary*, p. xxiiic-d.

26. Arnold, "Literature and Science," in *Discourses in America*, p. 82; Quint. *Inst. orat*. 12. 1. 25.

27. For the history of the *classic*, see Curtius, *European Literature and the Latin Middle Ages*, pp. 247-72, and Pfeiffer, *History of Classical Scholarship*, pp. 203-8.

28. Quint. *Inst. orat.* 10. 1. 20-131.

29. Cic. *De orat.* 1. 6. 20.

30. Quin. *Inst. orat.* 12. 1. 1.

31. Ibid., 1. proem. 9-10.

32. For a good survey of the recent scientific and philosophical literature on this point, see Adler, *The Difference of Man and the Difference It Makes*, pp. 112-24.

33. Petrarch *Rerum senilium libri* 15. 1, p. 1046.

34. D'Alembert, *Preliminary Discourse to the Encyclopedia of Diderot*, pp. 92-93.

35. Eliot, *What is a Classic*, p. 31: "Our classic, the classic of all Europe, is Virgil."

36. Mill, "Inaugural Address at St. Andrew's," in *The Six Great Humanistic Essays of John Stuart Mill*, p. 327.

37. Bacon, *Novum Organum*, 1. 59-60. The Latin text may be found in *The Works of Francis Bacon*.

Chapter 2

1. St. Paul, 1 Cor. 1:19-20.

2. Augustine *Confessions* 3. 4. 7; 3. 6. 10; and 6. 4. 6.

3. Idem, *De doctrina christiana libri quattuor* 2. 42. 63.

4. Ibid., 1. 36. 40.

5. Ibid., 1. 10. 10 through 14. 14.

6. Ibid., 1. 39. 43 through 40. 44.

7. For a magisterial analysis of this indebtedness, see Marrou, *St. Augustin et la fin de la culture antique*.

8. Aug. *De doc. chris.* 1. 1. 1.

9. Ibid., 2. 11. 16 through 12. 17.

10. Ibid., 3. 29. 40-41.

11. Ibid., 2. 28. 42-43.

12. Ibid., 2. 29. 45-46.

13. Ibid., 2. 30. 47.

14. Ibid., 2. 31. 48-49.

15. Ibid., 2. 16. 25-26.

16. Ibid., 2. 36. 54.

17. Ibid., 2. 40. 60.

18. Aug. *Conf.* 7. 9. 13ff.

19. Idem, *De doc. chris.* 2. 40. 60.

20. Ibid., 2. 39. 58. The maxim quoted may be found in Terence *Andria* 1. 1.

21. Idem, *De doc. chris.* 4. 2. 3.

22. Ibid., 4. 6. 9 through 7. 21.

23. Ibid., 4. 3. 4.

24. Ibid., 4. 28. 61.

25. Ibid., 3. 10. 14.

26. Aug. *Conf.* 12. 31. 42 (Sheed translation).

27. Ibid., 13. 24. 37.

28. See Leclerc, *The Love of Learning and the Desire for God*, esp. pp. 23-26, where it is pointed out that *lectio* was usually out loud, "a real acoustical reading; *legere* means at the

same time *audire*;" and *meditatio* meant, in addition to reflection, "thinking of a thing with the intent to do it; . . . to prepare oneself for it, to prefigure it in the mind, to desire it, in a way, to do it in advance."

29. Hugh of St. Victor, *The Didascalicon of Hugh of St. Victor*, pref. p. 44.

30. Ibid., 6. 13, p. 151.

31. Ibid., 3. 1, p. 83.

32. Ibid., Taylor's introduction, p. 5.

33. Ibid., 6. 4, p. 141. This same structure is followed by Hugh in his *De sacramentis*, a theological work on the Christian faith.

34. Hugh, *The Didascalicon*, 2. 30, p. 81. See Taylor's note 87, p. 207.

35. My exposition follows primarily the interpretation of Van Ackeren, *Sacra Doctrinax*, and of Gilson, *Le Thomisme*.

36. Thus his first biographer, William of Tocco, in describing the impression Thomas made on his time, repeated the word *novus* and its cognates eight times within a few lines, as new in method, questions, arguments, inspiration, and so forth.

37. Aquinas *Declaratio 42 Quaestionum* no. 32.

38. See esp. Chenu, *La Théologie au douzième siècle* and *La Théologie comme science au XIII ͤ siècle*.

39. See idem, *La Théologie comme science*, p. 27.

40. Many are apparent from just the titles of the articles cited, but specific reference to the need for evidence is in *Summa Theologiae* 1. 1. 2, ob. 1; to lack of concern for singulars in l. 1. 2, ob. 2; to certainty in 1. 1. 5, ob. 1; to avoiding appeal to authority in l. 1. 8, ob. 2; against the use of metaphors in 1. 1. 9, ob. 1; against ambiguity and multiplicity of meaning in 1. 1. 10, ob. 1.

41. Aquinas *Sum. Theo.* 1. 1. 2c. See Chenu, *La Théologie comme science*, pp. 80–83.

42. Aquinas *Sum. Theo.* 1. 1. 8c and 1. 1. 7c.

43. Ibid., 1. 1. 2c.

44. Words used by St. Bonaventure in the prologue to his commentary on the *Sentences* of Peter Lombard, quoted in Chenu, *La Théologie comme science*, p. 54.

45. See Chenu, *La Théologie comme science*, p. 97.

46. Aquinas *Sum. Theo.* 1. 1. 7c.

47. Aquinas, *In Boetium de Trinitate*, 5. 4c (Maurer trans., pp. 44–45).

48. Aquinas *Sum. Theo.* 1. 1. 4c.

49. Ibid., 1. 1. 9, ob. 1. See infra, chap. 5.

50. Aquinas *In I de Anima*, chap. 1, lect. 8, no. 107.

51. Aquinas *Sum. Theo.* 1. 1. 3c. The crucial point is completely lost in some translations, as for example: "Because sacred scripture considers some things under the formality of being divinely revealed, all things which have been divinely revealed have in common the formality of the object of this science." (New York: Modern Library, p. 7).

52. Van Ackeren, *Sacra Doctrina*, p. 110.

53. Aquinas *Sum. Theo.* 1. 1. 2 sed cont., quoted Augustine's *De Trinitate* 14. 7.

54. Aquinas *Sum. Theo.* 1. 1. 8, ad. 2.

55. Ibid., 1. 32. 1, ad. 2. See *In De Coelo* 2. 17, no. 451.

56. Bochenski, *The Logic of Religion*, pp. 64–65.

57. See Van Ackeren, *Sacra Doctrina*, p. 120, and Gilson, *Le Thomisme*, p. 21.

58. Aquinas *Sum. Theo.* 1. 1. 5 sed cont.

59. For a defense of the article form, see my paper, "How to Read an Article of the *Summa*," *The New Scholasticism*, 27 (1953):129–59.

60. Pascal, *Pensées*, no. 283 (Brunschvicg, edit. minor).

Chapter 3

1. Whitehead, *Science and the Modern World*, chap. 3, p. 58.

2. Idem, *The Concept of Nature*, chap. 2, pp. 26-49.

3. *Aubrey's Brief Lives*, "Harvey," p. 130. Aubrey wrote *philosophy*, not *science*, but the two were not then distinguished. It might be noted that a recent biography is entitled *Francis Bacon: The First Statesman of Science* (by J. G. Crowther).

4. Bacon, *The Advancement of Learning*, 2. 1. 2, p. 85: "Historia Literarum"; 2. 23. 4, p. 219: "De negotiis gerendis." See infra, chap. 8.

5. See esp. Paoli Rossi, *Francis Bacon*, half of which is given over to a consideration of the influence of the rhetorical tradition on his work.

6. Bacon, *Novum Organum*, 1. 73. The Latin text may be found in *The Works of Francis Bacon*.

7. Ibid., 1. 124.

8. Ibid., 1. 129.

9. Ibid., 1. 124.

10. Ibid., 1. 74.

11. Ibid., 1. 78.

12. Ibid., 1. 79.

13. Ibid., "The Great Instauration," in *The Works of Francis Bacon*, pref., p. 14.

14. Ibid., 1. 95. Note that Swift uses the same metaphor but reverses it to make the moderns, including the new science, typified by the spider, and the ancients by the bee. See infra, chaps. 6 and 7.

15. Ibid., 1. 98.

16. Ibid., 1. 99.

17. Ibid., pref., p. 34.

18. Ibid., 1. 68, where the phrase "kingdom of man" appears.

19. D'Alembert, *Preliminary Discourse to the Encyclopedia of Diderot*, p. 74.

20. Ibid., p. 5.

21. Comte, *Introduction to Positive Philosophy* (Ferré trans.), p. 11; this introduction is a translation of the first two chapters of the *Cours de philosophie positive*.

22. Ibid., pp. 1-2.

23. Ibid., p. 2.

24. Ibid., p. 20.

25. Comte, *The Positive Philosophy* (Martineau), pp. 813-16.

26. Ibid., p. 816.

27. Comte, *Introduction to Positive Philosophy* (Ferré), pp. 17-18.

28. Ibid., pp. 24-25.

29. Ibid., p. 28.

30. Ibid., p. 29.

31. Comte, *The Positive Philosophy* (Martineau), p. 569.

32. Comte, *The Positivist Library of Auguste Comte*. Of the 138 authors included, 47 are in poetry and fiction, 32 in science, 30 in history, and 29 in philosophy and religion.

33. Comte, *The Positive Philosophy* (Martineau), p. 571.

34. Ibid., pp. 566-67.

35. Ibid., p. 686.

36. Neurath, Bohr, et. al., *International Encyclopedia of Unified Science*, vol. 1, no. 1: "Encyclopedia and Unified Science," p. 8.

37. Ibid., p. 18.

38. Ibid., pp. 73-74.
39. Ibid., p. 20.
40. Ibid., pp. 18-19.
41. Ibid., p. 61.
42. Neurath, Carnap, and Morris, *Foundations of the Unity of Science: Toward an International Encyclopedia of Unified Science.*

Chapter 4

1. Plato *Republic* 10. 607B and note of E. Chambry, Budé edition, p. 102.
2. Ibid., 10. 598D-E.
3. Ibid., 6. 509E-511E; see 7. 533C-534A.
4. The text does not specify the proportion, but there is a long tradition that it is the one Euclid, in the *Elements* (6. 30) called cutting a line into extreme and mean proportion and which later came to be called the golden section or divine proportion, i.e., the shorter is to the longer segment as the longer is to the sum of the two.
5. Plato *Rep.* 10. 596A.
6. Idem, *Timaeus* 54B-55B.
7. No mention is made of the mathematicals in Plato *Rep.* 10. 597E, where reference is made only to three makers—God, carpenter, and painter. It would thus appear that the painter and poet are at *two* removes from reality, not *three*, as Plato says. This discrepancy is sometimes explained by pointing out that the Greeks counted *inclusively*, and some translators even change the *thrice* to *twice*. But interpreting the passage in light of the divided line, and making explicit the place of the mathematicals, it is possible to retain the literal reading.
8. Plato *Rep.* 10. 605A-D.
9. Idem, *Seventh Letter* 342A-D.
10. Ibid., 341C-D.
11. Idem, *Symposium* 210E-211C; *Rep.* 7. 516B-517B.
12. Aristotle *Poetics* 1447b10.
13. Hulme, "Bergson's Theory of Art," in Adams, *Critical Theory Since Plato*, p. 779a.
14. Plato *Phaedrus* 275D.
15. Ibid., 276E-277A.
16. Arist. *Posterior Analytics* 97b37.
17. Aquinas *Summa Theologiae* 1. 1, ob. 1. See infra, chap. 5.
18. Idem, *In I de Anima*, lect. 8, no. 107.
19. Aquinas *In Boetium De trinitate* 2. 3, ad. 5 (Maurer, p. 52), and supra, chap. 2.
20. Horace, *Ars poetica*, in *Horace: The Complete Works* (Boston: Allyn and Bacon, 1901), v. 361.
21. The list is a conflation of many, including additions of my own. For such lists from literary critics, see the convenient summary in Adams, *The Interests of Criticism*, chap. 5, pp. 85-112.
22. James, *The Principles of Psychology*, vol. 1, p. 186.
23. Langer, *Mind*, vol. 1, p. 21, where the above James passage is also quoted.
24. Neurath, et. al., *International Encyclopedia of Unified Science*, vol. 1, no. 1, p. 23: One "may decide that in certain cases an emotional activity is more important than a scientific attitude. It is not the subject of a scientific explanation to support or oppose such a decision."

25. Mill, "Inaugural Address at St. Andrew's," in *The Six Great Humanistic Essays of John Stuart Mill*, p. 355.

26. Mill, "Thoughts on Poetry," in *Humanistic Essays*, p. 15.

27. Ibid., p. 23.

28. Ibid., p. 17.

29. Wordsworth, *The Prelude, or Growth of a Poet's Mind*, 13. 205; see 2. 296-303.

30. Such a compilation is provided by Marin-Sola, *L'Evolution homogéne du dogma catholique*, vol. 1, p. 363, which lists seventeen ways in which Thomas speaks of affective knowledge and ten for speculative knowledge.

31. Aquinas *Sum. Theo*. 1. 1. 6 ad. 3.

32. Ibid., 1. 43. 5 ad. 2.

33. Maritain, *Creative Intuition in Art and Poetry*, p. 118.

34. Ibid., pp. 184-85.

35. Ibid., p. 237.

36. Shelley, "A Defense of Poetry," in Adams, *Critical Theory*, p. 511b.

37. Aquinas *De veritate* 2. 6, ad. 3.

38. MacLeish, "Ars poetica."

39. Valery, "Poetry and Abstract Thought," in Adams, *Critical Theory*, pp. 920a, 919d, and 921d respectively.

40. Havelock, *Preface to Plato*, esp. chap. 3, pp. 36-60 and chap. 15, pp. 276-311.

41. Whitehead, "The First Physical Synthesis," in *Essays in Science and Philosophy*, p. 171.

42. W. T. Jones, *The Sciences and the Humanities*, p. 222.

Chapter 5

1. Edited and translated by Paetow.

2. Edited by Gompf.

3. The term *ars* was so used by Hugh of St. Victor in his *Didascalicon*. See supra, chap. 2 and infra, chap. 8.

4. See Kristeller, "The modern System of the Arts," in *Renaissance Thought II*, p. 184.

5. Kant, *Le Conflit des Facultés* ("The conflict of the faculties").

6. Supra, chap. 1.

7. Stahl, Johnson, and Burge, *Martianus Capella and the Seven Liberal Arts*, p. 234.

8. Ibid., appendix A, pp. 245-49, which is a "Bibliographical Survey of the Seven Liberal Arts in Mediaeval and Renaissance Iconography." See also Verdier, "L'Iconographie de Arts libéraux dans l'art du moyen âge jusqu'à la fin du quinzième siècle," in *ALPMA*, pp. 305-55.

9. Martianus Capella, *De nuptiis*, 1. 5-8. pp. 6-8.

10. Ibid., 1. 92, p. 39.

11. See Plotinus *Enneads* 3. 6. 19; Augustine, *De civitate Dei* 7. 14; and for fuller references, Pauly-Wissowa, *Real-Encyclopedie* under "Hermes."

12. See Stahl, et al., *Martianus Capella*, p. 37.

13. Martianus, *De nuptiis*, 2. 126, p. 56.

14. Ibid., 2. 136-39, pp. 59-60.

15. See supra, chap. 1.

16. Cicero *De republica* 2. 10. For the force of these expressions, see Marrou, *St. Augustin et la fin de la culture antique*, note A, "L'idée de culture et le vocabulaire Latin," pp. 549-60.

17. Joannes Scotus Erigena, *Annotationes in Marcianum*, p. 3.

18. John of Salisbury *Metalogicon* 1. 1 (McGarry trans., p. 11). For the history of the interpretation of the allegory, see Nuchelmans, "Philologia et son mariage avec Mercure jusqu'à la fin du XIIe siècle," in *Latomus* 16 (1957):84-107.

19. Martianus, *De nuptiis*, 2. 173-74, p. 71.

20. Ibid., 9. 998, p. 534.

21. Stahl, et. al., *Martianus Capella*, p. 231.

22. Diogenes Laertius *Lives of the Eminent Philosophers* 2. 79.

23. Clement of Alexandria, *Les Stromates* (French translation of *Stromata*) 1. 5. 30, where Philo Judaeus is also quoted on the relation of the "encyclical branches" to philosophy (Philo, *On Seeking Instruction*, 435).

24. *"Ordo artium,"* in *Mittellateinische Jahrbuch* 3 (1966):94-128, strophes 48-49.

25. Ibid., strophes 96-113.

26. Ibid., strophes 116-28.

27. See Paetow, ed., "The Battle of the Seven Arts," in *Memoirs of the University of California*, p. 34.

28. Ibid., lines 6-8 and 408-410.

29. Ibid., lines 55-56, 93, and 224-29.

30. Ibid., lines 79-80 and 88-90.

31. Ibid., lines 1-5.

32. Ibid., lines 314-15 and 396-97.

33. Ibid., lines 450-56.

34. See Weisheipl, "The Place of the Liberal Arts in the University Curriculum during the XIVth and XVth Centuries," in *ALPMA*, pp. 209-13 and Kristeller's comment on p. 258.

35. Aquinas *In Analytica posteriora* 1. 1.

36. Idem, *Summa Theologiae* 1. 1. 9, ob. 1. See supra, chap. 4.

37. This is the title of an essay by Cleanth Brooks in Adams, *Critical Theory since Plato*, p. 1033.

38. See Kibre, "The *Quadrivium* in the Thirteenth Century Universities," in *ALPMA*, pp. 176-77.

39. Paetow, "The Battle of the Seven Arts," p. 7.

40. See Bursill-Hall, *Speculative Grammars of the Middle Ages*, esp. pp. 24-36 and 340-41.

41. This position has been especially emphasized by McKeon, "The Battle of the Books," in Booth, *The Knowledge Most Worth Having*, pp. 175, 184-87, and 199-202, and Crane, *The Idea of the Humanities*, vol. 1, pp. 7-11.

42. See Delhaye, "La place des arts libéraux dans les programmes scolaires du XIIIe siècle," in *ALPMA*, p. 165, n. 10.

43. Weisheipl, *Friar Thomas D'Aquino*, pp. 333-38; Gilson, *History of the Christian Philosophy in the Middle Ages*, pp. 405-7.

44. Miles, *Religion and the Scientific Outlook*, p. 165.

45. Ibid., pp. 166-67.

46. Ibid., p. 171.

47. Ibid., pp. 217-18.

48. Ibid., pp. 218-19.

49. Kant, *Religion within the Limits of Reason Alone*, p. 142.

50. Gilson, *History*, p. 727, n. 50. See also idem, *Reason and Revelation in the Middle Ages*, pp. 58-63.

51. Shea, "Theology as an Academic Discipline," in *The Role of Theology in the University*, p. 84.

52. Freud, *New Introductory Lectures on Psychoanalysis*, lect 35, in *Great Books of the Western World*, vol. 54, p. 880b.

53. Aristotle *Metaphysics* 4. 4. 1006a35ff.

54. For an analysis of these positions from typical representatives, see Gilson, *Reason and Revelation*, and Niebuhr, *Christ and Culture.*

55. Pascal, *Provincial Letters*, no. 18, in *Great Books of the Western World*, vol. 33, p. 163b.

56. Ibid., pp. 163b-164a.

57. See Gilson, *Le Thomisme*, pp. 209-213.

58. Pascal, *Pensées*, no. 277.

59. Ibid., no. 282.

60. Ibid., no. 278.

CHAPTER 6

1. See Sandys, *A History of Classical Scholarship*, vol. 2, p. 403.

2. Ibid., p. 404.

3. "A Full and True Account of the Battel Fought last Friday Between the Antient and the Modern Books in St. James's Library," pp. 224, 235-37, and 244. It is perhaps surprising to find Aquinas and Scotus among the moderns, although they were so in their own time. Harvey, however, might have considered it a slur, for, if Aubrey is to be believed (*Aubrey's Brief Lives*, "Harvey," p. 129), he "did call the Neoteriques shitt-breeches."

4. Ibid., pp. 225 and 238 respectively. The fable of the spider and the bee is found on pp. 229-235.

5. Jebb, quoted in Sandys, *Classical Scholarship*, vol. 2, p. 405.

6. D'Alembert, *Preliminary Discourse to the Encyclopedia of Diderot*, p. 60.

7. Ibid., p. 63.

8. Ibid., pp. 65-66.

9. Ibid., p. 68.

10. Ibid., pp. 70-71, 74, 77, 81, and 83.

11. Pascal, *Scientific Treatises concerning the Vacuum*, in *Great Books of the Western World*, vol. 33, p. 355.

12. Ibid., pp. 355-56.

13. Ibid., p. 356.

14. Ibid., p. 355.

15. Marione, Guala. *Tutti i verbi greci.* Milan: G. Principato, 1961.

16. Charles Perrault, in his *Parallèle des anciens et des modernes* (1693), cited in Kristeller, "The Modern System of the Arts," in *Renaissance Thought II*, p. 195.

17. Pound, *ABC of Reading*, p. 13.

18. Joyce, *Ulysses*, chap. 14.

19. This is the position taken by Thomas Kuhn in *The Structure of Scientific Revolutions*. It has been strongly criticized by Toulmin in *Human Understanding*, vol. 1, pp. 98ff.

20. Supra, chap. 1.

21. Kant, *Critique of Pure Reason*, 2d edit., pref., par. 1.

22. Gilson, *The Unity of Philosophical Experience*, p. 306.

23. Toulmin, *Human Understanding*, p. 282.

24. I owe this metabolic metaphor to Dean Frederick J. Crosson of the University of Notre Dame.

25. For this analysis of tradition, see Congar, *Tradition and the Traditions*, p. 307.

26. Toulmin, *Human Understanding*, p. 282.

27. Holton, *Thematic Origins of Scientific Thought*, p. 414.

28. Congar, "Tradition in Theology," in *The Great Ideas Today 1974*, p. 5.

29. Toulmin, *Human Understanding*, p. 395ff. It should be noted that Toulmin here develops this distinction in order to discriminate more sharply than is usual between "disciplines" and "nondisciplines," whereas he uses the expression "rational enterprises" for what I am calling here and throughout a "discipline."

30. Ibid., p. 232.

31. Collingwood, *Speculum Mentis, or the Map of Knowledge*, p. 82.

32. Supra, chap. 1.

33. Crane, *The Idea of the Humanities*, vol. 1, p. 89.

34. Supra, chap. 3.

35. The classic on this subject remains Newman's *An Essay on the Development of Christian Doctrine*, although the theology of the subject has not yet been very fully elaborated, even though the principle was endorsed by the second Vatican Council.

36. Kurt Vonnegut.

37. Bacon, *Novum Organum*, 1. 56. The Latin text may be found in *The Works of Francis Bacon*. The same explanation is given by W. T. Jones in "Philosophical Disagreement and World Views," *Proceedings of the American Philosophical Association, 1969-1970*, p. 29.

38. Rigault, quoted in Paetow, "The Battle of the Seven Liberal Arts," in *Memoirs of the University of California*, p. 5. See also R. F. Jones, *Ancients and Moderns*, p. 146.

39. See McKeon, "The Battle of the Books," in *The Knowledge Most Worth Having*, p. 177.

40. Snow, "The Case of Leavis and the Serious Case," *Times Literary Supplement* no. 3,567, pp. 739-40.

Chapter 7

1. Thus Snow noted that the bibliography of publications on the topic between 1964 and 1968 alone already contained eight-eight separate items. ("The Case of Leavis and the Serious Case," *Times Literary Supplement* no. 3,567, p. 737.)

2. Leavis, " 'Literarism' versus 'Scientism'," *Times Literary Supplement* no. 3,556.

3. Snow, "The Case of Leavis."

4. Ibid., p. 739b.

5. Idem, *The Two Cultures*, p. 11.

6. Ibid., p. 12

7. Ibid., p. 17.

8. Idem, "The Case of Leavis," p. 739c.

9. Arnold's and Huxley's essays were originally published in 1882 and are reprinted in Cornelius and St. Vincent, *Cultures in Conflict*, which contains a representative selection of statements on the early phase of the Snow-Leavis controversy.

10. Snow, *Two Cultures*, p. 23.

11. Ibid., p. 20.

12. Ibid., p. 27.

13. Ibid., p. 89.

14. Idem, "The Case of Leavis," p. 739a-b.

15. Idem, *Two Cultures*, pp. 12 and 20.

16. Leavis, *Two Cultures?*, p. 47.

17. Snow, "The Case of Leavis," p. 739-c.

18. Vico, *On the Study Methods of Our Times*, 4, p. 23.

19. Idem, *The New Science*, no. 331, pp. 52-53.

20. Dilthey, *Introduction à l'étude des sciences humaines*, pp. 14-15. (French translation of *Einleitung in die Geisteswissenschaften*.)

21. Idem, "Abgrenzung der Geisteswissenschaften," in *Gesamelte Schriften*, 7, p. 79 (translated in Rickman, p. 68).

22. Snow, *Two Cultures*, pp. 66-67.

23. Dilthey, "Abgrenzung," pp. 79-81 (Rickman, p. 68).

24. Ibid., p. 85 (Rickman, pp. 70-71).

25. Ibid., p. 136 (Rickman, p. 79).

26. Thus, for example, it is claimed that the logical system of Polish logician S. Lesniewski is superior to that of Russell and Whitehead precisely because it does not have to assume the existence of at least one object in the world, while the latter does, as is explicitly noted by Russell in his remark in the *Principia Mathematica* with regard to theorem no. 24.52.

27. Dilthey, "Abgrenzung," p. 86.

28. Ibid., p. 71 (Rickman, p. 97).

29. Levi, *Literature, Philosophy, and the Imagination*, p. 2. See also his book, *The Humanities Today*, p. 52.

30. Levi, *Literature*, p. 46.

31. Supra, chap. 4.

32. Levi, *Literature*, pp. 5, 29, and 257 respectively.

33. Ibid., pp. 5, 196-98, and 205 respectively.

34. Ibid., p. 2.

35. Ibid., pp. 5 and 1 respectively.

36. Levi, *Humanities Today*, p. 56.

37. Ibid., p. 52.

38. Veatch, *Two Logics*, p. 11, n. 18.

39. Ibid., pp. 171-72. The quotation from Lewis is from *Mind and the World Order*, p. 119.

40. Veatch, *Two Logics*, p. 265.

41. Ibid., pp. 11-16.

42. Spencer published an essay of that title in 1859 ("What Knowledge is of Most Worth"). The title was also used for the collection of essays edited by W. Booth, published in 1967.

43. Leavis, *Two Cultures?*, p. 48.

44. Luke 10:42.

45. Veatch, *Two Logics*, pp. 133, 238, 265, and 275 respectively.

46. Aristotle *Nicomachean Ethics* 1. 1094b24-25.

47. Wittgenstein, *Philosophical Investigations*, 1. 88.

48. Chew, "Impasse for the Elementary Particle Concept," in *Great Ideas Today 1974*, pp. 119-20.

49. See Church, *Introduction to Mathematical Logic*, p. 47.

50. Veatch, *Two Logics*, p. 26: "It provides no means either for saying or for thinking what anything is."

51. Haecker is quoted to this effect in Toulmin and Janik, *Wittgenstein's Vienna*, p. 179.

52. Skinner, *Beyond Freedom and Dignity*, pp. 191-92.

53. Blanshard and Skinner, "The Problem of Consciousness," *Philosophical and Phenomenological Research* 27 (1967):319 and 334.

54. "Common experience" is preferred by Adler, *The Condition of Philosophy*, p. 121; "experience in general" by Lewis *Mind and World Order*, pp. 33 and 36; "macroscopic experience" by Dewey, *Experience and Nature*, pp. 2-3, 5-7, 9-10, and 28; "naive experi-

ence" by Whitehead, *Science and the Modern World*, p. 111; "public experience" by Santayana in *Scepticism and Animal Faith*, p. x; "primary objectivity, originary evidence, and elementary experience" by Strasser, *Phénoménologie et sciences humaines*, pp. 99 and 275-76.

55. Eddington, *The Nature of the Physical World*, pp. 5-6.

56. Veatch, *Two Logics*, pp. 232-33 and 259-60 respectively.

57. Husserl, *Ideen III*, quoted in Spiegelberg, *The Phenomenological Movement*, vol. 1, p. 87.

58. Sartre, *L'Existentialisme est un humanisme*, p. 22; see also p. 78.

59. Heidegger, "What is Metaphysics," in *Existence and Being*, postscript (Brock edition, p. 355).

60. Aquinas *In Metaphysicum Aristotelis Commentaria* 1. 3, no. 60.

Chapter 8

1. See Flint, *History of the Classification of the Sciences*, and Mariétan, *Problème de la classification des sciences d'Aristote à St. Thomas*, for accounts of the many and various classifications of knowledge.

2. *Encyclopaedia Britannica*, "Propaedia," p. 6b-d.

3. Ibid., pp. 6h-7a.

4. Ibid., p. 698g-h.

5. 20 U.S.C. §952, quoted in Levi, *The Humanities Today*, p. 27.

6. See supra, chap. 7.

7. See Aron, *Essai sur la théorie de l'histoire dans l'Allemagne contemporaine*, esp. pp. 275-87.

8. Supra, chap. 7.

9. Dilthey, *Einleitung in die Geisteswissenschaften*, 1. 386ff. (French translation: *Introduction à l 'étude des sciences humaines*, p. 475.)

10. Bacon, *The Advancement of Learning*, 2. 25. 3, p. 253. See 2. 5. 1, p. 105.

11. See the plan included in D'Alembert, *Preliminary Discourse to the Encyclopedia of Diderot*, pp. 144-45.

12. Bacon, *Advancement*, 2. 1. 1, p. 85.

13. Ibid., 2. 4. 1, p. 101.

14. Ibid., 2. 5. 2, pp. 105-7.

15. Ibid., 2. 5. 2, p. 105.

16. Ibid., 2. 7. 1, p. 111.

17. Ibid., 2. 9. 1, p. 130.

18. Ibid., 2. 12. 3, p. 149.

19. See supra, chap. 1.

20. Bacon, *Advancement*, 2. 17. 9, p. 173.

21. Ibid., 2. 23. 2, p. 217 and 4, p. 219.

22. See supra, chap. 2.

23. Hugh of St. Victor, *The Didascalicon of Hugh of St. Victor*, 1. 4, p. 51.

24. Ibid., 2. 1, p. 61.

25. Ibid., Appendix A, p. 152.

26. Ibid., Appendix A, p. 153, for a succinct statement; for a detailed account, see 2. pp. 61-82.

27. Ibid., Appendix A, pp. 153-54.

28. Ibid., 1. 4, p. 51.

29. Aristotle *Poetics* 1451b6.
30. Idem, *Metaphysics* 6. 1025b19-1026a21.
31. Ibid., 6. 1025b29–1026a16. See idem, *Physics* 2. 193b22–194a12.
32. Idem, *Metaphys.* 6. 1026a27; see 11. 1064b8.
33. Idem, *Nicomachaean Ethics* 6. 1141b24–1142a11.
34. Ibid., 1. 1094a1-18 and 1094b12-27.
35. Idem, *Politics* 8. 1337b4-32.
36. Idem, *Parts of Animals* 1. 639a1-13.
37. Idem, *Politics* 8. 1337b23-26.

Chapter 9

1. Galileo, *The Assayer* in *Discoveries and Opinions of Galileo*, p. 121 (Drake trans., pp. 237-38): "Philosophy is written in this grand book, the universe, which stands continually open to our gaze. But the book cannot be understood unless one first learns to comprehend the language and read the letters in which it is composed. It is written in the language of mathematics, and its characters are triangles, circles, and other geometric figures without which it is humanly impossible to understand a single word of it; without these, one wanders about in a dark labyrinth."
2. See Kristeller, "The Modern System of the Arts," in *Renaissance Thought II*, p. 178.
3. See under "college" (Hoyt, Cassiere trans.), p. 37.
4. Richards, *Interpretation in Teaching*, p. 3.
5. Einstein, *Relativity* (Lawson trans., pref.): "In the interest of clearness, it appeared to me inevitable that I should repeat myself frequently, without paying the slightest attention to the elegance of the presentation. . . . Matters of elegance ought to be left to the tailor and to the cobbler."
6. Plato *Apology* 17B-C.
7. See supra, chap. 4.
8. See G. Patzig, "Syllogistic," in *Encyclopaedia Britannica*, 15th edition, vol. 17, pp. 890-98; or for a more extensive but still elementary treatment, see my book *Syllogistic and Its Endeavors*.
9. Supra, chap. 7.
10. Thus, for example, Frye emphasized especially literature and literary criticism, Levi, literature and philosophy, and Dilthey, history.
11. Supra, chap. 1.
12. *Scholastics* was a fitting name insofar as they addressed their work not to the common Christian, but to those in the schools, i.e., to academics, and highly specialized ones.
13. Supra, chap. 7.
14. Arnold, "Literature and Science," in *Discourses in America*, esp. pp. 101-5 and 135-37.
15. Comte, *The Positive Philosophy* (translated by Martineau), p. 788. See Gusdorf, *De l'Histoire des sciences à l'histoire de la pensée*, vol. 1, p. 103.
16. Descartes, *Discours sur la méthode*, 2d part, p. 18.
17. The *Discourse on Method* forms only the introduction to three long essays—the Dioptrics, Meteors, and Geometry—some 78 pages out of a total of 413.
18. Adam Smith, *The Wealth of Nations, bk. 1, chap. 1.*
19. Toulmin, *Human Understanding*, pp. 395-97; see supra, chap. 6.
20. Toulmin and Janik, *Wittgenstein's Vienna*, pp. 256-60.

21. Holton, *Thematic Origins of Scientific Thought*, pp. 15 and 19.

22. See supra, chap. 4.

23. See supra, chap. 6.

24. Holton, "The Mainsprings of Discovery," *Encounter* 43 (April 1974):89.

25. Popper, *Objective Knowledge*, p. 185.

26. Stahl, Johnson, and Burge, *Martianus Capella and the Seven Liberal Arts*, p. 239; see p. 232.

27. Cicero *Tusculan Disputations* 5. 23. 64-67.

28. See H. M. Jones, *One Great Society*, p. 64.

29. Stahl tends to be guilty of this in his concluding strictures against the humanities. See Stahl, et. al., *Martianus Capella*, p. 243.

30. Supra, chap. 7.

31. Mill, "Inaugural Address at St. Andrew's," in *The Six Great Humanistic Essays of John Stuart Mill*, p. 319.

32. These terms were first used for this purpose, as far as I know, by Whewell in *Of a Liberal Education in General*, p. 5.

Chapter 10

1. Diogenes Laertius, *Lives of the Eminent Philosophers*, "Speusippus," p. 375.

2. See Havelock, *Preface to Plato*, p. 111.

3. Ibid., p. 153; see p. 100.

4. Ibid., p. 155.

5. Collingwood, *Speculum Mentis, or the Map of Knowledge*, p. 39.

6. Ibid., p. 41.

7. Ibid., p. 42.

8. Ibid.

9. Ibid., pp. 46-49.

10. Ibid., p. 306.

11. Ibid., p. 307.

12. Ibid., p. 309.

13. Ibid.

14. Ibid., p. 160; see pp. 233 and 218 respectively.

15. Supra, chap. 3.

16. Collingwood, *Speculum*, pp. 81 and 254.

17. Supra, chap. 7.

18. Supra, chaps. 5 and 7.

19. Richards, "Notes toward an Agreement between Literary Criticism and Some of the Sciences," in *Speculative Instruments*, p. 8.

20. Ibid., p. 11.

21. Ibid., pp. 11-12.

22. Ibid., p. 12.

23. Ibid., p. 7.

24. For an eloquent indictment on these grounds, see Arrowsmith, "The Shame of the Graduate Schools, *Harper's Magazine* 232 (March 1966):51-59.

25. See, for example, the paucity of laws claimed to have been established by the empirical social sciences in Berelson and Steiner, *Human Behavior*.

26. See Stahl, Johnson, and Burge, *Martianus Capella and the Seven Liberal Arts*, quoted supra, chap. 9.

27. See Gilson, *The History of Christian Philosophy in the Middle Ages,* pp. 408-10, and supra, chap. 5.

28. Newman, *The Idea of a University,* pp. 37-38.

29. For this formulation in terms of restricted and unrestricted knowledge, see Pantin, *The Relations between the Sciences,* pp. 18-20.

30. Monod, *Chance and Necessity,* p. 180.

31. Ibid., p. 4.

32. Ibid., p. 175.

33. Ibid., p. 174.

34. Ibid., pp. 172-73.

35. Ibid., pp. 176-77.

36. Plato *Republic* 7. 537C.

37. Richards, *Speculative Instruments,* p. 124. The Platonic text is quoted on p. 108.

38. Supra, chap. 7.

39. Leavis, *Two Cultures?,* and especially the essay by M. Yudkin in the same book, pp. 54-55.

40. Supra, chap. 7.

41. See, for example, Holton, *Thematic Origins of Scientific Thought,* pp. 467-71.

42. Leavis, *Two Cultures?,* p. 49.

43. See supra, chap. 3.

44. H. M. Jones, *Education and the World Tragedy,* pp. 155-57.

45. Adler, *Dialectic,* pp. 235-42, and the later statement in his *The Idea of Freedom,* vol 1, pp. 10-17.

BIBLIOGRAPHY

Adams, Hazard, ed. *Critical Theory since Plato*. New York: Harcourt, Brace, Jovanovich, Inc., 1971.

_____. *The Interests of Criticism*. New York: Harcourt, Brace and World, Inc., 1969.

Adler, Mortimer J. *The Conditions of Philosophy*. New York: Atheneum, 1965.

_____. *Dialectic*. London: Kegan, Paul, 1927.

_____. *The Difference of Man and the Difference It Makes*. New York: Holt, Rinehart and Winston, 1967.

_____. *The Idea of Freedom*. 2 vols. Garden City, N.Y.: Doubleday, 1958, 1961.

Alembert, Jean Le Rond d'. *Preliminary Discourse to the Encyclopedia of Diderot*. Indianapolis: Bobbs-Merrill, 1963.

ALPMA. See *Arts Libéraux et Philosophie au Moyen Âge*.

The American Heritage Dictionary of the English Language. Boston: Houghton-Mifflin, Inc., 1969.

Aquinas, Thomas. *Declaratio 42 Quaestionum*.

_____. *De Veritate*.

_____. *The Division and Methods of the Sciences*. Questions 5 and 6 of *Commentary on De Trinitate of Boethius*. Translated by A. Maurer. Toronto: Pontifical Institute of Mediaeval Studies, 1963.

_____. *Expositio super Boetium De Trinitate*.

_____. *Aristotelis librum De Anima Commentarium*.

_____. *In libros De caelo et mundo expositio*.

_____. *In Metaphysicam Aristotelis Commentaria*.

_____. *In Primum librum Posteriorum Analyticorum Aristotelis*.

_____. *Summa Theologiae*.

Aristotle. *Metaphysics*.

_____. *Nicomachean Ethics*.

_____. *Parts of Animals*.

_____. *Physics*.

_____. *Poetics*.

_____. *Politics*.

_____. *Posterior Analytics*.

_____. *Rhetoric*.

Arnold, Matthew. "Literature and Science." In *Discourses in America*. London: Macmillan & Co., 1885; also in *Cultures in Conflict*, edited by D. K. Cornelius and E. St. Vincent (see entry below).

Aron, R. *Essai sur la théorie de l'histoire dans l'Allemagne contemporaine*. Paris: Vrin, 1938.

Arrowsmith, William. *"The Shame of the Graduate Schools." Harper's Magazine* 232 (March 1966):51-59.

Arts Libéraux et Philosophie au Moyen Âge: Actes du Quatrième Congres International de Philosophie Mediévale. Montreal: Institut d'Études Mediévales, 1969 (cited as *ALPMA*).

Ashley, B. M. *The Arts of Learning and Communication*. Dubuque, Iowa: Priory Press, 1961.

Aubrey, John. *Aubrey's Brief Lives*. Edited by A. Clark. Oxford: Clarendon Press, 1898.

Augustine. *De civitate Dei*.

——— *Confessions*. Translated by F. J. Sheed. New York: Sheed & Ward, 1943.

——— *De doctrina christiana libri quattuor*.

——— *On Christian Doctrine*. Translated by D. W. Robertson. Indianapolis: Bobbs-Merrill, 1958.

Bacon, Francis. *The Advancement of Learning*. Edited by W. A. Wright. 5th edition. Oxford: Clarendon Press, 1900.

———. "The Great Instauration." In *The Works of Francis Bacon*. Latin text of *Novum Organum* edited by J. Spedding, R. Ellis, and D. D. Heath. New York: Hurd and Houghton, 1869.

——— *The New Organon and Related Writings*. Edited by F. H. Anderson. Translated by R. Ellis and J. Spedding. Indianapolis: Bobbs-Merrill, 1960.

Berelson, Bernard, and Steiner, G. A. *Human Behavior: An Inventory of Scientific Findings*. New York: Harcourt, Brace & World, 1964.

Bird, Otto A. "How to read an Article of the *Summa*." *The New Scholasticism* 27 (2 April 1953):129-59.

——— *Syllogistic and Its Extensions*. Englewood Cliffs, N.J.: Prentice-Hall, 1964.

Blandshard, Brand, and Skinner, B. F. "The Problem of Consciousness—A Debate." *Philosophy and Phenomenological Research* 27 (1967):317-37.

Bochenski, Joseph M., O. P. *The Logic of Religion*. New York: New York University Press, 1965.

Booth, Wayne C., ed. *The Knowledge Most Worth Having*. Chicago: University of Chicago Press, 1967.

Brooks, Cleanth. "The Heresy of Paraphrase." In *Critical Theory since Plato*, edited by H. Adams (see entry above).

Bursill-Hall, G. L. *Speculative Grammars of the Middle Ages*. Paris: Mouton, 1971.

Capella, Martianus. *De nuptiis Philologiae et Mercurii*. Edited by A. Dick. Leipzig: B.G. Teubner, 1925.

Chenu, M. D., O. P. *Nature, Man and Society in the 12th Century*. Translation of *La Théologie au douzième siècle* by J. Taylor and L. K. Little. Chicago: University of Chicago Press, 1968.

——— *La Théologie comme science au XIIIe siècle*. Paris: Librairie Philosophie J. Vrin, 1969.

Chew, G. "Impasse for the Elementary Particle Concept." *In Great Ideas Today 1974* (see entry below).

Church, Alonzo. *Introduction to Mathematical Logic*. Princeton, N.J.: Princeton University Press, 1956.

Cicero, Marcus Tullius. *Cicero on Oratory and Orators*. Translation of *De oratore* by J. S. Watson. Carbondale: Southern Illinois University Press, 1970.

——————— *De oratore*.

——————— *De Republica*.

——————— *Tusculan Disputations*.

Clement of Alexandria. *Les Stromates*. Translation of *Stromata*. Paris: Editions du cerf, 1951.

Collingwood, R. G. *Speculum Mentis, or the Map of Knowledge*. Oxford: Clarendon Press, 1924, 1970.

Comte, Auguste. *Introduction to Positive Philosophy*. Translated by F. Ferré. Indianapolis: Bobbs-Merrill, 1970.

——————— *The Positivist Library of Auguste Comte*. Edited and translated by F. Harrison. New York: Burt Franklin, 1971.

——————— *The Positive Philosophy*. Translated by H. Martineau. New York: Calvin Blanchard, 1855.

Congar, Yves. "Tradition in Theology." In *Great Ideas Today 1974* (see entry below).

——————— *Tradition and the Traditions*. Translated by M. Naseby and T. Rainborough. New York: The Macmillan Company, 1967.

Cornelius, David K., and St. Vincent, E., eds. *Cultures in Conflict: Prespectives on the Snow-Leavis Controversy*. Chicago: Scott, Foresman and Co., 1964.

Crane, R. S. *The Idea of the Humanities*. 2 vols. Chicago: University of Chicago Press, 1967.

Crowther, James G. *Francis Bacon: The First Statesman of Science*. London: Cresset Press, 1960.

Curtius, Ernst R. *European Literature and the Latin Middle Ages*. Translated by W. R. Trask. New York: Bollingen Foundation, Inc., 1953.

Delhaye, Philippe. "La Place des arts libéraux dans les programmes scolaires due XIIIᵉ siècle." In *ALPMA* (see entry above).

Descartes, René. *Discours sur la méthode*. Edited by E. Gilson. 2d edition. Paris: Vrin, 1930.

Dewey, John. *Experience and Nature*. Chicago: Open Court, 1925.

Diderot, D. Alembert, J. d', et. al. *Encyclopedia: Selections*. Translated by N. S. Hoyt and T. Cassirer. Indianapolis: Bobbs-Merrill, 1965.

Dilthey, Wilhelm. "Abgrenzung der Geisteswissenschaften." In *Gesamelte Schriften*, vol. 7. Leipzig: Teubner, 1921.

——————— *Introduction à l'étude des sciences humaines*. French translation of *Einleitung in die Geisteswissenschaften*. Paris: Presses Universitaires de France, 1942.

——————— *Pattern and Meaning in History*. Translated by H. P. Rickman. New York: Harper Torchbooks, 1961.

Eddington, Sir Arthur. *The Nature of the Physical World*. London: J. M. Dent & Sons, 1928, 1947.

Einstein, Albert. *Relativity: The Special and General Theory*. Translated by R. W. Lawson. New York: P. Smith, 1920.

Eliot, T. S. *What is a Classic*. London: Faber & Faber, 1945.

Encyclopaedia Britannica. 15th edition. Chicago: Helen Hemmingway Benton, 1974.

Euclid. *Elements*.

Flint, R. *History of the Classification of the Sciences*. Cambridge: University Press, 1935.

Freud, Sigmund. *New Introductory Lectures on Psycho-analysis*. Translated by W. J. Sprott. New York: W. W. Norton & Co., 1933.

Frye, Northrop. *Anatomy of Criticism*. Princeton, N.J.: Princeton University Press, 1957.

Galilei, Galileo. *The Assayer*. In *Discoveries and Opinions of Galileo*. Translated by S. Drake. Garden City, N.Y.: Doubleday Anchor Books, 1957.

Gellius, Aulus. *Noctes Atticae*.

Gilson, Etienne. *History of Christian Philosophy in the Middle Ages*. New York: Random House, 1955.

_____ *Reason and Revelation in the Middle Ages*. New York: Charles Scribner's Sons, 1938.

_____ *Le Thomisme*. Paris: Librairie Philosophique J. Vrin, 1948.

_____ *The Unity of Philosophical Experience*. New York: Charles Scribner's Sons, 1937.

Great Books of the Western World. 54 vols. Chicago: Encyclopaedia Britannica, Inc., 1952.

Great Ideas Today 1970. Chicago: William Benton, 1970.

Great Ideas Today 1974. Chicago: Encyclopaedia Britannica, 1974.

Gusdorf, Georges. *De l'Histoire des sciences à l'histoire de la pensée*. 5 vols. Paris: Payot, 1966–1971.

Havelock, Eric A. *Preface to Plato*. Cambridge: Harvard University Press, 1963.

Heidegger, Martin. "What is Metaphysics?" In *Existence and Being*, edited by W. Brock; translated by R. F. C. Hull and A. Crick. Chicago: Henry Regnery Co., 1949.

Henri d'Andeli. "The Battle of the Seven Arts." In *Memoirs of the University of California*, vol. 1, no. 4, 46. Edited by L. J. Paetow. Berkeley: University of California Press, 1914.

Holton, Gerald. "The Mainsprings of Discovery." *Encounter* 42 (April 1974):85-92.

_____ *Thematic Origins of Scientific Thought*. Cambridge: Harvard University Press, 1973.

Homer. *The Iliad*.

Horace. *Ars poetica*.

Hugh of St. Victor. *The Didascalicon of Hugh of St. Victor*. Translated by J. Taylor. New York: Columbia University Press, 1961.

Hulme, T. E. "Bergson's Theory of Art." In *Critical Theory since Plato*, edited by H. Adams (see entry above).

Huxley, Thomas Henry. "Science and Culture." In *Cultures in Conflict*, edited by D. K. Cornelius and E. St. Vincent (See entry above).

Jaeger, Werner. *Paideia: The Ideals of Greek Culture*. 3 vols. Translated by G. Highet. Oxford: Basil Blackwell, 1939.

James, William. *The Principles of Psychology*. 2 vols. New York: Dover Publications, 1950.

Joannes Scotus Erigena. *Annotationes in Marcianum*. Edited by C. E. Lutz. Cambridge: Medieval Academy, 1939.

John of Salisbury. *Metalogicon*. Translated by D. D. McGarry. Berkeley: University of California Press, 1955.

Jones, Howard Mumford. *Education and the World Tragedy*. Cambridge: Harvard University Press, 1946.

_____ *One Great Society*. New York: Harcourt, Brace, 1959.

Jones, Richard Foster. *Ancients and Moderns*. 2d edition. Berkeley: University of California Press, 1965.

Jones, W. T. "Philosophical Disagreement and World Views." *Proceedings of the American Philosophical Association, 1969-1970*, pp. 29-42.

_____ *The Sciences and the Humanities: Conflict and Reconciliation*. Los Angeles: University of California Press, 1965.

Joyce, James. *Ulysses*. New York: Random House, 1934.

Kant, I. *Le Conflit des facultés*. Translated by J. Gibelin. Paris: J. Vrin, 1955.

_____ *Critique of Judgment*. In *Great Books of the Western World*, vol. 42 (see entry above).

_____ *Critique of Pure Reason*. In *Great Books of the Western World*, vol. 42 (see entry above).

_____ *Religion within the Limits Reason Alone*. Translated by T. M. Greene and H. H. Hudson. New York: Harper & Row, 1960.

Kennedy, George A. *The Art of Rhetoric in the Roman World, 300 B.C.–A.D. 300*. Princeton, N.J.: Princeton University Press, 1972.

Kibre, Pearl. "The *Quadrivium* in the Thirteenth Century Universities." In *ALPMA* (see entry above).

Kristeller, P. O. "The Modern System of the Arts." In *Renaissance Thought II*. New York: Harper & Row, 1965.

Kuhn, Thomas S. *The Structure of Scientific Revolutions*. Chicago: University of Chicago Press, 1962.

Laertius, Diogenes. *Lives of the Eminent Philosophers*. Translated by R. D. Hicks. Cambridge: Harvard University Press, 1938.

Langer, Susanne K. *Mind: An Essay on Human Feeling*. 2 vols. Baltimore: Johns Hopkins Press, 1967.

Leavis, F. R. " 'Literarism' versus 'Scientism'; The Misconception and the Menace." *Times Literary Supplement* no. 3,556 (23 April 1970):441-44.

Leavis, F. R., ed. *Two Cultures? The Significance of C. P. Snow*. New York: Pantheon Books, 1963.

Leclerq, Jean. *The Love of Learning and the Desire for God*. New York: New American Library, 1962.

Levi, Albert William. *The Humanities Today*. Bloomington: Indiana University Press, 1970.

_____ *Literature, Philosophy, and the Imagination*. Bloomington: Indiana University Press, 1962.

Lewis, C. I. *Mind and the World Order*. New York: Charles Scribner's Sons, 1929.

Mariétan, Joseph. *Problème de la classification des sciences d'Aristote à St. Thomas.* Paris: Alcan, 1901.

Marin-Sola, Francisco. *L'Evolution homogène du dogme catholique.* 2 vols. Fribourg, Switzerland: Imprimerie et Librairie de l'oeuvre de Saint-Paul, 1924.

Maritain, Jacques. *Creative Intuition in Art and Poetry.* New York: Pantheon Books, 1953.

Marrou, Henri Irenée. "Les Arts libéraux dans l'antiquité classique." In *ALPMA* (see entry above).

——————. *Saint Augustin et la fin de la culture antique.* Paris: Bibliotheque des Écoles Françaises d'Athenes et de Rome, 1938.

McKeon, Richard. "The Battle of the Books." In *The Knowledge Most Worth Having,* edited by W. C. Booth (see entry above).

Miles, Thomas Richard. *Religion and the Scientific Outlook.* London: Allen and Unwin, 1959.

Mill, John Stuart. "Inaugural Address at St. Andrew's." In *The Six Great Humanistic Essays of John Stuart Mill.* New York: Washington Square Press, 1969.

——————. "Thoughts on Poetry." In *The Six Great Humanistic Essays of John Stuart Mill* (see entry above).

Miriam Joseph, Sister *Shakespeare's Use of the Arts of Language.* New York: Columbia University Press, 1947.

Monod, Jacques. *Chance and Necessity.* Translated by A. Wainhouse. New York: Alfred A. Knopf, 1971.

Neurath, Otto, Bohr, N., Dewey, J., Russell, B., Carnap, R., and Morris, C. W. "Encyclopedia and Unified Science." *International Encyclopedia of Unified Science,* vol. 1, no. 1. Chicago: University of Chicago Press, 1938, 1952.

Neurath, O., Carnap, R., and Morris, C. W. *Foundations of the Unity of Science: Toward an International Encyclopedia of Unified Science.* 2 vols. Chicago: University of Chicago Press, 1969, 1970.

Newman, John Henry Cardinal. *An Essay on the Development of the Christian Doctrine.* New York: Longmans, Green and Co., 1903.

——————. *The Idea of a University.* New York: Holt, Rinehart and Winston, 1966.

Niebuhr, H. R. *Christ and Culture.* New York: Harper & Row, 1956.

Nuchelmans, Gabriel. "Philologia et son mariage avec Mercure jusqu'à la fin du XIIe siècle." *Latomus* 16 (1957):84-107.

"Ordo Artium. Edited by Ludwig Von Gompf. *Mittellateinische Jahrbuch* 3 (1966):94-128.

Paetow, L. J., ed. "The Battle of the Seven Arts." (See entry above under "Henri d'Andeli.")

Pantin, C. F. A. *The Relations between the Sciences.* Cambridge: University Press, 1968.

Pascal, Blaise. *Pensées et opuscules.* Edited by L. Brunschvicg. Paris: Hachette, n.d.

——————. *Provincial Letters.* In *Great Books of the Western World,* vol. 33 (see entry above).

——————. *Scientific Treatises concerning the Vacuum.* In *Great Books of the Western World,* vol. 33 (see entry above).

Perelman, Chaim. "The New Rhetoric." In *Great Ideas Today 1970* (see entry above).

Perelman, Chaim, and Olbrechts-Tyteca, L. *The New Rhetoric.* Translated by J. Wilkinson and P. Weaver. Notre Dame, Ind.: University of Notre Dame Press, 1969.

Petrarch, F., *Rerum senilium libri*. In *Opera Omnia*. Basel: Henricus Petri, 1554 (reprinted Ridgewood, N.J.: Gregg Press, 1965).

Pfeiffer, Rudolph. *History of Classical Scholarship*. Oxford: Clarendon Press, 1968.

Plato. *Apology*.

――――――. *Phaedrus*.

――――――. *Republic*.

――――――. *Seventh Letter*.

――――――. *Symposium*.

――――――. *Timaeus*.

Plotinus. *Enneads*.

Popper, Karl R. *Objective Knowledge: An Evolutionary Approach*. Oxford: Clarendon Press, 1972.

Pound, Ezra. *ABC of Reading*. London: George Routledge & Sons, 1934.

Quintilian. *Institutio oratoria*.

Richards, I. A. *Interpretation in Teaching*. New York: Harcourt, Brace, 1938.

――――――. "Notes toward an Agreement between Literary Criticism and Some of the Sciences." In *Speculative Instruments* (see entry below).

――――――. *Speculative Instruments*. Chicago: University of Chicago Press, 1955.

Rigault, Hippolyte. *Histoire de la querelle des anciens et modernes*. Paris: L. Hachette et cie, 1856.

Rossi, Paolo. *Francis Bacon: From Magic to Science*. Translated by S. Rabinovitch. Chicago: University of Chicago Press, 1968.

Russell, Bertrand, and Whitehead, Alfred North. *Principia Mathematica*. 2d edition. Cambridge: University Press, 1950.

Sandys, John Edwin. *A History of Classical Scholarship*. 3 vols. New York: Hafner Publishing Co., 1921, 1967.

Santayana, George. *Scepticism and Animal Faith*. New York: Dover Publications, 1955.

Sartre, Jean-Paul. *L'Existentialisme est un humanisme*. Paris: Les Editions Nagel, 1946.

Shea, F. X. "Theology as an Academic Discipline." In *The Role of Theology in the University*. Milwaukee: Bruce Publishing Co., 1967.

Shelley, Percy Bysshe. "A Defense of Poetry." In *Critical Theory since Plato*, edited by H. Adams (see entry above).

Skinner, B. F. *Beyond Freedom and Dignity*. New York: Bantam Books, 1971.

Skinner, B. F., and Blanshard, Brand. "The Problem of Consciousness—A Debate." *Philosophy and Phenomenological Research* 27 (1967):317-37.

Snow, C. P. "The Case of Leavis and the Serious Case." *Times Literary Supplement* no. 3,567 (9 July 1970):737-40.

――――――. *The Two Cultures: And a Second Look*. New York: The New American Library, 1963.

Spencer, Herbert. "What Knowledge is of Most Worth." In *Essays on Education, Etc.* London: Everyman, 1911.

Spiegelberg, H. *The Phenomenological Movement*. 2 vols. The Hague: Martinus Nijhoff, 1965.

Stahl, William H., Johnson, R., and Burge, E. L. *Martianus Capella and the Seven Liberal Arts.* New York: Columbia University Press, 1971.

Strasser, Stephen. *Phénoménologie et sciences de l'homme.* Louvain: Universitaires de Louvain, 1967.

Swift, Jonathan. "The Battle of the Books." In *A Tale of a Tub,* edited by A. C. Guthkelch. Oxford: Clarendon Press, 1958.

Terence. *Andria.*

Toulmin, Stephen. *Human Understanding.* vol. 1. Princeton, N.J.: Princeton University Press, 1972.

Toulmin, Stephen, and Janik, A. *Wittgenstein's Vienna.* New York: Simon and Schuster, 1973.

Trinkaus, Charles. *In Our Image and Likeness.* 2 vols. London: Constable, 1970.

Valery, Paul. "Poetry and Abstract Thought." In *Critical Theory since Plato,* edited by H. Adams (see entry above).

Van Ackeren, Gerald F. *Sacra Doctrina.* Rome: Catholic Book Agency, 1952.

Veatch, Henry B. *Two Logics: The Conflict between Classical and Neo-Analytic Philosophy.* Evanston, Ill.: Northwestern University Press, 1969.

Verdier, Philippe. "L'Iconographie des arts libéraux dans l'art du moyen âge jusqu'à la fin du quinzième siècle." In *ALPMA* (see entry above).

Vico, Giambattista. *The New Science.* Translated by T. G. Bergen and M. H. Fisch. Ithaca, N.Y.: Cornell University Press, 1948, 1970.

_____. *On the Study Methods of Our Times.* Translated by E. Gianturco. Indianapolis: Bobbs-Merrill, 1965.

Weisheipl, James A. *Friar Thomas D'Aquino: His Life, Thought, and Work.* Garden City, N.Y.: Doubleday, 1974.

_____. "The place of the Liberal Arts in the University Curriculum during the XIVth-XVth Centuries." In *ALPMA* (see entry above).

_____. "Philosophy and the Two Cultures." *American Catholic Philosophical Association Proceedings* 38 (1964):1-10.

Whewell, William. *Of a Liberal Education in General.* London: John W. Parker, 1850.

Whitehead, Alfred North. *The Concept of Nature.* Cambridge: University Press, 1920.

_____. "The First Physical Synthesis." In *Essays in Science and Philosophy.* New York: Philosophical Library, 1948.

_____. *Science and the Modern World.* Cambridge: University Press, 1933.

William of Tocco. "Hystoria beati Thomae." *Sancti Thomae Aquinatis Vitae Fontes Praecipuae.* Edited by A. Farua. Alba: Editiones Domenicaue, 1968.

Wittgenstein, Ludwig. *Philosophical Investigations.* Translated by G. E. M. Anscombe. The Macmillan Co., 1953.

Wordsworth, William. *The Prelude, or Growth of a Poet's Mind.* London: Oxford University Press, 1956.

Yudkin, Michael. "An Essay." In *Two Cultures?,* edited by F. R. Leavis (see entry above).

INDEX